Clare Campbell is an author and journalist. She writes regularly for the *Daily Mail* and is a contributing editor to *Marie Claire* magazine. Her critically acclaimed book, *Out Of It*, was published in 2007. She is married to the author and historian Christy Campbell, and lives in London with her husband and twelve-year-old son. She has grown-up twin daughters.

TOKYO HOSTESS

Inside the Shocking World of Tokyo Nightclub Hostessing

CLARE CAMPBELL

SPHERE

First published in Great Britain in 2009 by Sphere
This paperback edition published in 2010 by Sphere

A CIP catalogue record for this book
is available from the British Library.

ISBN 978-0-7515-4099-4

Typeset in Caslon by M Rules
Printed and bound in Great Britain by
Clays Ltd, St Ives plc

Papers used by Sphere are natural, renewable and
recyclable products sourced from well-managed forests and certified
in accordance with the rules of the Forest Stewardship Council.

Mixed Sources
Product group from well-managed
forests and other controlled sources
www.fsc.org Cert no. SGS-COC-004081
© 1996 Forest Stewardship Council
FSC

Sphere
An imprint of
Little, Brown Book Group
100 Victoria Embankment
London EC4Y 0DY

An Hachette UK Company
www.hachette.co.uk

www.littlebrown.co.uk

For Christy

Author's note

On a warm spring day in early May 2007, I pulled up in front of a timber-clad house surrounded by soaring pines in the backwoods of Pennsylvania. A swing and climbing frame painted in primary colours showed evidence of small children. In the dappled midday light it seemed a happy, secure place – the sort of American home where nothing bad could ever happen.

So why the double-padlocked security, the guards at the gate and the brisk shakedown for visitors? It was as if the people I had come to see were in a witness-protection programme. But then I remembered why I was here.

Samantha Ridgway was no ordinary suburban house-wife. Her only sister, Carita, had been abducted, raped and killed by a Japanese business tycoon. He had been tried for the alleged murder of a young, blonde British nightclub hostess called Lucie Blackman, and the month before my visit, he had been found not guilty in a Tokyo court. The story was a press sensation at the time and had been revisited many times since as the drawn-out process of criminal justice, Japanese-style, ran its course. His prosecutors suspected that he had also drugged and then raped as many as two hundred other young women. In the end he had been tried in the matter of ten of them. How he had been brought to justice at all, as I would discover, was an amazing story. But it was the killing of Carita, Samantha's sister, that had earned him a sentence of life imprisonment.

I was here to interview Samantha as a journalist on commission for a magazine. But I, myself, already knew something about sibling loss under dramatic and tragic circumstances. Seven years earlier I had found my own older brother, also a journalist, dead from the effects of crack cocaine. He, I would eventually discover, had been on the fringes of a criminal conspiracy. As a consequence, I had had years of dealings with suspicious law-enforcement officials before I had got anywhere close to the truth. I hoped, almost sensed already as I walked up the path to the modest house, that Samantha and I would understand each other.

A smiling, beautiful woman in her late thirties came to the door, long blonde hair pushed back off her face. Taking me through into a large, open-plan room filled with toys and finger paints, Samantha introduced me to her husband,

Richard, an Italian-American in his early forties, and their two exceptionally pretty children.

As we sat down and started to talk, Samantha reached out to a folder beside her and showed me a photograph of her sister, Carita, then aged twenty-one, taken shortly before her death. Gazing at this strikingly attractive dark-haired girl (their mother was a model), I was struck again by the horrific way her life had ended. I remembered the throwaway remark in a diary kept by this man, Joji Obara, alongside Carita's name – the evidence that had judicially linked him to her death: 'Carita Ridgway – too much chloroform.'

The stories of two young women from opposite ends of the earth, Carita and Lucie, both aged twenty-one, had come together in the seaside apartment of a middle-aged Japanese businessman.

Their families, divided and feuding as they were as relationships fell to pieces, seemed at least to have been united in their grief and outrage at the loss of a child in young adulthood. Were it not for the tenacity of Carita's and Lucie's families, Obara might indeed have got away with it.

Lucie's mother Jane felt unable to meet or communicate personally with me. And why should she rake up for yet another pushy journalist the trauma of Lucie's death? Meanwhile, her determination to first find, then secure justice and retribution for the man accused of causing the death of her daughter was evidently as strong as anyone else's.

In March 2007, two months before my trip to see Samantha, it had all seemed to be happening again. The battered body of another young woman, English-language teacher Lindsay Hawker, from Brandon, Coventry, was found buried in a bathtub filled with sand on the balcony of a Tokyo apartment. She had been strangled and bludgeoned to death, apparently by a Japanese male aged twenty-eight who had persuaded her to give him a one-off English lesson. He had evaded capture and disappeared – but there was lots of press speculation about this new killer and his grisly motivations. One Tokyo-based reporter was asked by his news editor in London: 'Are there any new developments? It is simply impossible to overestimate the degree of interest there is in this *creature* with his fascination for white women.' There was a renewed feeding frenzy as the racial stereotype of perverted oriental and pale-skinned female victim was revisited. It naturally served to heighten media interest in the trial of the original sex-monster-in-chief, Joji Obara (who of course had nothing to do with this new tragedy), about to reach its climax in a Tokyo courtroom.

The legal process had been going on for seven years and

it was still not over. Obara's testimony throughout had been bizarre to say the least. He came across as cunning, but also intelligent. And he was not considered 'mad' in a judicial sense. In spite of the nature of his crimes, no court-appointed psychiatrist (as might be expected in say a British or American jurisdiction) had been asked to comment on the activities of someone who seemed to have realised the fantasies of subjection and rape that were already the everyday fare of the countless 'image clubs' and *hentai* (pornographic comics) for which Japan was infamous. Perhaps such things were considered unremarkable.

Obara called it 'conquer play', and the basis of his defence was that the women he had 'played' with had done so consensually. They were prostitutes who did such things for money. That they were 'foreign' and took drugs, as he insisted they did, seemed to absolve him from any guilt. I had it in mind to explore further the party scene into which these young women so lightly dipped on their carefree global travelling – and to see for myself that party capital of Japan, if not the world, Roppongi.

It was in a Roppongi nightclub that Lucie worked as a hostess selling, as one girl put it, 'a fantasy love affair each night'. She was not and was never expected to be selling sex. Her tragedy was that one customer thought differently.

I became fascinated by the parallels in the Obara case

between what actually happened to his victims and the erotic fantasy landscape that so many Japanese seemed to inhabit. Why was real sex crime and rape so much lower than in my own country, when Japanese pornography seemed the most violent and sadistic I had ever encountered?

Back in London, I found I could not forget the stories of Carita, Lucie and Lindsay. Each of them had felt safe in Japan. Yet they had not been. I remembered Samantha's words in particular: 'Neither of us were too worried. At the time I was only twenty-three, Carita eighteen months younger, and I think both of us naively believed we understood Japanese culture. I knew men were fascinated by Western girls, and did not appreciate that this might sometimes be dangerous.' Now I found myself wondering whether they had been misguided, unlucky or just childishly innocent.

I also wanted to know just why so many girls chose to go to Japan, either to work as teachers, hostesses or frequently both. What was going on? I did not for a moment believe I could ever fully comprehend Japanese culture and sexuality, or how the two interacted so perversely and tragically as in the case of Joji Obara and his victims.

But I wanted to find out more – about the three girls, about Joji and, most of all, about Japan. So I went there. This book is about what I found.

Acknowledgements

I would like to thank the following for the help they gave me in writing this book – firstly my husband Christy, for his enthusiasm, energy and support; my daughters Maria and Katy, and my son Joseph, for not objecting when his mother upped and left him to trawl hostess bars. Bridget Freer at *Marie Claire* for sending me to New York in the first place; Roberto, who chaperoned me from New York to Pennsylvania; Samantha Ridgway, her husband Richard and their family, and Robert Finnigan for kindly giving their permission for me to write about Carita; Tim Blackman for talking so frankly to me about Lucie; and to Amanda Stocks for putting me in touch with the Hawker family.

To Joy Ingerson for her affection and hard work in helping with this project; Barbara and Dominic Allen for their help and hospitality in Tokyo; Professor Jim Farrer; BBC journalist Ilana Rehavia; and Hideki Toyama and Hanami San for their insights into Japanese culture. Stephen Haynes, who acted as my tour guide through Japanese clubs and bars; the bar staff at Flowers, Geronimo and Gas Panic; Shannon and Aimee for sharing their experiences of life as a hostess. I would also like to thank Justin McCurry and the Press Club in Tokyo; Simon Wood and Simon Lavender of the FCO; Kenichiro Suzuki of Paradise TV; Yukari (we didn't meet but tried to); Natsumi Ikoma and Tsukazi Nobuyuki; the incredibly helpful and courteous staff at Shibuya Granbell Hotel; and the old Japanese man in a local fruit shop who insisted on giving me an orange every single day of my visit, as well as the many Japanese people who offered their help and guidance.

I am also grateful to my agent Vivienne Schuster, her assistant Felicity Blunt, and to my publisher at Little, Brown, David Shelley, and his colleagues Zoe Gullen, Hannah Torjussen and Emma Stonex. And lastly but never forgetting Harry and the Whitakers, who looked after Joseph while I was away.

PROLOGUE

Den-en-Chofu, Tokyo, October 2000

The house had something creepy about it for years. That's what the neighbours said, anyway. It wasn't especially old. It was a big, luxurious place with a gated drive, arranged on three floors with a kind of glazed observatory on the roof. The mansion – you would have to call it that – was set within a substantial garden, a fabulously lavish expanse by Japanese standards. This was where someone rich and important lived.

Or maybe they had done once. Rust stains bloomed through the rendered concrete. Tiles flaked from the walls exposing bare cement. At the gate, a surveillance camera blinked indifferently at the street. Grimy plastic bags flapped like stranded jellyfish in the unkempt bushes. The decrepitude of the house was emphasised by the neatness of its neighbours in this wealthy suburban enclave of well-tended gardens and topiary, private academies and discreet clinics, where even the little railway station had its own koi carp pond.

Detectives from the Keishicho, the Tokyo Metropolitan Police Department, used heavy wire cutters to get through the steel gate. It bore a little name plate. Two uniformed officers stood at the end of the street to keep the curious away, not that anyone on this October morning in the wealthy suburb of Den-en-Chofu would ever think of prying into their neighbour's business. This was where the wealthy sought seclusion and a certain anonymity – bankers, society surgeons, automotive industry chieftains. But there were some (or rather the servants and gardeners of the restless rich who used the place as a gilded dormitory) who had stories to tell about the house and the people who lived there.

The maid of an elderly couple who lived across the way had often heard dogs barking, but there was scarcely ever a sight of their owner, she said. Lights came on at night and sometimes during the day. There had been a rumpus a few years back. Men in dark suits had come and 'For Sale' signs were put on the gate – but no new owners had moved in. Then the place had gone back to sleep.

The house had apparently been in one ownership for

decades. Once, a long time ago, a young man had come to live here with a maid, but nobody knew what had become of him.

It was the rubbish that caught the detectives' attention: shards of broken furniture, shapeless bundles under the overgrown shrubbery. Then there were the cars – four of them – caked in grime and buried in ten seasons' worth of leaves, tyres flat, windscreens blackened like blinded eyes, going nowhere. A Maserati Mistral, a fastback Bentley Continental, a red (though it was hard to tell under the dirt) Rolls-Royce Silver Cloud, an Aston Martin DB5 – props from a long-ago Bond movie, glamour chariots from another age.

Guarding the side door was something stranger still, a life-size ceramic statue of a German shepherd dog, with bared fangs and a pink tongue.

The forensic team were in the garden, poking the ground, looking for disturbed soil, while in the house detectives picked their way through heaps of rubbish – newspapers and magazines, car batteries, old TV sets and dust-caked electronic equipment. In one room there was a large medical wall chart depicting the structure of the human brain. A chest freezer hummed in the basement; inside it were animal feed, a bunch of roses frozen solid and what appeared to be the cryogenically preserved corpse of a large animal.

3

There were boxes of letters, receipts, documents, notebooks dating back years. There were whiskery audio-cassettes and reels of Super 8 home movie. Then there were the videos. Hundreds of them, some stacked in their cardboard sleeves, labelled, others strewn in piles, magnetic tape spilling out in slippery coils. All were gathered by the investigators and sealed in evidence bags. It took a large panel van to take them back to Azabu police station. How much more of this stuff was there?

The land registry listed more properties in the name of the mansion's owner – a city apartment in the Akasaka district of Tokyo (a glitzy area of embassies and corporate headquarters), some sort of mansion in the hot-spring resort of Atami, eighty miles east of the capital, and two more properties a little apart from each other out on the coast, in Kanagawa Prefecture, south-east of Tokyo. They too would yield a strange harvest of evidence.

On the morning of 16 October 2000, at Azabu police station, a video player and monitor were set up so that the VCR evidence could be looked at by detectives. What was it they were looking at? Was this pornography? The lights were bright, the camera angle fixed. There was no music, no soundtrack. It featured a leading actor with an ever-changing cast of females. The show went on for hours with always the same plot: a middle-aged man, wearing nothing but a crude carnival mask, manoeuvring a succession of apparently lifeless, naked women on to a bed in some anonymous apartment. There were screw hooks on the ceiling and by the sides of the bed to which their flopping limbs were sometimes tied. All were then penetrated with fingers, dildos or other objects. Some were left lying insensate until the lights were clearly burning their naked flesh. Still they did not stir.

The leading man appeared unable to perform sexually himself – at least not in any normal sense. Instead, he cavorted around his inert companions for hours on end. If this was porn, it was for connoisseurs only.

The females cast in this repellent drama were not dead. In some sequences they could be seen moving, rising up sometimes before having their faces swaddled in some kind of cloth by their tormentor and returning to rag-doll compliance with his gruesome script.

It was clear to the policemen as they stubbed out their cigarettes. The naked figure with the goatee was the man they had been holding in the station's cells since his arrest three days before on suspicion of rape. He seemed to have had lots of names. The latest was Joji Obara.

PART ONE

CHAPTER 1

Lucie Blackman thought she was ordinary. Her self-judged ordinariness tormented her more than anything else. She would write about it in a diary which came into the public light in circumstances which were anything but ordinary.

'I constantly hate myself,' she wrote. 'I'm so average. Every single part of me from head to toe is completely average . . . I feel so disgusting and ugly and average . . . I hate the way I look, I hate my hair, I hate my face, I hate my slanty eyes, I hate the mole on my face, I hate my teeth, I hate my chin, I hate my profile, I hate my neck, I hate my boobs, I hate my fat hips, I hate my fat stomach. I am so fucking up to my neck in debt and so badly need to do well.'

In short, Lucie Jane Blackman's self-esteem was as shaky as that of any other twenty-one-year-old, not long fledged from gawky adolescence into young-adult woman-hood. She drank too much, spent too much, hated her body (on the whole) and true love was hard to find. So yes, in all of that she was pretty normal. But she had already done some things in her life which, for a girl from Sevenoaks, Kent, were altogether remarkable.

She wrote her self-deprecating statements in Tokyo, capital of Japan, party capital of the world. Fate, ambition and curiosity had brought her there – like many hundreds of Western women – in the early summer of 2000, to have a good time and pile up some quick cash. She worked in a hostess bar. She was a gaijin girl, whose blonde foreignness Japanese men were supposed to find especially alluring. They would pay enormous sums, it seemed, just to sit with these girls in tacky clubs, make conversation in fractured English, have their drinks poured and cigarettes lit. Nothing else was expected or demanded. It was safe, safe, safe.

And it was fun, supposedly so. But right now, three weeks into her new career as queen of the Tokyo night, Lucie Jane Blackman thought she was completely crap at the job.

Getting work had been a breeze, just as her fellow traveller and best friend from school, Louise Phillips, had said it would be. Lucie and Lou had done everything together – left school and gone to work in London at the same boring bank. Then they had both got into British Airways as flight attendants. Louise had become as restless and bored with it as Lucie. But Louise thought she had found a way out. And now they were fluttering their eyelashes in Casablanca, a club in Roppongi. Every night Lucie was expected to laugh at the (mercifully incomprehensible) smutty jokes of middle-aged men, keep the whisky and tequila flowing and generally be as *genki* (lively) as possible.

Only she wasn't feeling *genki* today. Why was she still here? The cell-like room in the gaijin house in Sendagaya, their tiny toehold in teeming Tokyo, was spinning. Pain shot through Lucie's head as she reached her hand out for the furry rabbit-shaped alarm clock. Why did everything have to have cute animals on it? Everything in Tokyo was cute.

But not her. Lucie didn't feel at all cute. Her mouth was parched. She couldn't remember how much she'd had to drink the night before, only that it was a lot. She wondered how many calories there were in a glass of wine. At least, so she comforted herself, she hadn't had much to eat. If only, if only they hadn't decided to go out clubbing after her shift had ended at the club. But that's what they always did. They'd done Geronimo's, Wall Street, Hama's and then some. What time had they got back? It was daylight anyway, with those big, glossy Tokyo crows pecking at the bags of rubbish in the street. The taxi fare had been gouging – as always.

Now it was already well past midday. Grabbing a

bathrobe from the pile of clothes on the floor, Lucie gazed at it in disgust. It looked like it had been made for a ten-year-old. She didn't know which of the others it belonged to. Her body felt stiff from sleeping on the floor.

Looking in the mirror, she was certain she saw the raised red tracing of a spot starting under her nose. She scrabbled through the pile of cosmetics on the table to try and find the tube of Dr.Ci:Labo. She knew someone had some. It was brilliant stuff (all the Japanese girls used it), but really expensive. All the girls borrowed one another's stuff, and if she got good tips tonight she'd pay them straight back.

She could hear Louise in the shower ahead of her. Her friend had grabbed the next slot in the diminutive bathroom as the other girls in the house – dancers, models, teachers, hostesses, whatever – also blinked, scrubbed and cosmeticised their way into the challenges of an already passing Tokyo day. Tokyo had been Louise's idea; or rather she was following the trail blazed by her older sister, Emma. Why was it always that way? Why did Louise always get there first? It was the same at the club. All the customers seemed to ask for Louise especially.

Still, Lucie told herself, if her best friend could get the hang of 'Tokes', so could she.

Lucie Blackman was already a seasoned traveller. She had left school aged eighteen, with three A levels. She was bright, intelligent, attractive. Going to university for another three years of studying was not on her agenda. She wanted to get out into the world as soon as she could.

Lucie's parents had married young (Jane was twenty-two, Tim only a little older) and they had clambered up the social ladder as her self-employed builder father found financial success in property development. It had been a bumpy journey.

Jane had had more than her fair share of tragedy in her young life. At the age of thirteen she lost her own mother, Marie, to a brain tumour. Lucie, or Lula, as her mother called her, had been born in 1978 when Jane was barely twenty-five. Her younger sister Sophie was born two years later and her brother Rupert arrived in 1983. There were family holidays in Spain and on the Isle of Wight where Tim, a keen member of the classic and vintage yacht club, kept a boat – a beautiful thirty-three-foot Bermudan sloop, all teak and gleaming brass, called the *Bettine*. Jane, meanwhile, sought a post-parenting career, training in reflexology. She had qualified in 1991, the alternative therapy suiting her interest in the spiritual aspects of life.

Lucie's home life was like a war zone. It had been for a long time. Her parents split rancorously in 1995, when Lucie was seventeen, after Tim had an affair (one of several, he would later confess) and headed for the door. Things got a bit quieter after that but not altogether. The

13

truncated family soldiered on, remaining (on the whole) loyal to Jane. Lucie hardly saw her father for the next two and half years. He shuffled off (in penury, he would claim) to the Isle of Wight, where he found new love with a new partner – Jo Burr, a blonde divorcee with four young children. He had known Jo for ages; her sister had been his teenage sweetheart.

Lucie's late childhood and adolescence in a household at war was typical – there was nothing unusual about parental discord or mix-and-match families in late nineties Britain to scandalise the neighbours or set the school bullies on her. It was just that Lucie, as the eldest child, had to grow up that much quicker – her parents perhaps spending too much time picking each other to pieces to be able to worry about what she might be up to. According to her father, 'Lucie's independence of spirit stood her in good stead within the family dynamics. Where Sophie and her mother would meet head-on in an argument, Lucie quietly managed to defuse the situation.' She was hard-working and as self-sufficient as she could be – she babysat, worked in Pizza Hut and went out to spend her hard-earned money on her own kind of fun.

In her father's words: 'No one was telling her what time to go to bed at night, she could go anywhere she liked, drink in bars, have sex with her boyfriends, do whatever she liked.' Which was to see more of the world than just

Sevenoaks. Aged eighteen she went to work at the office of the French bank, Société Générale, in the City of London, where her already good French became even better. Then she quit the bank job to try her luck as a flight attendant with British Airways.

Lucie passed the assessment and written exam with ease. To begin with, it was all terrific, but the short-haul regime of to-and-fro trolley-dollying quickly palled. Then Lucie was promoted to long-haul. There were new destinations – Moscow, Nairobi, Kingston, New York. But the permanent jet lag, the two-in-the-morning starts to get to Heathrow on time, day and night blurring into one, the overnights in a Crawley hostel, sleep snatched in some bleak crewroom – soon stripped life of any lingering illusions of glamour. When not actually working she still lived with her mother and younger sister and brother in the family home from which she was rarely away for more than a few days.

It was ironic really. Even if it was no longer glamorous in Europe, in Asia, at least, the image of the airline 'stewardess' still remained exciting and escapist. In Japan for example, with its otherwise male-dominated work culture, becoming a flight attendant was fantastically aspirational. There were magazines about it and dozens of training schools in Tokyo to help college-leaving girls (for that is what you had to be – no non-graduates or older women need apply) learn how to pour drinks, make light-hearted English-language conversation and bow correctly.

Lucie didn't do much bowing on BA. Her father confirms that the 'apparent glamour and social status of being an air hostess' was by now wearing distinctly thin. And despite criss-crossing the globe, she didn't actually feel she was going anywhere. 'One hotel room in one country is very much like another hotel room in another country,' she once told her father. But she had learned how to look after herself, and – in working the aisles at thirty thousand feet – how to flatter middle-aged men. That was going to prove useful.

Anyway, the whole business of being a flight attendant (no one in the business spoke of air hostesses any more) was changing. The brash new budget airlines were hiring kids and paying kids' wages – but it was like a gap year as far as they were concerned. Go wild and travel for a few months while you are young, that was their idea. Was she going to pursue a career with the airline then settle down? Or do some major partying before she became too much older? Lucie Blackman was never quite sure.

Then, quite suddenly, Lucie decided to quit. She'd simply had enough of being a flight attendant. Jane was concerned, of course, but inside she was ever so slightly relieved. Lucie got a job working in a local oyster bar. But another idea was forming for a new life of thrills and adventure, doing something a lot more exotic than asking the passengers in economy whether they wanted tea or coffee.

By now, Jane and Tim were not speaking on any level. Lucie took her mother's side, as did her younger siblings. But Lucie was discreetly making contact with her exiled father. He tells how, in the summer of 1999, she spent a cheerful weekend with him, water-skiing and relaxing on his boat on the Solent. It was like the old days. But an anonymous 'friend of the Blackman family' was quoted in a newspaper some years after the events with a much less sentimental depiction of their relationship. Whoever it was doing the talking clearly hated Tim – and seemed to know a good deal about his financial affairs. The 'friend' had this to say about father and daughter: 'To describe them as close is laughable. Lucie had built bridges with him before she went away because she was that kind of person. She didn't want to have bad feeling as she went on her travels . . . But she hated what he had done to her mother. [Lucie] used to tell me he had hidden his money well because he seemed to have rather a lot, but there was never any available for her mother or the children. She had very mixed feelings about having a relationship with him at all.'

In September 1999 Tim and his new partner went off to

17

America and bought another classic yacht, the *Josephine*, with the intention of restoring her to her splendid original condition in time to take part in the America's Cup Jubilee Regatta in summer 2000.

Whatever the truth of the matter, life in the backwash of Tim and Jane Blackman's divorce was clearly only a little less stormy than it had been when they had lived together as husband and wife, although the battleground had now shifted to their lawyers. Lucie wasn't earning much and her credit card was nudging the red line. But she really liked the idea of financial independence. She hated the mess her parents had made; when they communicated at all it was to row about money, and Lucie knew, from watching her mother, all about having to scrimp and save. That was certainly not her style. So, one day Lucie announced that she was going to pay off her debts and make lots of money. She was going to be a bar girl in Japan.

Just as it was for many girls who found themselves heading for Heathrow Airport with a Lonely Planet guide to Japan in their hand luggage (a good tip for getting through immigration at the other end; another was to dress like you really were a backpacker on a tourist visa and not like someone seeking work as a showgirl), for Lucie and Louise a more experienced friend or a big sister had been the ticket east.

Louise's older sister Emma had just come back from far-away places. She had worked as a 'hostess' in Tokyo. It was safe and it was fun. Some girls signed up with recruiting agencies in London, but there was no need for that. They just had to go to Narita Airport and pick up *Tokyo Classified* magazine. There would be loads of job ads – they could take their pick. You were supposed to work in a place for three months minimum – but some clubs would hire for shorter periods or even offer a couple of nights' trial. It would be easy.

Lucie's mother would one day tell a newspaper reporter: '[Louise] told us it was safe – that there was no hidden agenda to the job, no sexual element. I knew Louise would never do anything silly.'

Lucie herself was just as reassuring. From what she'd been able to find out, it was all a big laugh with loads of money thrown in. As a girl she would meet in Tokyo would put it: 'Where else can you get paid so well for working six hours a night and basically party and have a good time?' One girl described it as being a 'conversation prostitute', while the United Nations International Labor Office, no less, in a special report on sex-workers in Japan defined hostessing as being no more than 'conversation, pouring drinks, lighting cigarettes, but involving no physical contact or sex service'.

But telling either of her parents the whole truth was

clearly difficult. Lucie had told her father that she would be working in a bar and staying in a flat owned by her friend Louise's 'aunt' – who conveniently enough was Japanese and lived in the capital. They'd get cheap tickets courtesy of her old employers, British Airways, and be in and out of Japan on a ninety-day tourist visa. She'd be home by the beginning of August. Or maybe she'd go and see more of Asia – get to Thailand and end up in Australia. She told her younger sister that she would be back before anyone knew she'd even been away, and after that she was going to train as a primary school teacher – maybe. Anyway, whatever happened, she would earn enough in Japan to pay off her debts and then some. It was all going to be fantastic.

Japan appealed to Lucie. She liked what she'd heard of its consumer glitter – the huge shopping malls and department stores in Shibuya, Tokyo, filled with achingly fashionable young people and every kind of electronic gadget. Japanese stuff was expensive. But it was cute. Hello Kitty and the other cuddly denizens of the Sanrio character merchandising empire had long since pushed Barbie and My Little Pony out of many a nice English girl's bedroom. You could even get a Hello Kitty mobile phone. Lucie would like a flash phone – just as she liked expensive clothes, shoes, handbags . . .

As her sister Sophie would say: 'The idea that she was a

backpacker is laughable. When Lucie decided to go on a trip she'd buy matching suitcases. The night before she left, I was helping her pack and she was trying to decide how many pairs of shoes she'd need for three months in Japan. Twenty? Would that be enough?'

Although the very idea of doing what Lucie and Louise were planning might have seemed extraordinary in their parents' day, by the time Lucie was growing up, working as a Tokyo bargirl had become an established waypoint in globalised, young-adult culture. It was no more exotic (well, not much more) than clubbing in Ibiza or backpacking in Ko Samui. Lucie at the age of twenty-one was just embarking on her party years. Why not make loads of money at the same time?

But was it dangerous? Did you really get paid all that money and not have to do anything sexual? Apparently not – so Lucie had heard anyway. The literature around hostessing – novels and academic books – was enough to make it seem like Lucie would be an esteemed player in an ancient tradition rather than some kind of sex-worker. The exquisite image of the geisha rather than the grounded flight attendant fluttered round the whole business. If you were a reasonably attractive Western woman, you could make big money just drinking and talking – you didn't even have to speak Japanese. You would need 'conversational skills' and a 'bubbly personality', but Lucie had both of those – she'd shown that working the aisles with boring old British Airways. Now she'd be earning five times as much, just sitting and talking in a bar. She was made for it. So was Louise. What could possibly go wrong?

CHAPTER 2

When Lucie told her father about her plans to work as a Tokyo bar hostess, 'she certainly didn't say to me: "Hey, Dad, I'm going out to Japan to work on the fringes of the sex industry",' so Tim Blackman recalled. But that is precisely where she was headed, to try her hand at the nicer end of what was sometimes quaintly called *mizu shobai* (the 'water trade') – the night-time entertainment business involving female company and alcohol in varying degrees. But that harmless-sounding phrase had long ago been supplanted by the tougher label, *fuzoku*, encompassing every variation of paid-for carnality.

The word was derived from the 'Public Morals Business Laws', or *fuzoku eigyoho*, which passed into Japanese law over fifty years earlier and were still in force. They were originally enacted to try to keep prostitutes out of dance halls. Things had moved on a long way since then.

Lucie and Louise had done some research. But the exquisite differentiations between what was selling sex in Japan and what was not were far more complex than a magazine article or recruitment advert in an expat freesheet could possibly explain. You could only find out, it seemed, by actually doing it.

All jobs in the water trade involved drinking and sex in some form. But the higher the class of the operation the less actual sex there was – that's how it seemed to work. And once you were on the scene, there were all sorts of local distinctions as to what was expected, depending on where you were working. Roppongi was not Akasaka which was not Ginza which was certainly not Kabuki-cho – the prime red-light district of the capital.

There were all sorts of girls working the *fuzoku* business: Brazilians, Filipinas, Thais, Chinese, Colombians, Russians, Ukrainians, Romanians. But in fact the majority were Japanese. An unashamed gaijin sex tourist had this to say not long after Lucie's arrival on a (very) informed website about J-girls who charged for sexual services: '[They are] above the legal age, they are not starving, they are not addicted to hard drugs and most do not seem to have been forced into this line of business. A lot of girls are simply trying to earn spending money,' he said. 'I have met a lot of *fuzoku* girls who are attending universities, two-year women's colleges and special vocational schools. Therefore, a lot of *fuzoku* girls are fairly intelligent and culturally aware.'

A special slice of the trade seemed to be reserved for English-speakers – Aussies, Kiwis, Canadians, Americans and, presumably, Brits. Most of the girls were in their early twenties, although some were a lot older. They were a mix themselves: posh adventuresses, suburban rebels, emo-runaways, abuse-refugees, hard-core partiers, bored professionals and old-style hippies, the sort you were as likely to meet over again on the Kathmandu, Marrakesh, Goa, Phuket trail. Tokyo was just another stop on the circuit, but a special one, a place to boost the finances with a little light hostessing. It was horribly expensive just to live, but the trick was to keep some of what you earned in Japan back for later.

Lucie and Louise knew the kind of water traders they were going to be. Or they thought they did. There were these supposedly super-exclusive nightclubs where girls just had to listen to men's jokes, light their cigarettes and smile. The idea was to lure a rich catch into a fantasy love affair while the bill was discreetly settled on a corporate expense account.

That was not the same as *kayabajura* (cabaret clubs), where *kyabajos* (club girls) were expected to befriend whoever walked in and get their wallets opened pretty quick.

Slightly below that were the 'snack girls' who worked the *sunakku*, the more humble bars where cocktails were mixed and booze poured out as rapidly as the attentive female staff might manage. You could find these places dotted all over Japanese cities. Below that – well, there was a lot below that.

The writer Angela Carter went to Tokyo in the early seventies, leaving her husband to be a 'foreign hostess' – one of the very first. Aged thirty-two at the time, she seemed to have been rather good at it. Middle-aged Japanese men went weak at the knees at her very gaijin-ness. She went on to write a magazine article about her experiences, which was published almost a decade before Lucie was even born. It may have been ages ago, but her pioneering adventures were still relevant when it came to the big question. How far were you expected to go?

Carter described a typical evening in Butterfly, a classy establishment, all chandeliers and pale wood, in Ginza, Tokyo's swishest district:

One customer's English was limited to the single word 'masturbation', which he pronounced very frequently and with a singular relish. Another raptly muttered the phrase, 'sexual intercourse', over and over again . . . while another grasped my thighs quite unexpectedly and then announced: 'I want you tonight.'

26

It is no good turning wrathfully on the poor things and crying: 'What do you think I am? A prostitute?' They know you aren't a prostitute.

That is how it was meant to be, in 1972 anyway. And that is how it was still meant to be almost thirty years later when Lucie and Louise bought their air tickets for Japan. But what about the *men* – the clients they were supposed to entertain, the ones who somehow *knew* you weren't a prostitute?

There was a general received wisdom passed on from girls who were veterans of the hostessing scene after just a few months. Any female flight attendant could recognise that the Japanese man liked to be treated as a pampered little boy. It could be explained quite easily – at home the wife was in charge. He gave her his salary and she gave him money with which to go out and have fun in the evening – with hostesses, more likely than not. It was all understood. Between them, the women made sure he was taken care of from morning to night.

But only fantasy women were allowed in the night-time world. They had to be players in a myriad individual fantasies. Lucie was intending to be one of them. Did she have the slightest idea what she was really going into?

On 3 May 2000, Lucie slept fitfully in her bedroom at home in Argyle Road, Sevenoaks. She had already stripped the room as if she wanted the break to be absolute this time. Posters were taken off the walls, books and cuddly toys packed away. Every record of her childhood and teenage years she'd ever kept had been thrown out or banished to the loft, it seemed. Her mother fretted. Are you sure you're going to be all right? Are you sure it's safe? The more Jane fussed, the more determined Lucie was to go.

Jane Blackman had written off to get a gas-powered rape alarm from the Suzy Lamplugh Trust (which had been established by a mourning mother who had lost her daughter to a mysterious attacker). She put a card with guardian angels on it in her daughter's handbag and scattered New-Age healing crystals in her luggage just to be on the safe side. Lucie shrugged. That's how Mum was.

In the early hours Sophie climbed into bed with Lucie for a sisterly cuddle. She'd intended to give her a good luck card, but instead it had turned into a sixteen-page letter to be read on the plane. Lucie was as reassuring as she could be in return. Of course she'd be OK, she'd ring or e-mail every day; or so she promised.

It was the middle of the night when the minicab arrived to take Lucie to Heathrow, a journey she'd so often made before to set out across the world. Only now she was a paying customer, and so was Louise Phillips. They found it funny that their previous employer's bitter rival, Virgin Atlantic, would be getting their business.

It was 4 May 2000, a Thursday. London was electing its mayor. The new euro currency was in some sort of trouble and Coldplay were the chart sensation. It was goodbye to all that. But they'd bought return tickets, so it wasn't goodbye for ever.

The Virgin Atlantic Boeing 747 was packed, economy class full of eager young people – British, Japanese, Aussies. Lucie and Louise were being waited on for a change. The in-flight movies were that spring's hits: *Erin Brockovich*, *Gladiator*, and *The Beach*, 'a story about backpackers whacked out in Thailand'. That would be popular on this flight. This was going to be fun.

CHAPTER 3

Eight Years Earlier

Safe, safe, safe. That was the message about hostessing in Tokyo. It had been for years, since the first suburban adventuresses set out for the Japanese capital in the crazy bubble years. A girl could make enough money in three months to spend on seeing the rest of the world, or at least a big chunk of Asia, in another nine. Young Australians especially had blazed this trail as part of the post-hippy, no-worries, global travelling culture.

In 1987 a young, Liverpool-born English guy was setting off in the other direction. Aged twenty-two, he had gone travelling after school in 1984 to have as much fun and adventure as he could before his inner conformist won out (he would end up being a lawyer). His destination was Australia.

He met a beautiful girl in Sydney. Her name was Carita Ridgway and she had grown up with her older sister, Samantha, in Perth, Western Australia. As Robert would tell their story: 'We shared a large house with other back-packers. Within a few weeks of meeting we were sharing a room. We lived together in Sydney until late 1988 when Carita went to Japan for the first time with her friend Linda. They planned to be there for about three months, working as hostesses.'

It was the crazy, tottering height of the economic boom and times could not have been better for an attractive girl in her late teens looking to make money in Japan. Robert stayed in Australia, but he met up again with Carita in Hong Kong and their freewheeling love affair resumed. They criss-crossed the globe (spending new year in his native Liverpool), via California and Mexico, then went back to Sydney where Samantha came to live with them in 'a big house in Clovelly overlooking Coogee Bay'.

Robert went to college in Sydney to do his university entrance exams while Carita worked in a restaurant and took acting classes in the city. In early 1990 she and Linda returned to Japan for a second three-month stint as host-esses. She'd got a 'working holiday' visa so things were sort of legal (working in nightclubs was disbarred from the working-holiday programme that had begun as an Australian-only thing – but the police never checked). In 1991 Carita and Robert spent the summer together on Ko Samui in Thailand. Back then, the island was still the kind of place where backpackers partied till dawn on the beach. Conditions were primitive but both of them stayed remarkably healthy.

Samantha, meanwhile, had also left for Tokyo with the same working holiday stamp from the Japanese consulate in her passport, but not to work as a hostess. She had gone as that other gaijin-girl staple, an English teacher (for which that type of visa was specifically designed) and to be with her Japanese boyfriend, Hideki Toyama, whom she had first met while working as a hostess in a Japanese bar in Sydney where Hideki was head waiter.

In early December 1991, Carita flew in to Tokyo from Sydney to join her sister. They shared a double room at the Friendship House in Kichijogi, a gaijin hostel for teachers in Tokyo's western suburbs. There were eighteen young men and women staying there of all nationalities, most of them working for the big English-language school, Nova.

On this, her third stay in the city, Carita was looking for a teaching job, but the Japanese bubble was deflating rapidly and teaching jobs were all of a sudden at a premium. While Carita searched for work, Samantha took time out to explore the city with her sister. Carita was getting worried.

The Tachikawa branch of Berlitz where Samantha worked was not hiring. Nor right now was Nova. But the water trade certainly was. There was a page of small ads wanting hostesses in the English-language *Japan Times*. Carita could take her pick.

She found a job pretty fast at Club Ayakoji in Ginza. She was on a working holiday visa again so that was all right. In Samantha's words: 'Carita was like a cross between Winona Ryder and Kate Moss – ultra-feminine and sweet-natured. Men just melted.' The mama-san (den mother) took her on sight. Older and more experienced, she did well this third time round. Pretty soon she was going out on *dohans*, a kind of paid-for date where the customer took a girl out to dinner before bringing her back to the club. That was the way to make real money.

On the morning of Friday 14 February 1992, Samantha left the house in Kichijogi and went to work at the Tachikawa Berlitz. Carita went out early in the evening, heading as usual by subway for the Ayakoji club in Ginza. Samantha went straight from the language school quite late on the Friday evening to Hideki's house where, as she would recall: 'It was Valentine's Day and should have been a romantic evening. But instead we spent a lot of time arguing and trying to decide whether or not to stay together. I just couldn't see myself as an obedient Japanese wife.'

The tempests raged through Saturday night and on until Sunday morning, when she went back to the hostel, expecting to see her sister there. Instead, one of the housemates, an Italian girl called Santa Mautone, gave her the news that someone had rung and left a message for her. Samantha recalled its contents and how she felt when it was relayed:

'"Your sister, Carita, has gone away with friends." It was a man's voice, quite old sounding, no one [that Santa Mautone] recognised.

'Carita had only arrived in Tokyo eight weeks before. She didn't know anyone well enough to "stay" with them. Who were these mysterious friends? And how had whoever left the message got my name and telephone number? I felt very alarmed.'

Samantha spent the rest of the day in a state of increasing anxiety. The evening came and went with no word from her sister. 'By now I felt very worried indeed,' she recalled. 'After a sleepless night, I started getting ready for work, only to be interrupted at nine o'clock by a call from a nurse at the Hideshima Hospital saying: "Your sister has been admitted to hospital suffering from severe food poisoning. Can you come immediately?"'

Samantha scrambled to get to the Kichijogi Emergency Hospital – part of the vast Hideshima Hospital in Mushashino City. Nursing staff told her in broken English what seemed to have happened. The story was garbled, bizarre, like a mad thriller plot. She was told that a Japanese man had dropped her sister off in the early hours of the morning, saying that she had eaten 'bad shellfish'. Yes, he had left his name. It was Akira Nishida. He had then left without giving any further details, but had at least given Samantha's name and phone number to the hospital. That is how they had been able to ring her. How had he got that information? Who was this man? Who was Akira Nishida?

But then such questions were irrelevant. She had to see Carita – whatever state she was in. 'The doctor warned me that he had given Carita a painkiller that would make it difficult for her to speak,' Samantha recalled. 'The doctors did not want me to see her. I had to insist. But nothing prepared me for the shock of seeing how ill she looked. I kept asking her "Who is Nishida? Who is Nishida?" But she was so drowsy she couldn't answer.'

Within a few hours Carita lost consciousness completely. The diagnosis was hepatitis and acute liver failure. Samantha recalled the terror of it all. 'As I went to the telephone to call my parents to fly out to Japan as fast as they could, the doctor told me: "We think your sister might be dying."'

Samantha rang Robert Finnigan, who was 'absolutely distraught'. The medical team asked her if Carita took drugs. Their questioning was brusque, as if that was what they expected of a young foreign woman. Her answer was an indignant 'No!'

The doctor said Carita may have drug-induced hepatitis D. She asked him, 'How is that possible?' But Dr Nishi shrugged. Then, 'They changed their diagnosis to hepatitis E, but had no idea how she may have contracted it,' Samantha recalled.

Surprisingly, Nishida rang the gaijin house several times that evening, asking after Carita in 'a soft-spoken and persuasive voice'. He said that 'he had taken Carita to Kamakura [a popular tourist destination south of Tokyo], and she had got food poisoning'. Samantha was furious. Carita had hepatitis, not food poisoning, she told him.

Nishida tried to defend himself with various excuses, and told her that he'd had his own doctor give Carita an 'anti-nausea' injection before he took her to the hospital.

Samantha demanded to know what had really happened. What had he done? Who the hell was he? 'But he obstinately refused to tell me anything,' she said. 'Although I reported his calls to the police immediately, they took no action to investigate. So I asked Hideki to try to find him.'

On 19 February, Annette Ridgway and Robert Finnigan arrived in Tokyo. All they could do at Hideshima Hospital was to huddle helplessly at Carita's bedside, while doctors struggled with blood plasma transfusions. Nigel Ridgway, Carita's father, arrived soon after.

The next day, Thursday 20 February, a doctor tested Carita's responses by pricking her feet. There was no reaction. She was in a deep coma. At about six o'clock that same evening, Nishida called the Friendship House, this time asking to speak to Carita's mother.

Samantha asked Annette to take the call, to try to arrange a meeting with this weird guy so they could at least find out more – where he lived, who he was. Her mother spoke to whoever was on the line as pleasantly as she could. A meeting was suggested. If they could just get him to show himself, make contact physically, they might find out what had really happened. Carita was in a coma. Finding out could save her life. The mysterious Nishida agreed to a meeting at Haneda Airport Hotel on Sunday night, 1 March, with just Annette and Nigel there. Samantha, Hideki and anybody else of the younger generation would be too angry to make sense of it all, he explained. He was a good judge of character.

The meeting was more than a week away. Carita might be dead by then. Was there anything more they could do? What about the police? The days passed in increasing anguish and frustration. In the intensive care unit, Carita flickered between life and death, her brain swelling as her liver progressively failed to function, as if ravaged by some toxic substance.

On the Wednesday, the family went to the Australian Embassy. A consular official contacted the Tokyo Metropolitan Police Department. Samantha and Hideki went to the station at Mushashino City to try to get some action. The police ignored what they had to say, and in turn made accusations against Samantha and Carita. Did she take drugs? Did she work as a hostess? Was she working while on a tourist visa? They clearly had a well-worn agenda whenever a gaijin girl got into some sort of trouble. The housemates at Kichijogi were never questioned; the Nishida calls were treated as the product of an hysterical hallucination.

But they were real enough. Nishida called several times over the next few days. Samantha tried to get his number, his address, anything to find him. She tried the police once again. They were not interested.

In one of Nishida's creepy calls, Samantha demanded that he call the police himself to say what had really happened. Amazingly, he did ring the police, but he gave the same false name, and told them that he was a friend of Carita, the girl now lying in Hideshima Hospital, and that he had taken her there in good faith. Nothing untoward had happened, no crime was committed. It was food poisoning. Bad shellfish; nothing more.

In the meantime, Carita's condition had worsened. Ten days after being admitted to hospital, she was transferred to Tokyo Women's Hospital in Shinjuku. But by Saturday, 29 February, just three days short of Carita's twenty-second birthday, the consultant finally told her parents: 'Your daughter is brain dead.' He asked them if they wanted to switch off her life-support machine. They couldn't decide – not yet.

That evening, Carita's parents went to the Club Ayakoji in Ginza to talk, if they could, to the mama-san about Carita and Mr Nishida. She agreed to meet them – but claimed to know nothing. That's what they all said. She gave them Carita's outstanding pay.

Then Nishida called Samantha again – this time at Hideki's apartment – offering one million yen to help pay for, as he said, 'the family's air fares from Australia and Carita's medical costs'.

'Although I was reluctant to accept anything from him, I did agree on condition that he deposit the money into my bank account. I thought this would be a way of forcing him to identify himself,' she recalled. But it didn't work out like that. He had carefully covered his tracks. This man, whoever he was, was clearly very clever at disguising his identity, at making calls and payments without leaving paper or electronic traces.

The next morning, a Sunday, the family returned to the

39

hospital. They had agreed it was right to withdraw life support, but Robert thought it appropriate that a sample of Carita's liver tissue be taken. Samantha recalled it in pin-sharp detail:

> Unable to speak for tears, my parents, Robert and I all hugged Carita, each of us touching one of her limbs until the doctors finally told us that she had died.
>
> We were asked to step out of the room for a while. The doctor took a liver sample for biopsy. When we came back, Carita had been dressed in a pink kimono and there were bouquets of flowers all over the bed. Her hair has been washed and a little make-up applied. She looked very beautiful.

Carita's body was taken to a Buddhist shrine in the building's basement. The intensive care staff all went to pay their respects; each one of them lit an incense stick. The candles burned all night as Annette and Nigel stayed with their daughter's body. There was no full-scale post mortem, no inquest – only the liver biopsy. 'On reflection, we realised that we should have insisted on an autopsy, but we were too overcome with grief and tiredness to think straight,' said Robert Finnigan.

The ordeal continued. Sunday evening came, and with it the hour of the promised meeting with Mr Nishida.

Hideki, who had accompanied Annette this far, thought that this man was some sort of criminal, certain that yakuza (organised criminals) were stalking the lobby and the rest of the hotel. Annette was convinced he would have some kind of heavy or bodyguard with him in the room.

In the event he was alone. The immaculately dressed man in early middle age made a vague reference to the yakuza before offering a rambling story about how Carita had become sick after eating oysters. 'He was sweating profusely and mopping his face with a handkerchief the whole time,' Annette Ridgway would later recall. 'I could not imagine for a moment that a young girl as lovely as my daughter could possibly have been with this man.'

Finally, he said to them: 'I loved your daughter and I wanted to spend much more time with her,' insisting that they accept a diamond necklace and ring that, so he said, he had planned to give Carita on her birthday. Then he disappeared.

Carita's body was cremated at 5 p.m. the next day, after which the family took a taxi back to Friendship House in Kichijogi. They all flew to Perth the next day, 3 March 1992. It would have been Carita's twenty-second birthday.

A Christian memorial service was held in Perth for all of Carita's family and friends. Her remains were laid to rest in the memorial gardens at Karakatta Cemetery.

The family had been promised the results of the liver

41

biopsy within a matter of days but they were never received. Was it ever even examined? It did not seem worth making a fuss. For now it was time for the family to mourn their loss and to bury all thoughts of how the police had shown what appeared to be a wilful reluctance to investigate how their dying daughter had been deposited at the emergency hospital like some piece of roadkill.

Nishida faded into memory like a bad dream. The police were not interested in finding him; they never had been. The case of the dead gaijin girl was closed. It was almost as if Carita Ridgway had never even existed.

For Samantha Ridgway, her boyfriend was that suddenly problematic thing: a Japanese male. Her relationship with Hideki Toyama ended. She went back to Australia. Her sister was dead – by some tragic mischance. All she might do was mourn.

CHAPTER 4

Louise Phillips and Lucie Blackman stepped off the Virgin Atlantic flight from London at Narita Airport on 4 May 2000. They navigated their entry into this new world with the confidence of former airline employees and knew exactly what to say. They were tourists here to see the sights of fabulous Japan. Of course they were. The immigration inspector looked dispassionately at the two young English women before wearily stamping each passport. They were in.

Telling lies had been part of the crazy plan from the moment Louise had first thought of it. There had been no discounted flight tickets courtesy of British Airways, nor was there an apartment in which to stay with Louise's 'aunt'. There never had been. Lucie had been more than economical with the truth in whatever she had told either of her estranged parents.

And nor would Lucie and Louise be working legally. Both of them were on tourist visas, like every other would-be gaijin bar queen. As Shannon, a Canadian and an established hostess at the club where Lucie would find work, explained:

> No one really cared and it was always a high turnover with new girls arriving every week. The trick was to do a visa run – usually a hop to Thailand – and then come back with a new permit to start all over again . . . after three months of partying you want a break anyway to regroup. After a few times going out and back you might get questioned at immigration as they knew what was going on; and the more you did it, the harder it was to get in and you might have been refused entry but that didn't happen often back then . . . Japan is a bizarre culture . . . it's like the dysfunctional functions and the illegal is a flexible legal.

Lucie was at the 'flexible legal' end of things. She needed money and quickly. But that really was not going to be a problem for long. As an English girl advised another eager ingenue at around the same time: 'You probably won't get much work and thus won't get money in your hand for a month but you will likely need a decent wardrobe – maybe you can borrow dresses.' Once you were in the door, though, the money would soon start to roll in. As a hostess explained:

How you get paid depends entirely on the club. Maybe every two weeks, maybe once a month, but weekly or fortnightly is more common. Expect an hourly salary of about three thousand yen [£15] – then you get money back when men buy you drinks (called 'drinkbacks'), money when you are asked for by name (called a 'request'), money when you have been on a date with a client (called a '*dohan*') and bring him into the club afterwards; there are loads of things like this.

Sometimes drinkbacks, etc, will be paid every night instead of with your wages. Wages are in cash because it is not a legal job.

Cash would have been handy for Lucie. Her credit card was already maxed out and Tokyo prices were jaw-dropping. But she and Louise found somewhere to rent pretty quickly, in a gaijin hostel, Yoyogi House at 4-17-2 Sendagaya. They'd be sharing a six-tatami room (six rush mats' worth of floor space – about ten square metres) in a two-storey block up an alleyway, sandwiched between the headquarters of the Japanese Communist Party Central

Committee and an electricity substation. They'd need a mobile phone, of course, but decided to rent one to share between the two of them.

Lucie and Louise paid thirty thousand yen a month for their Tokyo toehold with a communal kitchen and bathroom – a bargain by the city's standards. Even for seen-it-all Lucie it was a shock. Pay all this money and what do you get? The tiny amount of space you were expected to occupy was always a bit of a surprise for girls more used to leafy Bromley or the seaside suburbs of Sydney.

Still, many girls had come this way before, to wrestle with the rice steamer or get their long gaijin legs stuck under those low tables. There were no carpets, rugs or soft furnishings – just a futon to sleep on in a bare room – but Lucie soon began to appreciate the Japanese preference for minimalism as the summer heat and humidity began to rise.

Everything Lucie had ever heard or read about Tokyo, every cliché, seemed to be true. The city was vast, teeming, a megalopolis of forty million. The way people held themselves was different; their body language as they swooped and manoeuvred like huge flocks of starlings. Wherever you went there was the crowd. An intense, crackling energy drove the city day and night – on the streets and below it.

The subway was astonishing. What were they really thinking, all those salarymen and office ladies as they shuffled robotically around its underground labyrinths – the Kogals heading for Shibuya, the Loligoths, Bo' Peeps and myriad other fashion victims heading for Shibuya and Harajuku, and the young Japanese guys strutting round in leather jackets and dyed-orange hair like something out of an eighties disco.

And the Japanese grown-ups, if that's what they were – what did they think of the two young gaijin women whose height marked them out before anything else? On the subway, mostly, when space allowed, people read their comics or newspapers. But some people couldn't help staring at them fixedly. Were they being looked at in wonder or in contempt?

In her crash course in all things Japanese, Lucie had read of the conflict between *tatemae*, the public face of an individual, and *honne*, the real self of private thoughts and feelings that her hosts were so anxious to keep hidden. Hence the famous Japanese restraint and politeness, which made reading peoples' true intentions and understanding situations a bit difficult.

But right now just surviving was enough. 'We arrived in a shithouse, but slowly turned it into our home,' Lucie wrote in her diary. 'We have survived mass starvation and drunk any weight that dropped off right back on.'

Lucie and Louise headed for Roppongi. It was always

going to be Roppongi. Lucie knew all about it, or thought she did – Tokyo's entertainment district, the 'favourite haunt of young Japanese and expats out for a night on the tiles' as the guidebook oh-so-blandly put it. There was more to it than that, though.

Roppongi was a legend among BA cabin crew – or at least those with a few days off duty who might get into the city from Narita. Way out in the sticks, with its infamous 'truck' bar, a converted semi-trailer in one of the airport's vast car-parks, Narita was 'the best place on the planet for having fun after a long, long flight'. But the next-best place was Roppongi.

Roppongi was for hard-partiers not backpackers. It was always glittering, expensive, shiny. It had been for decades, caught in that weird cultural hinterland of America-worship with a uniquely Japanese twist. It had been the part of the city where the occupying US military had installed themselves after the war and had bloomed into a tacky Elvis-era strip of bars, restaurants and sex clubs.

The transformation had been kick-started by a former US Marine from New York named Nicholas Zappetti, who had come to Japan at the start of the Occupation and stayed around to work the black market and cut deals with the local villains. After a botched diamond robbery at the Imperial Hotel, he opened Japan's first pizza parlour – in Roppongi. According to his biographer, by the time he died in 1992, Zappetti 'was a frail and embittered old man who railed at all things Japanese, even telling American men visiting his restaurants to be sure not to marry their Japanese dates'.

Tokyo's reputation as a sleepless city began with Roppongi, where the bars and clubs had always stayed open late (the rest of the capital outside of Akasaka and Kabuki-cho was pretty snoozy until the seventies). When the great Japanese economic bubble really began to swell in the eighties, financial workers began to adopt a twenty-four-hour work culture into which some entertainment might be fitted in the early hours.

Now there was a McDonald's, a Subway, a TGI Friday, a Hard Rock Cafe – midtown USA meets midtown Tokyo with an elevated expressway cutting down the main drag.

Roppongi's clubs and bars, like everything else in the capital, followed the Japanese way of maximising all available space. There were thousands of these entertainment buildings all over the city, looking on the outside like prosaic offices, but for the cliffs of neon.

Each building might have fifty establishments inside – all dedicated in some way to the pursuit of pleasure. The big ones tended to be on ground or first floors or in basements, as a visitor from New York or London might expect, but there were plenty more perched one on top of the other, weird little karaoke 'boxes' and 'shot' bars, and something called 'image clubs' – the sort of places where only the real Roppongi aficionados might choose to go.

There were tales of dark happenings once you climbed those narrow stairs or rode in a lift the size of a kitchen cupboard to some waypoint within. A male gaijin visitor to Roppongi offered this handy guide on how to spend $4500 in a couple of hours in the shark-filled, high-rise reefs of the water trade:

Step one, he said, was to 'find some smiling black guys out on the street in sharp suits promoting their club'. Step two: 'Follow one of these nice guys to a place which usually has "gentlemen's" or "classy" in the name. It will be a small, dark, red, cramped room, with couch seating along the walls, no windows and the exit will be invisible.' Once in the door you could expect to find:

Hostesses: tired, half-dressed, Eastern European, Russian, African girls. No visas, no hope.
Staff: Nigerian, Ethiopian, Middle Eastern. More staff than customers.
Drinks: free for you, expensive for girls. Watch the wine and champagne.
No Japanese staff, no Japanese customers.

This gaijin guy's night out had begun to unravel when he was joined by a hostess – 'Princess' from Ethiopia. He ordered her a drink and when it came he was offered 'a free shot of a strange blue drink'. His advice on how to avoid his own big mistake is: 'Offer your girl the free shot. She won't accept it, she'll push it back to you. That's it, now you know you've got the drink with the date-rape drug in it.' He had, however, drunk it – then another, maybe a third. He could not remember how he got back to his hotel. Then he got the credit card statement.

OK, so every city has rip-off joints, and Tokyo had plenty. There was a name for them – *bottakuri*. But that was not the sort of place where Lucie and Louise were going to try to find work. And there was plenty more advice to be had – aimed not at would-be customers, but at the girls for whom they would be buying drinks. Not long after the two girls arrived, a well-informed Roppongi veteran posted this advice on a gaijin Internet forum for wannabe hostesses:

Each bar is gonna be a different story. Some have elegant girls some have trashy girls. Some are all-Japanese, some all-foreign, some mixed. Some are ridiculously expensive and others only mildly so. At some, girls will get fired if they date customers, whereas at others they might want a girl to do that now and then to ensure that a wealthy patron keeps coming back.

The hostess bar where one of my [male] friends works takes a lot of care to make sure the girls are safe.

51

The men that work there will wait with them outside for their ride to show up, walk them to their cars or drive them home themselves so that the girls don't have to go outside alone in their high heels and dresses (which are generally mid-to-long in length).

This not only means they don't have to walk around in the streets alone like that, but also, should a customer decide to try and wait for one to get off work and approach her, well, he'd have to think again. I've had a drink there a few times and the drunk-off-their-arse customers never seemed to do anything further than put an arm around a girl's shoulder.

Each bar was indeed a different story. Some establishments were discreet to the point of anonymity, their existence proclaimed by minimalist entrance-lobby plaques stacked up like credit cards in a bulging wallet. Others shrieked in neon of the excitements within and sent 'catchers' into the street to make sure customers knew it.

For all its neon-lit pretensions, Roppongi was not quite Las Vegas, but it was livelier than Sevenoaks on a Saturday night. During the go-go years the bubble babes had flocked to its clubs and bars – to the Velfarre, to the Kingyo with its transvestite cabaret, to the Lexington Queen or to Gas Panic, to Wall Street or to Geronimo's, the tiny first-floor bar near the central crossing where, on any night, investment bankers with English public-school accents would be drinking themselves into oblivion.

Roppongi was where gaijin men went, if not to find J-girls then to get smashed out of their heads. Roppongi was where J-men went to be entertained by gaijin girls and where Japanese women, who dressed up like schoolgirls tottering on stack heels, went to find gaijin boyfriends (who might, as a language teacher bemoaned, 'with some luck turn out be something other than the US Marines or English-language teachers who existed near the bottom of the sexual food chain, only just above Iranian telephone-card sellers'). But it was a much commented-on phenomenon that nerdy gaijin men could date stunning J-girls. Being a foreigner of any sort in Japan was like being famous.

Like almost everyone else, Lucie went to Roppongi to party. She wrote in her diary: 'We have drunk more alcohol in the last twenty days than I have ever consumed in my whole drinking lifetime. We have been on a neverending quest for . . . music (anything but Craig David), postcards and drugs!'

But they were there to get jobs, not just to get smashed. For a blonde girl from Sevenoaks speaking no Japanese whatsoever, finding work in Roppongi was not going to be a problem.

TOKYO HOSTESS

CHAPTER 5

By the start of the new millennium, the Japanese water trade's caste system of hostesses and snack girls was getting blurred. The country's economic recession was in its ninth turgid year. In response to a dwindling pot of salarymen's cash, the sex on offer had got cheaper – and dirtier.

When Lucie and Louise arrived, Tokyo was gripped by a new erotic sensation – strip bars and topless joints featuring 'Western' women, working not just as hostesses pouring drinks and making flirtatious conversation, but as exotic dancers. This was really something. American and European women dancing virtually naked would have been unthinkable just a few years before.

The new generation of strip clubs were in the same parts of town as the foreign hostess bars, often taking over the very same venues. New clubs were opening at the rate of about one a week. There was Dior in Shibuya, there were six Seventh Heavens scattered around Tokyo, there was Body Heat, Contact, Bachelor Party, two Maximuses in Yokohama, one J-Foxx and the most famous (or infamous) of all – One Eyed Jack in good old Roppongi.

There were those who mourned the dumping of the exquisite ritual of the simulated love affair in favour of something a lot more direct. As one habitué put it at the time: 'I'm not crazy about this whole gaijin stripper craze. I liked hostesses. You see, a hostess comes to Japan innocent and then has her heart broken. A stripper doesn't have a heart to break.'

The only rule for the customer at this new breed of club was to take what he could when he could, because who knew when the girl would move on to the next booth, straddling salarymen, pressing her breasts into flushed, drunken faces, grinding her buttocks into their groins.

But, in fact, it was all a big and very expensive tease. One Eyed Jack featured both strippers and hostesses. As a girl who worked there recalled: 'The stress at Jack's is on pleasure, but only on the surface – just as the dancers quickly drop their costumes, the hostesses are not positioned to be long-term companions. They are meant to look very good in the dim lighting of the club, but customers will get a closer look only in their imaginations. Not only will the men never get to have sex with these girls, they most likely won't even get to buy them dinner.'

One veteran Tokyo barfly lamented: 'That small hostess bar nicety, of meeting and greeting and pretending to be interested in more than sex, had been jettisoned. Here, you were greeted by a tuxedo-clad Nigerian who led you to a booth, took your drink order and asked you to pick out a girl. When she arrived, her top already open to disgorge a silicone-enhanced cleavage, she asked immediately if you would like a friction dance.'

Some of the new clubs had a production-line approach to hostessing, with girls 'rotating' every ten or fifteen minutes from table to table unless a premium was paid to keep them sitting and talking. And they consumed girls at an industrial rate. Scalphunters scoured gaijin houses to find the necessary. Female English-language teachers found themselves some ready cash on the side, as scouts scooped them up in the Arrivals lounge at Narita Airport or on the street. Huge cash bonuses were promised, plus cocaine, speed, whatever. Half-naked girls were shuttled through the night from club to club in panel vans to do their act. Girls were flown in by the planeload on cheap tickets from Toronto or Cleveland. On one famous day, 'two dozen midwestern strippers' arrived at Narita to be installed in a mansion in Gotanda (an otherwise perfectly respectable district of the capital).

An account by an American observer published a few

months before Lucie and Louise arrived in the city, described the scene:

They appeared, a vanquishing army of buxom amazons their first morning in that sleepy suburb of Tokyo as they made their way down in groups of twos and threes to the narrow shopping street that ran from the station. Blondes and brunettes, accustomed to travel and shacking up in less than luxurious accommodations, most of the girls had their hair tied back in ponytails and their sleepy, jet-lagged faces unadorned by make-up. Clad in sweatshirts and sweatpants that failed to obscure prominent busts and ample, muscular haunches, they sought coffee, cigarettes, croissants, orange juice, cold cream and tampons.

Gotanda gawked at these exotic new arrivals who in the morning rain failed to carry umbrellas and seemed to have no idea where they were going. To the foreign girls, whose profession was obvious perhaps only to the salarymen scurrying to buy newspapers and train tickets, even the simplest financial transaction, at the bakery, pharmacy or coffee shop, proved complex and laborious.

News travels fast in Tokyo, and the arrival of two dozen women ideally suited to the demands of topless and bottomless dancing did not go unremarked among the salarymen on their way to work that morning.

57

The same writer saw the 'Sindii Starrs, Dawns, Dixies and Renatas' at work – 'all big tits and shaved genitalia, thorough wax jobs and lacquered make-up'.

These were professionals, the best that the San Fernando Valley, capital of the US porn industry, had to offer. 'And they were here, in Tokyo,' he wrote, 'and they were the only ones who appeared to be cashing in on a downward economic spiral.'

Ah yes, the great Japanese slowdown – exulted over by (normally American or British) commentators who blamed ever more baroque sexual appetites on the drawn-out agony of a deflating economy. It had been so good for so long. For three decades, Japan's economic growth had been fantastic. Immigrant labour (much of it illegal) was sucked in to fuel the boom. That included women for sex – hundreds of thousands of them.

Then in 1990–91 the bubble burst. It took a couple of years of hissing rather than exploding in a climactic bang, but as company stock values and real estate prices tumbled, the great Japanese sex party was slower to stagger to a close. In fact the partying got harder as what would be a decade-long economic recession destroyed the certainties of the job-for-life salaryman and a new kind of emotional desperation kicked in. The new, hard, glossy clubs boomed. But even if Japanese tax laws still allowed entertaining to be written off as a business expense, everywhere the competition for clients' cash grew tougher. And the rewards greater.

It was the same in the *sunakkus* and hostess bars. The mama-sans got more demanding, the girls must hustle harder, they said. 'They tell you sit closer and closer to the men. They tell you to let them touch you a bit . . . and to go out on dates,' so a hostess told a reporter at the time.

Out on the streets the customer-pulling got more aggressive. Western women were no longer quite the knee-trembling novelty they might once have been back in the seventies when the first adventuresses blew into town, but still they were in big demand. Sexual appetites, meanwhile, were getting coarser.

A Japanese business magazine published in the early nineties explained it thus: 'In the flesh trade, deflation means that carnal desires are cheaper to satisfy, a fact that sparks growth. Cheaper services for workers on increasingly pinched wages have caused prices to plunge but overall revenues to rise. Part of this may be due to despair. Where people in other recession-ridden countries like Russia or Argentina are switching to hard liquor to console themselves, the Japanese are turning to sex.'

Not that they had not indulged frantically during the boom years – but, isolated from their family and anxious about the next round of corporate restructuring, those teeming hordes of salarymen put in more and more hours at the office. They deserved a little reward afterwards. The evenings would be filled by company leisure get-togethers or *tsukiai* – where faltering male self-respect would be revived by the fawning flattery of a beautiful young woman.

Not surprisingly, with a turf war raging to get gaijin girls into the revenue-earning firing line, there was a degree of crossover between the hostess clubs and the more blatantly sexual joints. The money could be fantastic. A friend of Lucie's explained:

> Sometimes girls moonlighted at strip clubs, like One Eyed Jack or Seventh Heaven. Here they would get 'kick-backs' from waiters for bringing in regulars from the Casablanca and encouraging them to buy drinks. There were always opportunities in Tokyo for making extra money, and since no one knew who you were, it was tempting to do things you maybe wouldn't have done at home.

Lucie's friend, for example, had found her first work in the city in casinos which, although they were illegal, were 'amazing – with the staff dressed in tuxedos, brass bar-rails, fountains and huge chandeliers, like something out of a Bond movie'. Gaijin girls greeting the customers and running the tables added to the glamour, even if these

miniature Monte Carlos really were as transient and illu-
sory as the film sets they emulated. She recalled:

> They spoiled us terribly, we lived in a huge apartment,
> vast by Tokyo standards, they took us on trips, to Onsen
> Park where they had hot springs, gold leaf sushi, amaz-
> ing food, geisha entertainment. They picked us up from
> home and drove us to work. A six-month life span is all
> that most casinos got. When I came back from the last
> visa run it had been busted and closed down.

The casino money had been 'great' but, as she described:

> The downside was that each time the casino got raided
> by the police, I'd have to find myself another job. I was
> usually helped in this by my boss, who I am certain was
> a member of the yakuza. Several of the men who
> worked for him had fingers missing and on one occasion
> I was forced to sit and eat my lunch while a man, who
> had been caught copying casino chips, was beaten up
> badly in an adjoining room. After the third casino I'd
> worked in closed down, I decided to get a job as a host-
> ess. It was then that I started at Casablanca.

So the sex business was an easier run than gambling. That
was the Japanese way. According to Lucie's friend, the

most blatantly full-on sexual clubs 'were those run by the Russians and the Eastern Europeans', who, by the time Lucie landed at Narita, were moving into the Tokyo sex trade big time – as just about everywhere else. The water trade was booming.

CHAPTER 6

Life at the gaijin house in Sendagaya was hardly glamorous – a mix of girlie party, permanent hangover and
cabin-crew hostel. Lucie and Louise spent the first few
days window-shopping in Shibuya and the nights bar-
crawling in Roppongi. They needed work. Whatever they
did, they were in this thing together. Just as they always
had been.

It was not difficult. The weekly freesheet for gaijin, *Tokyo
Classified*, was full of ads: 'Fun, exciting Club J F in
Roppongi,' for example, wanted '*genki* girls who can entertain
and like to enjoy themselves. Friendly staff and lively customers in a relaxed atmosphere. Y2500 an hour plus
drinkback and tips. Call. We're waiting. How can you resist?'
Well, they thought, they might resist that one.

Club Climax was looking for 'female dancers, hostesses, scouts, etc. Proper visa required.' That was a problem.

So how about 'Casablanca, now hiring Western hostesses. Very nice and friendly atmosphere Y3000–6000 per hour plus bonus. Great business clientele.' No mention of visas there – and they were offering good money. Casablanca was the place. Plenty of other girls said the same.

It was early evening. The girls had glammed up and were tottering up the narrow staircase in high heels before taking the lift to the top of the narrow building just off the Roppongi main drag to the club's entrance with its tuxedoed doorman. He let them in without a word. The manager, Tetsuo Nishi, eyed them professionally. These two were cool, exuding an air of having seen it all. He'd encountered this type many times before. What did they really know? But they might learn quickly enough. Neither Lucie nor Louise had work visas but what did that matter – they'd be gone in three months. Mama-san nodded her assent. They were hired.

The girls had struck lucky with Casablanca. It was one of the most popular (with Japanese men) clubs featuring foreign hostesses. The place was comparatively small, done up like an over-upholstered living room with black leather couches and dinky little tables, each just big enough for a bottle of whisky, a bottle of soda water and an ice bucket –

with the obligatory karaoke system parked in one corner. A girl who was working at the club when Lucie and Louise first showed up remembered it all clearly:

Back then it was all so bizarre, and so funny – that strange room up on the sixth floor, Ricky, the Filipino entertainer launching into a desperate chorus of 'Do the Locomotion', while we sat laughing in the Doggy Box, a low sofa over by the bar where we girls sat waiting for the men to pick us while they simultaneously ordered their sushi or mini pizzas.

But we were all there for one another, whatever happened. We'd talk for hours about boys, clothes, make-up and just the sheer oddness of it all.

All the management told me when I first started there was to 'create a party atmosphere'.

Which is just what Lucie and Louise were told. Make like it's a big party. They were getting used to that. The other Casablanca girls eyed the new arrivals with a certain suspicion. How long before they got to the top of the pile? 'New girls always stand out and were very popular with the customers,' recalled Lucie's friend. 'I chatted to Louise first, who seemed very relaxed and kind of in charge of herself. Then later in the evening she brought Lucie over. She was a very different type to Louise. She struck me as defensive, but at the same time very competitive.' She would need to be.

Lucie began on the nursery slopes of club work, as a *kyaku-hiki* ('customer-puller'), joining the other new girls as they handed out garish flyers in the streets, snuggling up to every drunk man walking by, trying to get him through the door with the strength of her bubbly personality. Lucie hated it. 'I'm never doing that again,' she told Louise. 'I feel like a prostitute standing on the corner, going: "Come to Casablanca. Have fun time."' But that's what they all did.

After a few days of this, she was pulled inside by the mama-san for the real thing. Was she going to have a hostess name? Some girls called themselves things like 'Passion' or 'Flame'. She'd stick with Lucie. It would be printed on a business card. Till then it would have to be handwritten on the Casablanca's own, along with her personal mobile number (she'd certainly have to get one of those) and e-mail address. Customers expected that.

By 7.30 p.m. Lucie must be in her seat with the other girls in the Doggy Box. Most clubs, and Casablanca was no exception, used a time-card system to ensure production line efficiency. No smoking or drinking, although conversation with the other girls was permitted and the really keen ones (there were not many of those) were allowed to read Japanese language primers while they waited for the action to begin.

There were plenty of dos and don'ts to learn. While at a table with customers, hostesses were not allowed 'private conversation'; indeed chatting in any language besides Japanese or English was forbidden. Make a mistake, break something, turn up late, and you'd be fined. Things like habitual leg-crossing (considered especially vulgar) could get you fired.

Getting paid to dress up, drink, feel special for a few hours – the hostess life might have seemed like the average girl's dream of stardom. But in fact, the arbitrary encounters with total strangers, all that dolling-up, then hours of hanging around and the whole day-for-night routine made it very much like being a flight attendant. Except the pay was five times as much. After a few days of it, Lucie e-mailed her sister to tell her that working in the club was 'like being an air hostess without the altitude'.

A resourceful journalist from *Time* magazine visited the club not long after Lucie's time there. Late on a Friday night he found an elderly Japanese 'giving a sick-dog rendition of John Lennon's "Imagine"' in the karaoke corner, while 'beside him a young blonde girl wearing a ruffly white dress smiles happily, her hands poised, ready to clap when her companion finishes his song'. At another table, a man wearing a custard yellow pullover and golf pants was flanked 'by two big-boned Nordic women. In halting English, he regales them with tales of how much he spent on a recent business trip. "Very much expensive" he repeats, as they dutifully nod.' On the other side of the room 'a powerfully built man in his thirties displaying the latest in Tokyo gangster style with his buzz cut and loud, metallic-coloured tracksuit sprawls on a couch, sleeping. A young blonde sits by his side staring into space.'

Casablanca *was* tacky, with its sozzled manager and Ricky's singing. Actually he wasn't too bad, considering he did five sets a night, six days a week. He didn't do much modern stuff as the older Japanese were not keen – even if the girls thought his cheesy old stuff was pretty rubbish. 'The clients liked him and always clapped,' according to a Casablanca girl. 'I liked him – he was the nicest person there.'

In fact, Casablanca and its exotic inhabitants was one of the most above-board establishments in Roppongi. For the most part, it treated its girls well. There were places, it was said, where girls had their passports taken off them, where their pay was docked for putting on weight, where coke and methamphetamine were relentlessly pushed as surefire ways of staying slim.

Casablanca's regime seemed more relaxed. The club's manager, Tetsuo Nishi, was 'a heavy drinker, an unhappy man who occasionally became aggressive and relied on Tahara, the head waiter, to do most of the day-to-day running of the club,' Lucie's friend alleged. 'The mama-san,

68

although she was meant to be there to look after the girls, in practice did nothing but sit, drink and chat with the customers.'

Every such establishment had its mama-san, more often than not an ex-hostess herself. There were mama-sans from China, Africa, Russia, Brazil – all over. Once past the age of thirty, twenty-five even, it was time for a hostess to start thinking about becoming one as a shrewd career move.

The mama-san understood the needs of men (although some might say she was almost as desexualised as her customers' wives) and what the girls in her charge had to do to satisfy them. A one-time hostess – a girl from Lancashire who had gone to Japan from university as a language teacher, but for whom the money in hostessing was too tempting, was told by the mama-san: 'Men are supreme . . . so you have to obey their every whim.'

'So we were as deferential as we could be,' she said. 'We were given all sorts of instructions about how to sit, how to hold ourselves. Poise was very important.' Mama-san was also meant to keep an eye on the girls' welfare, although at the Casablanca pastoral care seemed not to be a priority. 'But the club paid well and it was really Tahara who looked after us,' said a hostess who knew Lucie.

The Casablanca was in the same building as Seventh Heaven, Tokyo's largest strip club ('with over thirty gorgeous exotic dancers, the majority from America'), but that was something else altogether. Stripping was not expected of Lucie and Louise. Clothes were important, not bare flesh – a flash of cleavage or leg maybe, but not much more. Casablanca had its own rules on 'desirable and undesirable apparel', expressed in uncertain English:

> Skirts should either be a miniskirt or a long skirt. Shoes should cover the ankle and have heels with a minimum height of three centimetres or higher. T-shirts pant cardigans, sweaters and sandals are prohibited. Be aware of the dress code because violations will lead to a disallowable of work for that day (hint: party dresses are OK). If you have questions, ask a member of the staff or an experienced hostess.

There was this further sound advice from one such experienced girl for the newbies:

> Usually long dresses are what most girls wear; you will probably have to do something with your hair – if they don't insist that you have it done professionally every night (about five thousand yen) then you will have to make it look like you have made an effort anyway. The number of dresses depends on how many nights you are planning to work. Maybe start with four.

Then there was make-up – glossy, red Shu Uemura lipstick (not too dark, and nothing pale) and coloured eye-shadow (not too bright) – discreet earrings and blonde hair brushed out smooth, straight and long. There was a cramped dressing room which, at any time, a dozen or more girls would be trying to use at once in, as a hostess described it, 'a storm of flying bras, flashing compact mirrors and criss-crossing conversations in at least six languages'. Some girls preferred to do what they had to in changing rooms or washrooms of late-opening department stores on the way to the club.

Each hostess had her own standard survival kit. It was called the 'seven-pack' and contained lipstick, handkerchief, lighter, cigarettes (Marlboro Lights or a J-brand like Capri), memo pad, pen and mirror. Some added a shaver for their legs. The memo pad was important – Lucie would find out just why later.

Visible tattoos were a problem for a girl wanting a job. They were, so it was explained, a symbol of criminality or of being a prostitute. So was hair in a ponytail gathered in by a band or hairclip, but that was easier to fix than a tattoo. Hair held back from the face implied willingness to perform oral sex, and that was definitely not on a club hostess's job description. Not in this sort of club anyway.

Whatever Lucie might have said about not missing life as a permanently jet-lagged flight attendant, her new routine was as punishing as anything BA could have thrown at her. As one girl remembered,

> My nights (and days) as a hostess began to blur
> together: the hours of light banter and hard liquor, the
> clocking out at midnight and running to catch the last
> train (or being requested to stay late, which meant any-
> where from 2 to 6 a.m.) stopping at *kombini* or all-night
> convenience stores to load up on high-calorie snacks
> before making my way through the silent streets . . . to
> my six-mat room, sleeping until one or two in the after-
> noon, then heading to a café or aimlessly shopping.

And this was six days a week. Sundays they had off, most of the time. As it was explained by one English girl: 'The busiest days are on the twenty-fifth of the month, espe-cially if that falls on a Friday, because most people get paid on that day. The weekends can be a bit slow because most of the clients are married and have to spend time with their families, at least on Sundays . . . The main thing is to get enough rest. We only get two days off every month and with the Dracula-type hours it can be a bit tiring.'

But there were times when business was slow. There was an expression among experienced hostesses – '*ni-hachi gatsu*', meaning February and August, when the water trade for climatic reasons went still. February was too cold for salarymen to do anything but hurry home, while the heat and humidity of August made passions wilt.

But that was not all. They could also be working on weekends if they had a *dohan* (literally 'going with') – a ritual in which they went out with the customers in the evening to dinner or to play golf, perhaps.

To add to all of this, Japan in the first year of the new millennium was a dazzling digital playground of personal communications. The way the rest of the world said 'come back to my place' was still rooted in the Stone Age. But not in Tokyo. To be without a mobile phone was social suicide. And what were texts and e-mails but a new means of flirting? A hostess was expected to get out and hustle in cyberspace to get her customers coming back for more.

There were cute little chat-up lines to flatter Japanese men, at least those who understood English. It was part of the whole booming electronic sexual encounter phenomenon referred to in Japanese as *deai-kei saito* (dating sites) whereby things called 'telephone clubs' and 'two-shot dials' were ways for digital sex entrepreneurs to make money while staying within the law. What was dating and what was hooking? What was *dohan* and what was a compensated date? The distinctions were getting harder to draw. And every girl knew that there were customers who would pay for an evening of titillating flattery from a hostess, then go off to a prostitute for paid-for sex.

Lucie Jane Blackman never considered herself to be a prostitute. And she wasn't. But her tragedy was that it didn't matter what she thought she was. It was what one customer in particular judged her to be.

CHAPTER 7

Gaijin girls would naturally form little gangs based on nationality and language, as well as some instinctive sense of why they were doing it – often the difference between those girls who were there for fun and those who needed the money.

The fun-seekers came from privileged backgrounds in America or northern Europe, along with Israelis, Canadians and Australians all topping up their cash with a little bar work while on the global circuit. Learning the Japanese language was not a priority. There were some who were drawn by a restless curiosity or creative ambition and for whom hostessing was a way of subsidising their art. It was the old working-my-way-through-college-with-a-bit-of-waitressing-on-the side routine updated for glossier times. A girl from Canada who worked at Casablanca recalled:

It was like working at the UN there were so many nationalities – Vera Svechina for example was a cool photographer and artist from Russia who spoke Japanese. She was hostessing on the side to make ends meet as she established her art in Japan. Another girl, Angela, was a friend and she played violin and did hostessing on the side.

I tended to hang out with these kinds of girls who were in Tokyo for the long term. Once you get over the party-shopping-clubs-bars-drinking scene, you move on.

Some of the more recent arrivals in Tokyo, especially the Russian girls, who had started coming this way in the mid-nineties, were in the business for more mercenary reasons and longer term. It would be their career, or at least a way of piling up a load of cash to take home eventually. Speaking Japanese was a revenue-earning advantage. As an American one-time hostess explained:

I didn't understand how it was possible until I discovered that the Russian girls often had been hostesses in the suburban sticks until they had perfected their Nihongo [Japanese language], then moved to Tokyo to cash in. It gave them the competitive edge over native English speakers who were sometimes younger and prettier, but who would eventually return to their lives in London, Sydney or Chicago. They were in it for the long haul, and whatever that might entail.

The story of Vera Svechina was slightly different, in that she saw hostessing as a way of getting out into the big world to fulfil her ambition of being a photographer and film-maker. Her story, as she told it, begins with her childhood, mother a teacher, father an engineer. They lived in Obninsk, a shabby Soviet-era provincial city miles from anywhere whose inhabitants tended a nuclear research plant. In 1993, aged nineteen, Vera was looking for adventure as the world as she saw it on a post-Communist TV screen opened up like a miraculous box of capitalist delights. She was told by a friend that they could make huge money in Tokyo working in a bar.

She went to an 'audition' in Moscow held by 'New Russian businessmen' alongside a solitary Japanese. She was accepted and given a ticket to Narita Airport along with her friend. The plane was crowded. In her words, 'Shimidzu-san, the Japanese man we met in Russia, met us at the airport and took our passports, promising to give them back after three months of work. The other girls started to worry, but I didn't care. I was ready and open to new adventures and didn't plan to go back to the homeland sooner than six months anyway. We ate huge caramel-covered ice cream bars and got into a minivan.'

They arrived at a 'cute little club' in Roppongi where, 'as it was explained, our job was to talk with customers, mix them drinks, light up their cigarettes, stand by them when they came to the stage to sing karaoke and clap after they finished their song. All night we changed tables and were introduced to the customers. The Japanese men were very friendly. "What a cutie!" they would say to us in Japanese. "Oh! Russia! Moscow! Big breasts!"'

Actually, she was not from Moscow but a place a hundred kilometres south-west. And Lucie Blackman was from suburban Sevenoaks. No matter, they were both foreign and had blonde hair. They were just what the customers wanted.

An American hostess (a postgraduate student in English Literature at Berkeley who hit the Tokyo bar scene a few months before Lucie) recorded her experiences for the online magazine *Salon*. She landed a job at Verdor's, an exclusive club in Akasaka, which she had found, just like Lucie, by answering an ad in *Tokyo Classified*. As she recalled:

The girls were hand-picked to create an eclectic group of young women. At any given time, the club featured a dozen girls from around the world. While I was there we had a Brazilian samba dancer, a Lithuanian jazz singer, two British students, some part-time models from Canada and the US, an Australian artist preparing for her first international exhibition, a Romanian ex-engineer and a New Zealander who was opening a bar in Roppongi with one of her customers. Most could speak at least a little Japanese, a few were fluent, but a couple of girls spoke none at all.

Fortunately for them, many of the customers spoke English – enthusiastically if not correctly. In any case, not understanding Japanese can be a blessing, at times, particularly when the men begin to talk among themselves about matters better left to the imagination.

Japanese men loved being with these 'foreign girls', all wide-eyed attentiveness and breathy giggles. But even in the racial melting pot there was an implicit if unspoken racism. As one girl recalled: 'There were never any African-American hostesses hired, even though they sometimes would come in to apply . . . apparently Japanese men like mostly Caucasian gaijin for hostess clubs. In all my time and clubs there, never did I see a black hostess hired.'

Although they could have been conversing in their native tongue with beautiful Japanese girls who were just as eager to please, these men – loads of them – were here in the Casablanca, trying to understand the dirty jokes of some blonde from Leeds. Why? Why did they spend so much money on overpriced whisky and inane conversation? Why did they keep coming back for more?

There was no shortage of observers of the scene asking the same questions. All sorts of psychosexual and cultural reasons had been offered over the years. It seemed a uniquely Japanese phenomenon. These apparently gaijin-obsessed men for the most part were in their forties and fifties, but often considerably older. To these men, the girls were like something from imported American TV shows of the sixties – the perfect girlfriend or hi-honey-I'm-home wife who is always up for a drink or a flirt, who never scolds or criticises.

In the men's eyes, Filipina or Thai girls worked the water trade for money. So, presumably, did the Russians. And why else would a Japanese girl do it except that she needed the cash? (In fact, Japanese hostesses were paid marginally more than their American or British counterparts.) But from the customers' point of view, these freckle-faced fantasies from Sevenoaks or Seattle *chose* to do it. They were nice girls from good families. They must really, really like them.

And the illusion had to be protected. Sometimes a party of men would turn up with foreign business partners in tow to celebrate a deal. But it never seemed to work. The play acting was too obvious – ludicrous even – especially if the customer came from somewhere near home. One girl from Yorkshire, who had gone out to Japan as a teacher, but found the water-trade money too tempting, recalled how 'Western businessmen were sometimes brought into the club but they'd always be uncomfortable, however drunk they got – especially about white women having to play subservient to the Japanese, getting them towels, lighting every cigarette, doing the ultra-deferential bit. They'd look at the floor, not talk to you out of embarrassment. And what were we supposed to do with them? Go through our laugh-at-every-joke routine?'

In fact, the really upmarket clubs discreetly barred 'Western' customers altogether. In that, they were like the rougher end of the trade, the 'soaplands' and massage parlours where male gaijins were forcefully kept out. Some frustrated would-be customers protested about such blatant 'racism' but any such discrimination against anyone the management did not fancy was perfectly legal under Japanese law.

Many explanations have been offered for this eagerness to keep foreign men out. It might have been shame, a collective desire for secrecy – or a feeling that tainted outsiders would introduce disease or act outside the rules. Or was it just so obvious that the girls who were selling themselves were so desperate?

When an American expatriate made a very public fuss about being barred from a Japanese-only sex club, a proprietor told a newspaper that he needed to 'supervise' the foreign female dancers sent to him by an entertainment agency. 'Foreign customers and dancers can converse in English, and they may even get together outside the club and start a relationship,' he explained.

But did the smart executives and ageing playboys who routinely bought the company of blonde gaijin girls in hostess bars for a little ego-boosting flattery seek something else and pay for it just as readily? Of course they did. Sex, real sex, must be in it somewhere.

The American girl at Verdor's, the club in Akasaka, recalled that the biggest-spending customers stopped first at a traditional geisha establishment 'before coming to our place. I thought this testified to their cultured tastes.' But just how cultured were they really? 'One had enthroned my friend Sandra and me as his favourites . . . small, dapper and white-haired, he seemed harmless enough, even sweet, until he started propositioning me.

'"You can become my mistress, earn very good money in a short time," he told me. He repeatedly offered me twenty thousand dollars to sleep with him – a high figure, but not out of line with the sums that get thrown around in such places . . . But my final answer every time he broached the subject was no!'

Lucie heard such stories over and over again. She and Louise would laugh about them. But what would happen if it got real? How far would either of them go? Would Louise get the call and not Lucie? The whole club system ran on competition. Wasn't getting a big pay-off the whole point?

What would Lucie Blackman do in return, if asked often enough – if a customer offered her twenty thousand dollars? Would her answer always be no? For now, she'd have to navigate this exquisite distinction between paid-for sex and a fantasy love affair with the skill of a Hollywood actress. But the trouble was, she was a flight attendant from Sevenoaks.

CHAPTER 8

If a Japanese man wanted paid-for sex, there were much cheaper ways of getting it than at a hostess club. But just as everyone can agree that the Japanese are the world's most ingenious nation when it comes to packaging sexuality for commercial reward, it was also clear that Lucie's job selling fantasy love at Casablanca was a part of it.

While the Western girls worked the hostess clubs and the new wave of strip joints, such establishments represented only the more stylised end of a vast sex industry of staggering variety (not to say perversity) in which thousands of girls from less privileged backgrounds than Lucie Blackman toiled.

It could mean a blowjob in a soap parlour down by the railway tracks. It could mean a multimillion-yen night

spent in a platinum-plated hostess club in Ginza, or something marginally cheaper in Roppongi. It embraced the
huge adult video industry, print and Internet pornography . . . the sex business in Japan was big business.

The rougher end of Tokyo's sex trade was and remained
clustered around the Kabuki-cho district in Shinjuku with
its sticky alleyways full of ramshackle bars, yakitori chicken
joints and massage parlours. 'Piss Alley' squeezed between
the railway tracks was where old men clustered in tiny bars
to drink beer. It was always a *sakariba* ('lively place') for
salarymen looking for sex on their way to or from work,
conveniently located as it was near the sprawling Shinjuku
station used by two million people every working day.

If you were an attractive female – Japanese, gaijin, it
didn't matter – just going to Kabuki-cho was an invitation
for fast-talking touts to pounce on you. These young men,
known as *kyattchi* ('catchers'), with their mobile phones
and fancy hairdos, accosted young women on the street
and attempted to recruit them for club work or porn. It
was seen as a commercialised version of *nampa*, the art of
picking up a female stranger in the street.

Kabuki-cho was sleazy, but there were never many votes
for the politicians who every so often promised to clean it
up. Much of it had somehow survived Tokyo's multiple
property-boom makeovers. The yakuza, for the most part, kept
out of sight. The public face of the sex-trade 'management' was

a middle-aged mama-san, a Nigerian tout decked in gold-chained bling and baseball cap or a Japanese *chimpira* (meaning 'little prick') – petty criminals posing as gangsters with their permed hair. The police also kept their distance on the whole. Unless there was a stabbing or a shooting, which was very rare, official Japan watched the goings-on in Kabuki-cho from the shadows. But unofficially, corruption and pay-offs determined which clubs would stay or go, how long a casino might operate for and the timings of the occasional sweep when all of a sudden there was a clampdown on overstayed visas.

Lucie Blackman did not go to Kabuki-cho. She had no reason to. It may never have occurred to Lucie and her friends that they had anything in common with the girls from Mindanao and Bogota who did go there to find a different way of making money. It was where men went to buy the cheapest sex available. Everything was on the menu.

An English visitor to Tokyo who found himself by accident in a tiny Kabuki-cho bar (one of those places for Japanese customers only) at 2 a.m. recalled:

At each table, in the dimmest light imaginable, gun-toting women playfully forced their weapons down middle-aged men's throats while having their breasts fondled. On stage, a dancer gyrated over a large sheet of paper. 'Look no hands,' she gestured, revealing a perfectly-shaped Mount Fuji drawn in felt-tip to a bespectacled man. He rejoiced in the erotic masterpiece, and she thanked him by urinating into his glass. He dispatched the contents with satisfaction.

Despite all of this, no sexual monsters seemed to lurk there. No muggers or rapists clustered in its shadows. In fact, good old Kabuki-cho was as famously 'safe' as anywhere else in the capital. 'Girls going to the nightclubs in the centre of it all usually walk from Shinjuku station on the last train at 1 a.m., dressed in next to nothing, alone – and there is nothing to make them think to be especially careful,' said an online forum post about Kabuki-cho at the time. 'The equivalent districts in any other city, even a modestly dressed woman would be insane to walk alone,' he said. And he was absolutely right.

Lucie Blackman knew most of this before she decided to get on the plane to Narita. She knew she would be 'safe' in Tokyo, and had emphasised just that to her mother and sister from the very beginning. Of course there were the famous subway gropers and some of the porn was pretty weird – but that was just a laugh, wasn't it? What Lucie could not know was just how permeated Japanese society was by an eroticism which was both centuries old and rampantly modern. And often it was not quite clear which was which.

The travellers' tales and urban myths were all true. There really were vending machines dispensing school-girls' knickers (Lucie heard about them once she got to Tokyo, even if she'd yet to see one). There actually were magazines on sale in the convenience stores featuring ten-tacled monsters ravishing schoolgirls in tiny tartan kilts. There really were 'maid cafés' where waitresses dressed as cartoon characters tended customers. There were love hotels and image clubs. Bukkake, sex with eels, you name it, the Japanese did it.

As Lucie and Louise travelled to work on the subway or went shopping in Shibuya, in-your-face eroticism was everywhere – young women clip-clopping along on high heels, in plaid micro-skirts and loose white socks like schoolgirls, salarymen reading porn-manga on the subway without any evident embarrassment, *pink-chirashi* (post-cards advertising sexual services) stuffed in every domestic letterbox or floating round the pavement gutters, little packets of tissues being handed out on street corners with bizarre sexual come-ons on the wrappers.

If the Japanese liked to keep their inner feelings hidden (as people said), there was certainly no coyness about the desire for and the availability of sex. And it seemed to be aimed at kids. Everything was aimed at kids. Packets of condoms featured a cute cartoon monkey on their packag-ing. What was that about?

But at the time Lucie and Louise arrived in Tokyo, the nation was going through one of its episodic moral panics about sex – especially underage sex (although 'underage' was a loose term, the age of consent at the time being thirteen). In a way the Internet was to blame – it had alerted the rest of the world to the wilder excesses of the water trade and especially Japan's astonishing output of child pornography. American magazines and TV ran exposés, Interpol and UNICEF stepped in; the whole thing became an acute diplomatic embarrassment. But, shockingly, the nation's youth seemed to be offering themselves for sexual exploitation quite willingly.

The children of the nation's affluent, showered in wealth from the bubble years, were meanwhile going through the kind of cultural upheaval and 'age-gap' panic that their counterparts in America and Western Europe had experienced two decades earlier. Youth tribes had arisen, like the Kogals (young women who effected a pastiche schoolgirl-meets-hooker fashion style) or the Loligoths (a combination of pre-pubescent Lolitas and Transylvanian families who clustered round the Harakura district of Tokyo).

What really got things going was the phenomenon known as *enjo kosai* (variously translated as 'supportive relationship' and 'assisted dating') in which schoolgirl-hookers became a reality, or so it seemed. Teenage girls were dating older men for money.

It began in the early nineties with so-called 'telephone clubs', where girls' phone numbers were given out. Originally, a man could pay a fee and then wait in a room for a call from a young girl, then arrange to meet for an *enjo kosa*. But these clubs diversified rapidly in the age of mobile phones and the Internet with so-called 'two-shot dial' telephone cards that allowed men to call from anywhere and be connected with girls and young women.

An interested customer simply typed in a cash offer for 'dinner and sex', left a phone number or e-mail address, and waited for a reply. A computer did the actual match-making. It was all part of the *deai-kei saito* phenomenon. Nor was it just a means for miniskirted teenagers to make money to buy glossy brand-name goods. Housewives and office ladies started doing it too. It seemed to be legal.

When the schoolgirl-sex-for-sale issue first gained widespread public attention in the late nineties, there was a media frenzy in Japan and around the world. To many outside observers it was inconceivable that young, middle-class girls were apparently selling sex. And they did it willingly. How was such a thing possible?

Although it was far less prevalent than it was at first being hysterically reported, 75 per cent of schoolgirls in one Tokyo-based survey admitted to being solicited by older men. The thing that emerged was not that the girls were part of some new millennial wave of moral decay, but that they were doing it because they craved expensive designer clothes and make-up. They wanted the latest NTT DoCoMo mobile phone, adorned with Hello Kitty trinkets and sheathed in a fluffy Gucci case.

As one commentator wrote:

There seems generalised astonishment at the fact that these girls have so little regard for their bodies and their sexuality that they would sell them for such superficial gains. For the girls themselves however, the gains are far from superficial.

In a youth culture and media saturated with unattainable ideals and images that make self-esteem conditional and so hopelessly pinned to physical appearance, is *enjo kosai* any more extreme than young girls in the west with eating disorders?

Lucie Blackman was not selling herself for designer trinkets. But she was going into a business where self-worth was pinned to financial performance. How much money you made in a hostess bar depended on how many men asked for you. Lucie thought she was tough, but her self-esteem was as fragile as any other twenty-one-year-old's. It would take a pounding.

A little extra flattery, a little extra gift was not to be ignored. A handbag, jewellery, perfume. There was always something new in Japan, thought Lucie. Something with some amazing trick to it. Something that everyone simply had to have. Especially something like a mobile phone with a tiny camera that actually took pictures. They had such things here. Nobody in Sevenoaks had anything as cool as that. What did you have to do to get one?

CHAPTER 9

The Japanese appetite for paid-for sex, the cultural toler-ance shown across society towards prostitution (*baishun* in Japanese, which translates as 'selling youth') and an intense political reluctance to legally interfere have long been commented upon by outsiders.

Japanese men – ordinary men with families – thought that resorting to prostitutes was nothing special. Wives did not ask or seemed not to care. Or at least that was the pop-ular perception. Much more shaming for a heterosexual man than seeking sex outside marriage was being over the age of thirty and still single. There were stories of men being banned from visiting home by their ageing mothers because their unmarried status was a disgrace. A single man might be disbarred from promotion or even renting a flat – on the grounds he would be incapable of keeping it in any kind of order.

So being married was good. Having sex on the side was not all bad. Indeed it was where the Japanese talent for sensuality could be legitimately pursued.

Commentators who take the long view offer various theories as to why. Erotic and sexual themes had been a traditional part of Japanese culture for centuries, with none of the shame or religion-based sinful aspect associated with sex in the West.

A Japanese writer concluded in 1802 that half of Kyoto consisted of brothels. It was called *ukiyo*, 'the floating world', and the depiction of its inhabitants and distractions in woodblock prints became Europe's first real window on Japan.

A general licentiousness, if that is what is was, remained widespread even with the rapid modernisation of Japan in the second half of the nineteenth century, when some of the West's comparatively restrictive sexual mores were grafted on by a government anxious that the nation should not look uncivilised or backward. For example, nudity and mixed bathing were forbidden in public bathhouses – or at least those in cities. Homosexuality became much more generally stigmatised. As for depictions of sex in art and literature (and more basic forms of communication), the term 'obscenity' (*waisetsu*) appeared in the penal code for the first time in 1880 and a quarter of a century later a legal sanction of fines or imprisonment was given for those 'selling or distributing obscene materials'. Just what was obscene, however, remained ill-defined.

Actual prostitution meanwhile had been subject to some form of official control for centuries. Prostitutes and courtesans were licensed as *yujo*, 'pleasure women', and ranked according to an elaborate hierarchy, with so-called *oiran* at the top. They wore elaborate hairstyles and white make-up, but tied their *obi* (the sash worn with a kimono) at the front so that it might be untied easily.

The 'pleasure districts' were shut off and guarded. The prostitutes were not let out, except once a year to 'see the cherry blossom or to visit dying relatives', according to a history of the period.

There was another historical phenomenon, the so-called *Karayuki-san* (China-bound woman) who were the daughters of impoverished peasants who were driven into prostitution to work in Japanese-run brothels far overseas. A hundred years later when the bubble boom started sucking in girls from Thailand and the Philippines they were mockingly known by the derogatory term *Japayuki-san*, or 'Japan-bound woman'.

These women and their like were not geisha – the exquisitely mannered, doll-like women to whom hostesses were sometimes compared, being described as the modern version. Geisha were trained, according to one definition: 'To entertain their customer, be it by reciting verse, playing musical instruments or engaging in light conversation . . . [which] may include flirting with men and playful innuendos; however, clients know that nothing more can be expected.'

In that sense the hostess–geisha comparison was accurate. As it was explained further: 'In a social style that is uniquely Japanese, men are amused by the illusion of that which is never to be. Geisha do not engage in paid sex with clients.' It was also traditional for geisha to take a *danna*, or patron – an older man, sometimes married, who was wealthy enough to support their training. He did not expect, nor did he get, sex with his favoured one as a reward for his generosity.

But he would with a prostitute. Just as it was in nineteenth-century Chicago, Paris or London, prostitution in urban Japan was practised on an industrial scale. The closed Yoshiwara district of the capital was reckoned to hold over nine thousand women. Many of them had been sold to the brothels by their parents when as young as seven years old.

There are quaint photographs from the 1900s of dolled-up girls sitting behind wooden screens on the streets of Yoshiwara, waiting for dusk and the arrival of their customers. If a girl was lucky, she would become an apprentice

to a high-ranking courtesan. The girls were often only contracted to the brothel for about five to ten years, but debt
bondage kept them there for their entire lives.

The authorities had moved to regulate Yoshiwara and
sex-for-sale generally in the first years of the twentieth
century, but prostitution was never actually made illegal.
The place was levelled by the Great Kanto Earthquake of
1923.

Then came political ultra-nationalism and war, during
which domestic pornography production was banned outright while Japanese troops went on an infamous rampage
of gang-rape and enforced sex-slavery across Asia.

The United States forces occupying the defeated nation
imposed Western ideas of morality and law – conservative
in some ways and permissive in others. This new version of
East meets West was not *Madame Butterfly*, nor even *Miss
Saigon*. Something called the Recreation and Amusement
Association (organised jointly by the Tokyo police and the
capital's bar owners) provided thousands of girls as sex partners for the occupiers immediately after the first Allied
troops arrived in a devastated Tokyo in September 1945.

It was depicted as an act of selfless patriotism, to shield
the rest of Japan's women from sexual ravishing by the
conquerors. After a year of frenzied activity it was shut
down. Then the Korean War brought a renewed wave of
US dollars and sex-hungry soldiers across the Pacific. A

kind of wild decadence flourished into the fifties as the self-loathing Japanese abased themselves before all things American.

The sexual etiquette was difficult to navigate at first. 'A kiss is virtually equivalent to the sex act, and if a girl gives a kiss, she automatically gives permission for intercourse.' So a young US officer wrote in his private journal. 'In the traditional circles and villages, even if a girl gives a man her hand she grants permission for fucking.'

The so-called *pan-pan* girls, teenage amateur prostitutes who teemed in the bombed-out cities, were less coy. 'They are all highly motivated sexually, and go out for it in what can only be described as irrepressible girlish glee,' wrote the same soldier, a junior officer in his early twenties. He went on:

> They come out in the best dresses as soon as twilight falls, and compete with one another for the men, as if it were no different than picking up dates at the corner drug store in the States. What is behind the phenomenon is hard to say – something of the sort always existed in Japan. But the magnitude and garishness of the present situation is unheard of. In Shinjuku [district of Tokyo] alone there must be at least three thousand of these kids.

It all got wildly out of control. Huge sex factories sprang up before all brothels were declared off-limits to GIs. The *fuzoku* laws of 1947, which sought to regulate dance halls and the like, were enacted, bringing in with them the first moves to proscribe prostitution. To get round them, the former brothel keepers became 'special purveyors of beverages' and the girls 'waitresses' and things carried on pretty much as before.

Ironically, it was American women who pushed things further. They were the wives of occupation officials who had come to live in Japan (temporarily) and who were outraged at what they saw. There was enormous pressure for a law banning prostitution outright. Which is what happened.

The new legislation of 1956 made it illegal both to publicly solicit and to keep an establishment where *honban* (literally, the 'real thing', or penetrative vaginal sex) was on offer in exchange for money. But that was more or less it. *Honban* was not illegal if the deal was between the man and the woman, with no broker involved, and the girl was aged eighteen or over. But government-licensed prostitution was meanwhile officially at an end. From now on it would become the domain of the yakuza, and the number of (now illegal) prostitutes actually rose.

When Lucie hit town, all those long-ago arguments about *pan-pan* girls, public morality laws and what was prostitution were ancient history. Japan had enriched itself beyond imagination, and instead of GIs getting laid in

Shinjuku backstreets by *pan-pan* girls, now it was salary-men who bought the favours of wide-eyed blondes from England.

Hostesses could try to reassure their families in all honesty that they were not prostitutes, but what about the men whose cigarettes they lit and drinks they poured? What did they think they were? What other sexual services, other than a pretty gaijin girl laughing at their jokes, did they spend their money on? They bought sex – real sex, and on a mind-numbing scale.

A gaijin male sex-tourist in Roppongi wrote the following in a revealing blog about finding what he was looking for in Tokyo, around the time Lucie arrived in the city: Roppongi girls 'all say "massaji, massaji". You would think that by the way the whole situation is set up that there would be a lot more than a massage at stake. Take my word for it – don't go with these girls (unless you actually want a massage) . . . I have tried on a number of occasions, but the most you can score is a really expensive handjob.'

Much more like it was the sex supermarket beneath the Keihin Kyuko line at Koganecho station, Yokohama, forty minutes or so by train from Shinjuku, where 'mouth-watering girls in sexy attire lined up practically shoulder to shoulder, for several blocks on either side in the narrow pedestrian roads that run parallel with the tracks,' so the traveller discovered. Some two hundred and fifty *chon-no-ma* ('quickie joints') lit by pink neon lights were open for business twenty-four hours a day.

Most of the women at Koganecho were Taiwanese or mainland Chinese, so he found, plus some Russians and Colombians who were 'generally more well endowed that their Asian counterparts, but also more expensive'.

And gaijins were not barred from such places here. 'They stand outside their small drink bars and will either nod or say "*asoboyo?*" [Want to play?] to attract customers,' the visitor reported. 'Some speak English and may say, "Hello!" In any case, positive reaction from these women is a sure sign they are willing to play with a foreigner . . . There are some women who will have nothing to do with foreigners (they are the ones who avoid looking at you or return inside the bar and close the door as you pass).' For this customer, however, being a gaijin turned out to be no problem:

There were girls for every taste: short, tall, thin, plump, no boobs, big boobs, school uniforms, etc. The little doorways they stand in are the doors to these little fuck shacks; tiny buildings which seem to have been constructed for just this purpose.

The system is as follows: you go into the little doorway, they close the sliding door and take you to a tiny room with a futon on the floor and with the requisite supplies. She had a timer for twenty minutes.

Girls from all over Asia were brought to Japan during the bubble years to work in such places. Russians and eastern Europeans flooded in from the early nineties plus plenty of Latin Americans. Typically, they were flown in on so-called 'entertainer' visas, which were just that, then had their passports taken off them and were set to work in the sex industry to pay off the huge fee for being transported to Japan in the first place.

'How do you think Filipina and Russian women get into Japan?' asked an observer of the booming water trade not long after Louise and Lucie's arrival in Tokyo. 'Go to Otemachi Immigration Department at nine o'clock one morning and find the entertainer visa section. Look around you. The Japanese man with a fistful of passports and a group of around ten sexually charged women is a yakuza.'

The Japanese government would call it 'debt bondage'. Concerned welfare agencies did not hesitate to call such women 'sex slaves', but some of their more reflective clients (and some liberal politicians) thought they were doing something good with their money if a bit of it was sent home to some Manila or Taipei backstreet.

The profits for the traffickers were huge. A 1999 report estimated that a yakuza syndicate controlling ten Thai girls could make a billion yen in a year. Originally, control was in Japanese hands, but from the late eighties, Taiwanese steadily took over. The invasion gathered speed in the nineties, and Taiwanese or Chinese-run sex-trade establishments pushed out the Japanese, bringing Chinese organised-crime gangs with them. A big wave of Colombians followed.

The girls might be housed where they worked, in cramped, squalid conditions that were no better than those from which they were supposedly escaping. The luckier ones were lodged in apartments tucked into Tokyo's many crevices. But control over them remained absolute.

An American women's rescue charity tried to find out how an estimated 130,000 'show dancers' and 'singers' arrived in Japan each year fitted up with entertainer visas. The peak year was 2004: eighty thousand came from the Philippines alone. The corporation they investigated recruited 'foreign women to work at restaurants and clubs that cater to a Japanese male-only clientele. While their business license is for electronics, they are also registered with the Bureau of Immigration as a foreign entertainer recruiting company.'

Girls were promised four thousand dollars per month, investigators discovered. An agent in their home country was paid three thousand up-front and the company paid for the girls' air fares. What happened to them next went like this, according to Shared Hope International, a North American pressure group:

> The girls are told to arrive at a hotel in Roppongi. Afterwards, a facilitator transports them to an apartment and takes their passports 'for safekeeping.' When they arrive they are told that they will be performing sexual services. They are deceived into thinking they will work as high-class hostesses for rich business clients. The girls work a full shift at a sex parlour or as a prostitute and are paid a hundred dollars per day of which seventy-five is reclaimed by the handlers as 'fees'.

The water trade, in all its manifestations, flowed on.

CHAPTER 10

If paid-for, penetrative vaginal sex was technically illegal, everything else was allowed – anal, oral, handjobs, you name it. If you had the money you could buy it. And the result was a boom in bizarrely packaged live sex which reflected (in Western eyes anyway) the Japanese talent for both innovation and production-line efficiency.

There were 'lingerie pubs', 'take-out bars' and the ubiquitous 'soaplands' – all offering services that supposedly ended in the client's sexual fulfilment. It was called the 'ejaculation business'.

At the more basic end were the *ekimae sopu*, a kind of bath house literally located as the phrase implied, 'around train stations'. To dodge the law, soapland operators would claim their clients and their hired masseuses performed sex as couples who had grown fond of each other. Then there were the *nozoki beya*, 'peeping rooms', where strippers danced on a stage surrounded by small rooms in which the clients sat down, watched and masturbated. 'If you tip them enough, they put their hands into the little window to give you a handjob. The price is two thousand yen for fifteen minutes,' said a visitors' guide.

If time was of the essence, oral sex might be obtained at a 'pink salon' where, as the guide – produced for visiting football fans for the 2002 World Cup – explained: 'They take you to an empty booth and give you a service with hands and mouths. The cheapest one would be around two thousand yen.'

Or, 'if you are stuck in the hotel you can always call for *deriheru* or "delivery health", which "delivers" a woman to your place. They basically give you a blowjob or a handjob. The price is twelve thousand yen for forty minutes or more.'

There were 'fashion health clubs' which offered an attended shower, and a pricier variation called a 'mansion health club' where the 'action takes place in a relatively spacious condo or apartment'. A *nopan kissa* was a 'special kind of café where all the waitresses are almost naked. You are supposed to choose one and she takes you to a small room to give you a handjob or a blowjob. The price is three thousand yen (thirty minutes).' But no such physical contact was possible in a *shiru pabu* where naked women swam around in water tanks to be gazed upon by the excited clientele.

And still there were even darker fantasies than erotic fish-women that Japanese men could buy. A few months after Lucie and Louise began work at the Casablanca, a fire (it was supposed to have begun with a gas explosion in a mahjongg parlour) swept through a Kabuki-cho commercial block where numberless sex emporia were stacked, linked by lifts like an orgiastic department store. Forty-four people died in what was the city's worst post-war fire disaster, including twelve women in a fourth-floor club called Super Loose, where the speciality was lap dancers dressed as miniskirted schoolgirls.

That the dancers (they were Thais and Taiwanese) were dressed up as schoolgirls was no surprise, given the Japanese sexual obsession with 'underage' girls. As well as the assisted-date scene there was a whole industry – *burusera* – in which men collected not only schoolgirls' underwear but their socks and uniforms. The legendary vending machines may have been shut down in the nineties after a public outcry but not the *burusera* stores. In some of them customers (called *kagaseya*, or 'sniffers') were only allowed to browse the merchandise, but there were other establishments where the child prostitution laws (not introduced in any effective sense until 1999) were circumvented

107

by having the girls model underwear in a room next door while men watched through a one-way mirror.

If schoolgirls were not their thing, men could choose any number of *imekura* or 'image clubs', involving sexual role-play of a more extreme nature. These included encounters on crowded 'railway trains' (with sound effects) or in 'sexual-harassment clinics' (with girls dressed as nurses), in police interrogation cells or even with air hostesses.

Lucie would have laughed at that. A trip to Sky Heart, a 'sexy attraction pub' on one of Kabuki-cho's main streets, was not exactly like working the BA London–Manchester shuttle. The club's interior was decked out to look like an airline cabin – with economy, business and first-class seats – from which the paying customer could enjoy a selection of experiences, billed as 'high-jacking, panic and air-love times' among others. Passengers were advised to hold on tightly to a cabin attendant during air turbulence.

Where in the city the image clubs were clustered there were also 'love hotels', sex-trade establishments that also depended on erotic illusion. They were places where space could be rented by the hour to allow a couple to do what they wanted to do – a Japanese tradition, a necessity some might say, in a land where domestic space was limited and any kind of privacy hard to come by.

Money need not change hands between the participants

(apart from the hotel management – faceless hands accepting payment through a frosted-glass screen). In fact, many establishments actively barred prostitutes. The love hotel was a place to conduct an illicit affair or to rekindle marital passion with all the trappings of sexual 'play'. Some were plain and discreet, others had exteriors resembling castles, ocean liners or flying saucers, and special rooms decked out as clinics, schoolrooms or S&M dungeons.

Some observers of the love hotel phenomenon trace its origins and popularity to a much older tradition of surreptitious sex called *yobai* or 'night creeping'. This had long been a feature of rural Japan, whereby 'while a young woman slept, a silent intruder would creep into her room, slide behind her and make his intentions known. If she consented, they would have discreet sex until the early morning, when he would have to slip out of the house as stealthily as he had slipped in.' For added authenticity, the night creeper might wear a mask and urinate on the door hinges to stop them making a noise as he made his furtive entrance and exit.

The 1961 novella *'Nemureru Bijo'*, 'House of the Sleeping Beauties,' by the Nobel laureate Yasunari Kawabata, features *yobai* with a twist. An old man called Eguchi who finds himself no longer capable of physical sex seeks out a secret house where a beautiful naked woman, not yet twenty years old, is delivered to him. She has been drugged into deep unconsciousness – just how is not revealed.

'He was not to do anything in bad taste, the woman of the house warned old Eguchi. He was not to put his finger into the mouth of the sleeping girl, or try anything else of that sort,' wrote Kawabata. 'Some gentlemen seem to have good dreams when they come here,' the woman then tells the elderly client. 'Some say they remember what it was like when they were young.'

As Kawabata wrote: 'Because the girl would not awaken, the aged guests need not feel the shame of their years. They were quite free to indulge in unlimited dramas and memories of women. Was that not why they felt no hesitation at paying more [for a sleeping woman] than for women awake?'

The point of the transaction seems to be that the unconscious female should function as an aid to erotic memory and not as the fleshly equivalent of a blow-up rubber sex-doll.

Kawabata's story is not some ancient folk tale – its setting is mid-twentieth-century urban Japan. Eguchi returns to the house four times and each time the girl is different. Are they promiscuous? he asks. They are asleep, replies the woman, how can they be? They are all virgins and under these circumstances seem set to remain so. When Eguchi comes to understand that other men have 'slept' with the same girls in the same state, his anger is tempered when he realises 'of course that to take sleeping medicine regularly would only injure a girl's health'.

Sometimes the girls talk 'in their sleep' and he conducts a kind of conversation with one of them. At the end, girl number four will not respond and appears to be dead. He insists that she be brought back to consciousness but the madam tells him everything is as it should be. He departs into the night not knowing her fate.

Yobai had a 'respectable' cultural and literary tradition. The 'House of Sleeping Beauties' story has been filmed several times over by Japanese and European art-house and US porn directors. An off-Broadway play was produced and a ballet version staged in Japan.

The ballet's director and choreographer, Sakiko Oshima, explains that she was attracted to 'the strange form of eroticism in Kawabata's work [because] it made me think about what could cause the main character to wish for a relationship that was not sexual, but merely a desire to lie beside a sleeping young woman, who in that unconscious state was something close to a corpse'. Ms Oshima's previous (and critically acclaimed) work was a *burusera* version of *Swan Lake* in which schoolgirl-swans danced in an ever-expanding pool of discarded underpants.

Real-life *yobai* reportedly still happens in the more remote country areas of Japan, and there seems to be a wider nostalgia for the practice in towns and cities. There are clubs that offer special *yobai* services – providing prostitutes who pretended to be asleep while the client 'crept' up on them.

It goes like this: the customer peeps through a keyhole to see the girl fondling herself in an attempt to reach orgasm, but rather than moaning with pleasure she squeaks and mutters in frustration. With a final sigh, she puts on an eye mask and 'falls asleep'. The customer enters on all fours (essential, apparently, to the *yobai* 'play') and falls upon her. She never 'wakes up'. Everything is done to a sleeping form. 'It is really popular with our customers,' so a *yobai* image club owner told the *Shukan Jitsuwa* tabloid.

Yobai got the adult video treatment in a series called *Night Crawlers* in 1999. 'The series became our second most popular after *Female Pervert*,' a company spokesperson told a reporter from *Shukan Jitsuwa*. 'People find *yobai* exciting for its sheer depravity,' he added, 'since men today have such meek personalities, they are not aroused by the idea of violent rape. Rather, they are turned on by the idea of sneaking into a darkened room' – and having sex with an unconscious woman.

Image clubs, *yobai* and love hotels offer live versions of Japanese pornography – the fathomless perversity of which had long astonished outsiders. The laws of physical sex-for-sale were mirrored in its virtual counterpart in print and film. While depictions of genitalia, pubic hair and straight-forward intercourse were banned, almost everything else was allowed.

Once it was the case that so-called *pinku-eiga* ('pink movies') could only be viewed in special adult-only cinemas. But by the nineties, although the law still prohibited full intercourse from being shown, film-makers could depict anything else. Pornography production boomed while the obscenity laws began to be ever more feebly interpreted. Videos, personal computers, electronic games and the Internet revolutionised the means of production, distribution and consumption.

Makers of erotic 'art' movies found new freedom, even if they were soon to be overwhelmed by the tidal wave of porn. The veteran *pinku* protagonist Hisayasu Sato, for example, made a film in 1992 called *The Bedroom*. It begins with the main character, Kyoko, being ignored by her husband. After being rejected coldly, Kyoko returns (or goes for the first time – it is not precisely clear) to an exclusive sex-club referred to as The Sleeping Room, where all the young women use a drug called Halcion. The drug is both hallucinatory and numbs the senses, so that the women are unconscious when they are together with the men who act out fetishistic fantasies on their comatose bodies.

After a mysterious murder takes place at the club, Kyoko gets worried. Fantasies blur into reality, she discovers her detached husband is also on drugs and has violent sexual escapades of his own. Kyoko eventually stops taking Halcion so that she can watch what the club's clients are doing to her.

The movie scored an extra twist with the inclusion of Issei Sagawa in a cameo role as the enigmatic Mr Takano, 'who watches over the club'. When the film was made Issei Sagawa was Japan's 'celebrity cannibal' who, while studying in France, killed and then ate parts of a Dutch student in 1981. He was declared legally insane and deported back to Japan, where he spent fifteen months in a mental institution before walking free. Eventually, and perhaps inevitably, Sagawa produced an illustrated comic-book manga account of his gruesome exploits. 'My parents wouldn't let me read comics when I was young,' he told *Japan Today* newspaper when his book was published.

Sagawa was unusual in being a post-war Japanese male who was not a comic-book fan from childhood. The rise of manga and anime (film and television animation) for boys, girls and young adults was a national, cultural and uniquely Japanese phenomenon – with sexual elements entering the storylines in ever more bizarre and extreme ways as censorship faltered. It was sometimes called *hentai*, a word that has a negative connotation to the Japanese, as it is commonly used to mean 'sexually perverted'. Manga-porn, sexed-up comic books read with no apparent embarrassment by salarymen on the subway on their way to work, blurred the already indistinct cultural lines between child and adult.

Multiple pornographic subcultures, already bubbling semi-underground, burst into the open in the early nineties especially as adult video and *hentai*. They still have the power to astonish today. Take 'broken dolls', for example, a sub-genre of the already popular medical fetish in which young girls are sexually dominated in hospital beds, covered in casts, splints, gauze and fake bruises, and which usually involved rape and forced bondage. Or 'hammock fetish', where a man keeps a woman captive in a semi-transparent hammock suspended from the ceiling like some giant insect's cocoon. 'When he wants sex, he just cuts a hole in the hammock and goes at it. At all the times the woman is effectively faceless and limbless,' says an online dictionary of Japanese eroticism.

Then there's *goukan pure* ('rape play'), of which the most notorious example was an adult video called *Stalker*, which contains images of a woman going to work on the subway, coming home, being photographed through her window and then being violently raped.

While you might think that such extreme and graphic narratives would inspire real-life imitators, the incidence of actual rape remained historically lower in Japan than in equivalent developed societies. As indicated in academic surveys, it declined markedly in the nineties, just as porn became increasingly available and in ever harder-core variations.

Old-fashioned subway gropers accounted for most sex misdemeanour violations, according to official figures, but many of the cases brought to court now involved covert photos being taken up women's skirts (the first photo-capable mobile phones went on sale in Japan in 1999). A law was duly passed that mobile phone cameras must make an audible sound like that of a lens shutter clicking when used.

Some liberal commentators saw the porn boom as being directly responsible for a declining incidence of rape. The potential for sexual violence was sublimated in fantasy, they argued. As the English writer and Japan-watcher Lesley Downer put it: 'The Japanese attitude is that these [fantasies] remain in the world of the imagination and are therefore not a threat. If the imagination is free to roam, people do not feel the need to actually act out dark desires. There is a clear demarcation between fantasy and reality that doesn't usually get crossed. Tragedies occur in the rare instances when an individual doesn't understand that demarcation line.'

Others attributed it to internal restraint and self-discipline – part of the Japanese national character. But whatever the reason, it did seem to be true: the rate of sex crime was falling. A feminist advocate expressed the paradox thus: 'Japan has perhaps the most violent pornography on the planet; it has almost nothing to do with sex and a great deal to do with violence. Yet Japan reports one of the lowest sex crime rates in the world. Reporting of sex crime rates in Japan decreased in the eighties when one would have expected, with the emergence of feminism in Japan, reporting of sex crimes to have increased.' As this commentator realised, low incidence of sex crime can, of course, be the result of the reticence of the victim or a cultural taboo to tell her family or report it to the authorities.

Rape investigation units sensitive to women's issues were established in the nineties, when the police started public-awareness campaigns to encourage victims to come forward, and an internal attitude-adjustment campaign to persuade officers not to treat victims as if they were in some way to blame.

Safe, safe, safe. That was the message that Lucie and Louise had been given both before and after their arrival in the city. Even Kabuki-cho was safe. Low crime, safe streets. Public drunkenness was commonplace but was very rarely violent. There were plenty of law-enforcement patrols and *kobans* – miniature police stations on the main streets – but the cops were not in the business of making a real hassle over visas or work permits.

There were rumours, though, urban myths about girls

who had got it wrong somehow, taken too many drugs, couldn't handle the drink, tangled with the wrong guy. There were girls who had left without ever saying good-bye, slipping back on to the backpacker circuit or going home to Mum and Dad. Others went to Seoul or Bangkok to pull off the visa-renewal trick – then, for some reason, decided they had had enough of Tokyo. With the slump showing no sign of ending, some of the fairweather gaijins left town. But there were always more flying in to Narita. Like Lucie and Louise, they had not only come in search of supposedly easy money, but wanted to go to the big Tokyo party before it ended.

It never ended.

CHAPTER 11

Lucie and Louise had been hired. They set off for work at the Casablanca. The few days' trial, 'catching' in the street, had been passed. They were big girls now.

And they had actually got used to the Tokyo subway. The carriage on an early evening on the line to Roppongi was full, but not so full that when your stop came you couldn't get off the train, gasping and exhausted in a crush of bodies.

Lucie's eyes would flick over the girls on the other side of the packed carriage. At 6.30 p.m. the system was almost as busy as during the morning rush, only for a different reason. The salarymen (most of them) were heading home, while the city's late shift was going to work – barmen, waiters, bouncers, touts and every shade of female swimmer in the city's water trade.

There were Russian girls and Scandinavians, all sculpted cheekbones and arrogant blonde bobs. There were Americans, both the professional topless dancers heading for a night of crotch grinding and college-kid amateurs out to make some cash in the hostess bars. There were laid-back Australians and confident-looking English roses, all made in the Roppongi hostess eloi-image of slinky black cocktail shifts, Shu Uemura lips and expensively contrived blonde hair. Lucie recognised quite a few of them by now. They'd meet after work in Geronimo's or Wall Street.

Then there were the Japanese girls with names like aunties' cats – Mika, Yumi, Yukie. You saw their names and faces reproduced on the ubiquitous printed fliers. They looked pretty relaxed as they set out for work.

Travelling in the other direction were the strippers and handjob girls – sexually subjugated Koreans, Taiwanese, Thais and Filipinas heading for Kabuchi-cho. They did not look quite so up for it.

Take a typical evening in late May 2000. The streets of Roppongi are already buzzing. Music blares out from the bars, eighties karaoke hits, the Pet Shop Boys and George Michael playing against a backdrop of fast-food joints and flashing pachinko parlours. The building that houses the Casablanca is a just a few high-heeled totters from the subway station. Tetsuo Nishi time-clocks the girls in. He seems to be drunk already. Mama-san glares from the shadows. Her lips twitch in a smile of welcome, or perhaps something less approving?

The stage is set. The glasses are polished and the girls on their sofa make last-minute adjustment with lipstick and mirror. The first customers are arriving. All eyes turn to the door. It's show time. 'Just say "*irashimase*" ["welcome"] when a customer comes in and smile a lot,' Lucie is told. Which is what she does.

A visitor to the Casablanca, not very long after Lucie's time there, saw for himself:

Ten young women waiting to be selected by customers perch on couches. Nearly all of them are blonde, their average age perhaps twenty-two. They sit upright, jumbled together like a doll collection. Careful not to disturb make-up and hair, they move with exaggerated stiffness but their eyes flit eagerly when a new prospect enters the club. Soon each of the young women is sitting next to a total stranger. They hand out their business cards ...

Tetsuo Nishi or, if he was too drunk (which was quite often), Tahara, the head waiter, would lead Lucie over to a table, and introduce her with a certain formality to customers already seated. She must make a small bow and smilingly exchange *meishii*, business cards. That little sliver

121

of Japanese protocol was as important in a hostess bar as it was in a corporate boardroom, as a girl who worked with Lucie at the Casablanca explained:

> The most successful hostesses were those with the best memories and the best business cards. These were an art form in themselves, often featuring your picture alongside a favourite Disney or Star Wars character, which you got specially printed at Photoman.
>
> What you needed most of all was energy. The whole business was totally, mind-numbingly exhausting. You had to take something – drink, or drugs, just to keep you going. Alcohol was the easiest, and your tolerance grew the longer you were in Tokyo. I thought nothing of doing ten or twelve tequila shots before going out to dinner.

Tequila, brandy, whisky, you name it – keeping the drink moving was the most vital thing. Behind the bar were bottles of Scotch belonging to regular customers. When one of them arrived, a waiter would bring his bottle to the table and the hostesses must attempt to pour it all, so he would have to buy another. Some girls would go shot for shot with a customer. Not always a good plan: don't drink the whisky yourself, that was the general idea.

Sometimes a customer might buy champagne or wine,

but mostly he just ordered dinky little cocktails for the girls. These you *were* expected to drink. Some clubs offered 'drinkbacks', which meant a hostess would get a percentage fee for every drink she had bought, including her own. With a direct profit from each glass downed, girls in the drinkback system were more likely to get wrecked themselves. Some clubs had a scheme whereby the hostess ordered drinks on the customer's tab which seemed to be alcoholic but were actually watered down. Rum and coke without the rum. Of course there was nothing diluted about the price.

Whatever the tricks, it was hard to stay sober. There were stories of girls puking it all up in the toilet. That was one way of staying skinny, but just as dangerous as getting steaming drunk night after night.

There were no 'members' at the Casablanca (although some clubs operated on a rudimentary members-only basis). Customers came and went as their fancies changed. There were single guys and married guys, rich guys and not so rich, drunk, sober, reasonable-looking and ugly guys. But who were they?

The business-card ritual told its own story. A Casablanca hostess kept her collection in a little wallet, a time capsule of her Roppongi nights. There was a retired senior officer with the Self Defence Force, who was now head of a large company, lots of investment bankers, some advertising guys, oil exploration executives, a brace of Mitsubishi salarymen. Plus some Westerners – a Californian wind-farm promoter, and the owner of a Donegal wool mill on a sales mission (the Japanese liked tweed).

It was up to Tetsuo Nishi and the mama-san to decide who to let in and who to keep out. But it all seemed pretty loose. A Casablanca girl recalled: 'In fact, they let anyone in, they were so greedy. I never, ever saw them refuse anyone entrance only if it was full with no room actually to seat anyone. They had no idea for the most part who was coming into the club.'

Often there would be gaggles of men, noisy parties out on a *settai* (company outing) flushed with corporate solidarity. Steady drinking served to unravel office etiquette, allowing underlings to make jokes about the boss (it seemed to be completely acceptable, even obligatory – as was drinking to total insensibility). A good night out would end with men being physically carried out of a club by their colleagues with the last ones standing, still jigging around the dance floor, their ties around their foreheads.

Come the end-of-the-year *bonenkai* season when salarymen got their bonus cheques – and this would happen on an industrial scale – there would be an office party, then the after-office party. Light sexual banter with a hostess or three eased the way towards mass oblivion. But a keen hostess wasn't interested in a group. She must find the single customer with big money to spend – the one who would keep coming back for more. The one who was looking for love.

He would become the special target; she would sit next to him and do everything she could to enthral. A *sempai* (older mentor) would show her just how to do it: 'You say, "*Nomimono yoroshii desu ka?*" [Would you like to buy me a drink?] If he already has a bottle you take ice like this, pour whisky like this, then water, stir together . . . You dance when asked, light his cigarettes and swap the ashtray as soon as one cigarette has been put out in it. You make sure there are always four cubes of ice in a customer's *mizuwari* [whisky and water] and wipe off any condensation from the glass. If the customer needs the toilet, show them where it is, and wait for them with an *oshiburi* [warm towel] outside. Bow when they take it.'

But getting up close and personal with your target did not mean you had landed the catch. As a former hostess recalled: 'I didn't spend very long with any table, as the men always made a gesture with their arms, which meant "move her along". By then end of the evening I felt very ugly and unwanted.'

If a customer saw a girl he liked sitting at another table, he could ask for her. It was called *shimei* – 'choosing' or 'request' – and he must pay more for the privilege. In fact, there were two kinds of *shimei*, one when the customer already knew the girl before going into the club, the other, *jonai shimei*, is when a customer chose the girl after looking around. 'Request' was almost as good as *dohan*. It meant more money.

Sometimes a customer would suddenly get up and leave without ceremony. The implication was he was going to another club, with prettier and more seductive hostesses. Some men would visit four or five clubs in a single night. There was no shortage of choice.

There was an internal hierachy at the club, with a number-one girl who made the most money and various pretenders to the crown. The top girl would get regular customers asking for her by name. She would get money for each request, and a percentage of the takings for that table. The more champagne they bought, the more she made. She might ask other girls to join her in a little circle of giggling simulated infatuation. They would play charming younger sisters to the hostess whose customer it was, or be the funny friends of the customer's obvious favourite. They would get a lesser slice of the cake, but at least they were out of the Doggy Box.

The number-one girl got an extra cash bonus at the end of the month, and if she continued to bring in money she might be on track to become a chi-mama, a kind of apprentice mama-san. She could also make money by moving to another club, and taking her loyal customers with her. As a

(Japanese) hostess explained it: 'You know, in Roppongi, there are many bars, and every time a hostess moves from one to the next, there is an interview. At the interview, I tell the mama-san that I can bring in so many customers from my last job. I do this because my salary is based on this number of customers. So, of course, I lie a little bit to get a nice salary.'

A hostess club's internal incentive scheme could be as ruthless and punishing as those designed for the corporate executives they entertained. And it could do damage. Yes, the girls knew it was all an act, but in the club – that simulated theatre of physical attractiveness and sexual self-worth – it became real. As an ex-hostess put it, 'It is easy to begin self-hating if you have a few bad nights, or the customers don't seem to like you. Even though none of my customers were people whose opinions I would give two shits about outside of work, I found that while I was working, I did. I wanted to be good at the job and felt bad when I couldn't be.'

If nobody wanted you, if all the others had been 'chosen', you would just have to sit it out alone all evening on that sofa of shame until somebody did.

And there was more advice: project a personality, make yourself stand out. It wasn't just about the way you looked. Keeping the conversation rolling and acting *genki* was what mattered. After all, you're supposed to be more interesting than the women the men see every day – their girlfriends or their wives. In their minds, they always have room for one more woman. Would Lucie be the *genki* girl who laughed at every smutty gag? That kept the older guys happy? As a girl who knew Lucie recalled:

Hostess bars were all about illusion – pretend you're single, pretend you like your date and, for God's sake, pretend to be having fun. Men didn't come here to talk about their wives or their dreary lives. They came to the Casablanca to spend a few hours believing a fantasy: that they were sexy, handsome and that a whole bunch of beautiful girls wanted them.

In a way, the fantasists and smut-pedlars were to be preferred to the gloom-shrouded ones who would just chain smoke in silence. A hostess confessed: 'I would just talk and talk, pour whisky and smile, unsure if they could actually understand, but hoping at least they'd feel they were getting their money's worth.'

And Lucie herself e-mailed Sophie at home to tell her that sometimes her customers spoke English with such impenetrable accents, all she could do was nod and smile: 'I can't believe I am paid so much money just to pretend I am listening to them,' she wrote. Perhaps it was just as well she did not understand exactly what was being said, although she would surely have got the gist of it. As Angela Carter had noted long, long before in the seventies, working as a hostess in a city of pre-bubble innocence (though Tokyo was never *that* innocent): 'Double entendre, bawdy illusion and a constant reference to sexual performance and phallic dimension stoke the continuous conflagration of smutty mirth which will occasionally modulate into the authentic, empty, hysterical sound of the laughter of the damned.'

For a lot of the time the conversation was staggeringly banal. A Roppongi veteran of more recent times recalled its grimmer moments:

> I'd start with simple things ('What's your name? What kind of job do you do?') but if even these didn't get things going, I'd have to switch to a more absurdist track. 'I love Japanese food,' I'd say slowly and then proceed to list all the things I could think of . . . sometimes in a long, excruciating monologue met with only slight grunts or nods . . . At other times the customer would gamely play along, suggesting food words as if to ask if I had eaten them, or offering his own favourites.
>
> Thankfully, most of the customers did speak some English, and the waiters usually tried to seat them according to language ability – or at least rotate us out when it was clear that some distinguished corporate

executive was getting sick of the 'Do you like dog? *Inu*? Cat? *Neko*?' routine.

Some customers liked to talk about golf, lots and lots about golf. Some were painfully shy. Others droned on about the office, although talk about work, certainly among groups of men, was not generally acceptable. Everything had to proceed on a tide of smutty chuckles, not quite the laughter of the damned. There was absolutely no mention of home, of wives or children.

Some men got down to the *sukebei* (dirty) stuff immediately: Are you hairy? How many times have you had sex? Can you come and pee at the same time? Your breasts are non-existent. Your breasts are like melons. They would make crude remarks about the size of their penises, or the number of prostitutes they had had sex with. As an English girl recalled: 'One of the things that put me off hostessing was sometimes having to speak to really powerful, wealthy men who would want to talk about perverted subjects with you . . . one launched straight into asking me about weird, kinky sex . . . straight away . . . no chat about the weather first or anything. He told me he was a heart surgeon.' So many customers had stories about who they were and what they did. But this one really was a top doctor.

The fantasy stuff was often easy to spot, but not always. Everyone had a big important job, drove a Mercedes, had a weekend place out by the coast. But was it true? The guy who claimed to be a self-employed millionaire: was he for real or was he just another salaryman? A hostess's job was to find out pretty quick and keep the rich guy on the hook.

It wasn't all just conversation. There was karaoke, that Japanese gift to the world of entertainment. If there was a party of men, all its members were expected to sing. Not to do so was judged to be the height of rudeness. Some did their very best with a number they had clearly practised. Others delighted in being as bad as possible. Some addressed their outpourings to a favoured hostess, and as Lucie quickly discovered, however hilarious she found the efforts of a drunken middle-aged Japanese businessman singing 'Rhinestone Cowboy', it was all taken very seriously.

But it was not a girl's job to sing. As the Casablanca's house rules put it, 'The hostess's duties do not include karaoke. Doing so limits the times a customer can karaoke. Also realise that the customers do not come to listen to you sing. Hostesses should, however, sing along with a customer when a customer wants to sing a duet.'

As the boozing wore on the karaoke got more raucous, the jokes got coarser, the maudlin outpourings about first loves became more unintelligible. Hands began to wander. An American hostess (who was actually an academic researcher who had got work in Roppongi a little after

131

Lucie was working there) insightfully recalled the alcohol-fuelled balletics when she wrote:

> It was their job to try to touch us, our job to not let them. It was all a part of the game, the knowing laughter, the glow of mischief, the moment they nearly crossed the line just to make us draw it again. In many ways the hostess bar recreated the atmosphere of childhood, a space devoted to pure play and indulgence, but with the boundaries that allowed it to be pleasurable. The fact that the female manager of such a club is called mama-san is no coincidence. Taking care to mark the limits of the customers' desire relieved them of the responsibility to control it. And sometimes the touching just revealed the basic, fragile humanity of these men.

In fact, physical contact – if it happened at all – was transitory. As a girl from Casablanca explained: 'Kissing was frowned upon in the club as other customers in the room might want to "request" you. Request was more money for you and more money for the club. So no kissing and it was wise to never physically look attached. If my favourite did come in I might hold his hand and keep even that hidden. It was a case of do what you want after work.'

Lucie was taught by her mentor how to handle it when

things went beyond the 'boundaries'; how to deal with the sudden-tongue-down-the-throaters, the gropers, the biters, the comedy stranglers and the stumbling drunks. As a Filipina hostess told an American reporter: 'Take the guy's hands in yours and hold it in your lap. There will always be some aggressive guy who'll try to touch your arse or tits . . . But a good hostess can usually control her client. If a girl likes a guy she will let him get away with certain other things.'

It was all part of the routine: the customers going for a grope of bottom or breast, the girls batting them away with a squawk and the chastened groper resuming his blank expression as if nothing had happened. It was his hands, you see, they had a mind of their own. Pretend strangulation was another big laugh – if not for the girl on the receiving end.

It was all absolutely hilarious if you could keep up with the drinking. Some girls did cocaine or methamphetamine to keep going. Shannon, an established hostess who was at the Casablanca with Lucie, recalled:

Cocaine, although it was a sacking offence if the management caught you with it, was everywhere in Roppongi then. The dealers were mainly Iranian, and sometimes Israeli. You were lucky if you escaped getting hooked once you'd started down that path. Tokyo at night was just one long party, something happening in every bar, club or street you walked down.

As for Lucie, she kept going any way she could, until gone midnight and the very end when Ricky had finished his last song and the dancefloor was filled with hostesses clamped to their stumbling, swaying middle-aged partners who were trying hard to stay upright. It was funny some nights. It was fucking awful on others. Perhaps this was the time when she really should get home to bed. But the big Roppongi party was only just starting.

CHAPTER 12

Lucie was starting to get it now. Get this right, get the right guy, and you could make loads of cash. She phoned her mother once to tell her that a customer had offered her 'a fantastic sum of money to sleep with him'. Lucie said she had laughed off the proposal, reminding her mother that her job was to pour drinks, light cigarettes and 'discuss boring subjects like volcanoes'.

But there was more to be made than just the pay from the club. There were gifts and big tips for a favoured one. As a girl recalled, 'One hostess had a clever line – telling all of her clients that it was her birthday next week. She would get a Louis Vuitton handbag or a necklace every day.'

Then there was sex, or the offer of it, the deal on the side, an exchange of fluids and payment beyond sight of the club's management. But *makura eigyou* ('pillow business') was risky. In the high-class hostess world, not selling sex was more financially rewarding than giving it out. A customer kept coming to a club because of the chance that a hostess might one day say yes. The trick was to keep him coming.

Cynthia Gralla, an American, remembered how, in her incident-filled Akasuka hostessing career, she had managed, up to a point, to say no. But her big-spending admirer had 'also made overtures to Sandra, who was a more practical type'. She recalled what her friend and fellow-hostess had proposed they do:

'Look, Cynthia,' she said, 'it would be over in about five minutes. Maybe we could even get him to go higher.'

'Higher?'

'By offering to both sleep with him at once.'

She was serious about this. The way she described the hypothetical scene with this little snow-haired man was actually pretty comical. But in the end I just couldn't do it. It seemed too absurd – a grandfather paying two young girls a small fortune for an ephemeral pleasure. This wasn't the dream I wanted to create for this man or anyone else.

I talked Sandra out of accepting the big spender's offer for the time being, but when I left Japan, she was again considering his proposal . . . She wasn't in desperate need of money, so my guess is that she probably didn't go through with it. But who knows? Stranger things have happened to nice girls in that kind of place.

To keep things discreet, there was always the legendary 'secret handshake' whereby a customer would take the hostess's hand and move his middle finger to ask if sex was a possibility. If the girl did it back, the answer was yes. Girls were supposedly fired for that – shown the door as fast as if they'd been doing coke – or at least for being found out. As Ms Gralla said:

I know of only one girl at a top hostess club who did exchange sex for money. Amy was a New Zealander who worked for Toni, my friend's Spanish mama-san. Amy kept quiet about her transactions . . . Clearly she was smart, but her careful plans were spoiled when Toni discovered what she was doing.

Toni was furious and felt that Amy's behaviour was jeopardising her business. And it was true that after they got what they wanted, at least two customers stopped coming to the club . . . Toni couldn't afford to lose even one customer. What might have helped Amy in the short term was destructive for Toni's longevity in the business. It cheapened her image. Toni fired Amy, and no one seemed to know what happened to her after that.

An older girl who worked at the Casablanca with Lucie remembered the advice she would give the new girls who were never quite sure just how far they were expected to go. The rules were, it seemed, flexible: 'Because I was older than the other girls, and had been in Japan a relatively long time – nearly three years by then – the younger women had a million questions for me: "Am I expected to sleep with the customers?" was one of the most frequent. The answer was "No" – not unless you wanted to, and then a discreet deal could be done. I didn't.'

That was the really difficult bit – knowing how far to go. A year to the day from when Lucie landed at Narita, a twenty-two-year-old Californian girl wrote of her experiences as a Tokyo hostess. For her, faking it was the key to making it:

One night I was sitting with a youngish [European] customer, enjoying a break from the near-constant horniness of the older Japanese men, when he suddenly nodded his head towards Lisa, a British hostess. 'She's very good,' he whispered, his eyes filled with wonder and admiration.

I looked over at Lisa. That night she had arrived with

the customer we called 'the Cowboy', given his penchant for droning country and western songs all night long . . . Lisa, her hands on his shoulders, was gazing at the Cowboy in ecstatic adoration, or some perfect imitation of it.

'The way she looks at him, she looks like she's completely in love with him,' my customer said in a hushed voice. 'She's a very good hostess.'

She was. The ability to fake love may be the hostess's most important skill.

The writer of the memoir could not at first understand why she herself was proving almost as popular as her English friend Lisa. Then she realised how good an actress she too was becoming without knowing it – able to do a simple thing like put on a diversionary tantrum should a love-struck customer turn up at the club while she was fawning over a rival. 'To do well in this business, it's best to have two or three serious patrons at any given time,' she wrote. 'But having two customers at the club at once is like running an obstacle course in high heels. You have to come across as faithful, even though everyone knows that it's your job to not be.'

That's why a good memory was important. And that's where the memo pad in the hostess's survival kit came in. They'd use it to make discreet notes, bits of biography and little observations of likes and dislikes, so that each client could be afforded the special-one treatment when (and that was the whole point) he returned for more.

Mobiles and e-mails were established tools of the trade (by the time Lucie got to Japan there had been mobile phones operating in Tokyo for two decades). Clubs encouraged hostesses to give out their numbers – phone-flirting was a great way of bringing customers back for more. Trouble was, you were never quite sure who was calling. Was it work or was it social? Get it wrong and you could blow the whole thing.

One girl told the story of her great big mistake. A customer – a big-spending businessman – was infatuated with her and after seven hours spent drinking four bottles of Dom Perignon at the club (it was in Kitashinchi, the entertainment district of Osaka) one evening, she said she wanted to go home. To get things moving she told him that her boyfriend was waiting outside in his car. (In fact he'd been waiting for hours.) It was the end of her career:

I had never seen such a look of disappointment and disgust on the face of a customer . . . He told me that as a hostess I should never say I have a boyfriend. I had broken the cardinal rule of hostessing. He let me leave, but he never came back to the club while I was there. With him, although he may not have even had any wish

to move our relationship to a sexual level, once the possibility was eliminated, so was the point.

Another former hostess confessed how she too, in the end,
had found it impossible to keep up the pretence. As she
said:

> Sex was never really brought into it . . . The other girls
> told me you didn't need to have sex with these men and
> that it wasn't expected. If you did have sex with them
> you'd destroy the whole point of going to a hostess . . .
> The presents kept coming that way. The men want to
> keep the fantasy that you are their girlfriend. You must-
> n't have another boyfriend yourself.
>
> I wasn't very good because I always felt like I was
> doing something dishonest. I felt bad lying to men about
> my lack of a boyfriend, my plans to stay in Japan long
> term, my very interest in them. A good hostess doesn't
> mind the dishonesty, and sees it as part of the rules that
> even the customers understand. Which is true – the men
> are only as fooled as they choose to be by a hostess's
> smile.

A fantasy girlfriend was just that – not simply someone to
see in the club, but someone to take out, to show off, to
enjoy romantic dinners with or days out by the sea. That

was what *dohan* was all about. This was the money-shot, the ritual at the centre of the whole hostess thing as Louise's older sister Emma had explained it to them in the first place.

Dohan was highly ritualised. On their return from dinner to the club, the girls would cut through the Roppongi pavement as if they were turning up to some movie premiere, then stalk haughtily into the club on the customer's arm for the attention of whoever might still be interested.

After two *dohans* with a man he was 'her' customer, and then each time he came to the club, she got a cut of whatever was spent at his table. It was all meant to be terribly upmarket, but was not always so. As a Casablanca girl recalled: 'It depended on the status and wealth of the customer. One of my regulars was a doctor, who would take me on a *dohan* to Maxim's for steak and lobster. Or it could be ribs and a beer in Tony Roma's with a more downmarket salaryman.'

There was also something called 'afters' which was when the customer took the hostess out for more drinking when the club at last shut, to a karaoke joint or 'darts bar', somewhere to keep the dream of love alive for a few more hours until the first trains started running in the morning. The really, really keen girls would meet their besotted clients in Tully's coffee bar at lunchtime or the newly opened Roppongi Starbucks.

The clubs demanded a minimum number of *dohans* per month, usually four, and offered a bonus for more than twelve. Some had mandatory competitions for the girls to get the most customers – and posted scores in the dressing rooms just to heighten the tension.

Besides the tips, the gifts and the shopping trips, a successful girl might be offered out-of-town weekends by her enslaved admirer. This was a sensitive area but it was covered by the code. A committed customer might legitimately expect to meet his hostess on the weekend for dinner or an excursion outside of the city, so it was explained. They might go to Kyoto, the historic capital, or to Disneyland in Chiba. The truly smitten might take their object of desire to Singapore or Honolulu. Shannon and her friend Karen who worked at the Casablanca were taken to the island of Okinawa by a judge. She wondered how he managed to go without sleep until he told her his little cocaine secret. He 'brought it with him on the flight over and back, but he said, "Don't worry, they never check for drugs on domestic flights." He'd been doing it for years.'

There would be meals, treats, keepsakes, jewellery, handbags, watches, fancy telephones, credit card accounts, cars maybe. In the bubble years, so it was said, girls were bought apartments or *fuzoku* businesses and set up for life. The crash came, but the dream of the fantasy sugar-daddy never really went away.

Then there was golf, an activity for which middle-aged Japanese males felt the same passion as they did for Johnnie Walker whisky and karaoke. One hostess told a story about going on a golfing *dohan* with a customer who brought his son along. Very occasionally an older client would admit that yes, he did have a family. Some girls, so it was said, might be taken home to meet the adoring one's wife, to whom she would be introduced as his 'English teacher', the standard, made-safe narrative of Japanese man and gaijin girl. Everyone understood.

Vera Svechina, the provincial Russian girl who worked as a Roppongi hostess told the story of Mr Nishikawa, an old friend of the owner of the club where she worked. He too liked to play out his fantasy love affair in the bosom of his family:

They played golf together and after every game they would come to the club with a group of their friends. With a bald spot on his round head when Mr Nishikawa wore glasses, he looked like a *kolobok* [a spherical lump of bread that comes alive in a Russian folk tale].

What surprised me the most was how this older man would find time for me almost every day. He invited me to lunch and to go shopping where he would buy me huge bags of groceries.

Sometimes after golf, he would come to the club with

his wife and son . . . it made me feel very awkward. When his wife looked at me, I saw pain in her eyes. I wanted to tell her that I didn't have any feelings for her husband.

A *dohan* was not a date with a stranger, it was part of the drawn-out romantic fantasy. It was all safe. No sex; not if you didn't want to. You might be offered vast sums, but you could always say no. That's what people said, anyway.

But could Lucie do this kind of stuff? Could she keep some made-up story in her head and act her way through an award-winning performance every night? What about the memory tricks she had to perform, scribbling on that little pad, who was who and which was which?

The Japanese language remained impenetrable. Perhaps that was an advantage. All Lucie had to do was smile and nod her head, and keep smiling until it hurt. But just a few weeks of this strange, seemingly fast-forwarded existence were already feeling like a lifetime. Half a dozen courtship rituals might be conducted in a single night, 'romance' with a big-spending customer might blossom into commitment within a matter of weeks and a whole career trajectory, from naive street catcher to top girl, might unfold in just a month or two.

As one former hostess put it: 'At the same time, everything seems frozen, as one endless night broken briefly by daylight. The same little glasses of wine keep arriving, the same songs are sung on the karaoke system, the same relationship is played out over and over again by different actors.'

It was the party you could never leave. Like a Japanese animated movie, it was like being trapped in a mirror world of monsters you had somehow stumbled into without really meaning to, but for which you could not find your way back home.

Some girls tried to get out by going off sick or claiming a faraway crisis. Others just quit. For example, a young woman called Sarah Dale had left the certainties of her English suburban life as a solicitor for Thailand, in search of who knew what. When she ran out of money she took up hostessing in Tokyo. She lasted only two weeks. She set out her reasons for quitting in a collection of travel writing published a few months before Lucie set off on a similar trail:

I suppose what really got to me about hostessing was that I had put a price on my freedom. Ordinarily, when faced with a slobbering old man with a red face and a preoccupation with asking 'How big is your boyfriend's dick?' one might shout some abuse, turn away, and leave. In this situation, however, I had relinquished such rights; I had sold them to mama-san.

146

Sarah Dale set out to get the sack – crossing her legs, lolling around, eating sweets, talking back – but curiously customers seemed to like it. But mama-san didn't. Sarah got her final pay with a cash deduction for a fortnight's use of toilet paper. Some girls lasted a lot longer, of course – two tourist visas' worth – and got to be number one. As Sarah recalled:

> The loud fat one from Manchester left a few days after I arrived. Hostess with the mostest, she had been at [the club] the longest. Six months of hostessing had made her enough money to do an overland trip to Israel. On her last night she gave a sonorous rendition of 'My Way' on the karaoke and then gave me all her old clothes in exchange for a packet of condoms.

Lucie had by now lasted a little over a month and a half. She was doing her best, but in her terms she was failing. Whatever she was telling the family back home, the money was not enough. Three weeks into working at the Casablanca she confided to her diary: 'I'm in more debt than I imagined which means there is no way I am going home August 2nd. There's nothing I can [do] except deal with it and it's left me with a gutted feeling.'

The whole system was designed to incentivise by

humiliation in a non-stop contest with the other hostesses. Sure, there was loads of sisterly solidarity and girls'-night-out hilarity, but competition was what it was really about. As Louise Phillips would later recall: 'Every week a girl was sacked from the club. They had a chart on the wall detailing who had the most *dohans*. Lucie was about eleventh out of twenty girls and she felt under pressure . . . Although Lucie was so beautiful, she didn't have much confidence, so she fell for flattery. If only she could have seen herself as I saw her.'

But Lucie had just about had enough. She was tired of getting drunk every night and she was tired of having the same stupid conversations over and over again. She was tired of smelling of cigarette smoke and dragging some priapic *oyaji* ('dad') around the Casablanca's tiny dance-floor.

She performed the by-now achingly familiar routine of head bows and exchanging business cards like a grinning automaton. The appalling karaoke, moving from table to table, the smutty jokes, more karaoke, more inane conversation, cheeks aching from smiling so long, the gushing good nights to customers, extracting promises from them to return, swearing undying love as they exited, before rushing back inside to fall in love all over again.

Then going home – picking her way through the pools

of vomit and the suited figures passed out on the pavement next to their briefcases – to crash out herself at the gaijin house in Sendagaya. Only to start the whole thing over again.

Lucie had fits of uncontrollable crying, stomach cramps and an overwhelming feeling of self-loathing. 'I am so cried out, tears . . . only come exhaustively in waves,' she wrote. 'I can't pull myself out of this hole I've fallen into. I must have been kidding myself that I could make it out here . . . I feel so disgusting . . . It's not Tokes, it's me . . . I am so fucking up to my neck in debt and so badly need to do well. This is not a thing to do with Lou and I'm really happy for her – but I'm a crap hostess.'

Louise Phillips, meanwhile, was doing fine. As Lucie wrote:

I've had one *dohan* only because of Shannon. Another stood me up. I mean, how shit must you be for a *dohan* to stand you up? Louise gets men falling over themselves to request her. Nishi gave her a tip and she's being so fab about it, but she's just falling so well into it – making heaps of friends and as usual, wherever I am, I feel alone . . .

I'm so exhausted with feeling this shit and feeling so lonely despite being with Lou every day and feeling so

149

low and up to my eyeballs with debt – I sometimes really can't be bothered to wait and find out what happened. I just want to disappear.

Her wish would be granted.

CHAPTER 13

What you did after hours was big chunk of the hostess culture. Where did a bargirl who met men for a living go to
meet men? She went to another bar. Roppongi was where
gaijin guys came to drink, on a booze cruise through the
strip of pubs and clubs beside the Shuto Expressway that
was famous around the world. It was famous for lots of
things.

Posted on a website launched in Lucie's name is the story
of an anonymous girl from London. She'd never heard of
Roppongi when her narrative begins, but she'd soon know
all about it. Her story is tough and authentic, designed, as
the website says, to tell the 'truth about hostessing' – with a
view, it must be supposed, to warn young women off heading for Japan in search of easy money.

Thus our young hostess is more streetwise than Lucie. Her background seems a lot less privileged; she lives in London squats and seems to be on the run from dysfunctional family life rather than taking a long holiday from it.

Her conduit to hostessing was an advert in a London freesheet magazine: 'Attractive Hostesses Needed, strictly hostessing only.' It was placed by an agency which turned out to be operating from an address in prosaic Edgware. When she turned up there, ten girls were being assessed for their suitability by an older woman called Kay. She and her balding husband seemed to be running the UK end of things. There was a kind of beauty parade going on in the north London flat. Most of the girls were in their teens. She would make the grade, she was told, but only if she wore a wig. And her tattoos were going to be a problem.

The dramatic account of what happened next is full of incident. There are encounters with a 'bizarre-looking Japanese man in a garish suit', multiple cockroaches and plenty of Iranians pushing drugs (in that it was pretty accurate). It also describes partying in Roppongi. Some young people, naturally enough, might find her story an inducement to try it for themselves. Her hostess shift has just ended when:

We didn't go home. Me and six of the girls hit Roppongi town. We all reapplied our make-up, they smoked a bit of 'ice' [methamphetamine] and off we went to a bar called Harvey's. It was here that I found out a bit about Roppongi life. As hostesses we were entitled to free entry to all clubs, and free drinks in some.

Apparently we were entitled to lots of free drugs too, from what I saw that night. We ended up with a group of Iranian guys . . . They kept inviting me to go for a line, and putting pills in my hands. I kept saying no, which they didn't like. One of them sat with his arm around me, and I found him quite menacing. It was as though he had claimed me as his. We went to a few bars with them, and then eventually went home around 5 a.m. I was shattered and slept all day.

So hostesses took drugs. That was no surprise. And Roppongi was full of the stuff. That was no surprise either. As one commentator on the scene wrote: 'Tokyo's nightclubs, which, although bursting with drugs, are the safest of any city in the world.' What was surprising, perhaps, was that anyone should have any energy left after six or seven hours of drink and professional smooching at a hostess club to want to go on partying with her mates until dawn. But of course they did. That was the point of being twenty years old.

Like Lucie. At 2 a.m. or so on an average night, she might have been heading for home and the futon in the six-tatami room in Sendagaya. Or she might not.

Lucie Blackman and Louise Phillips were up for it. So were Mel and Shannon (who'd knocked ten years off her age to get a job at the Casablanca. Later, when at last interviewed by the police, Shannon said they were more interested in how she had changed her birth date on her passport by fiddling with a colour photocopier than they were in any information she had about Lucie.) And Angie and Hannah – and Rachael from Liverpool. They were all up for it.

The place to go was Envy, with its constantly cheerful owner, Hama, and the after-hours party on Thursday-thru-Saturday that lasted until dawn.

Lucie's diary entries gave an authentic glimpse into those hot Roppongi nights, bouncing from bar to bar in search of a good time. Of one (as it would turn out) special night Lucie wrote:

> . . . same old, same old until about 3 a.m. when we decided to quickly step into Wall Street to meet up with [friends]. While waiting for them to arrive, Lou spotted and allured a guy (v v cute one at that) named Scott. I got talking to him and we just really hit it off . . . We then decided to go to Lexington Queen. By this point I was wrecked and really trying to keep my cool self together.
>
> We left at around 7 a.m. . . . Scott came home with me. I kissed him, [but] never let him upstairs with me.

At first I think he was a bit disappointed, but at the end of the day anyone can have a load of one-night stands but really all of us want someone to love, and have someone to love us back.

It was an endearingly honest sentiment in the context of what she was paid to do at the Casablanca.

The routine of partying till dawn, somehow making it home, crashing at the gaijin house, then starting all over to go to work by seven the next evening was no less punishing than it had been at the start. But now there was a guy, Scott, the US Marine, and Lucie was clearly smitten. 'Average day and average night made fantastic as I was walking on air', she wrote in her diary for Monday 22 May. 'Had a request of . . . photo-man and Joe – who got absolutely wasted – worst night so far in my opinion! Dragged Lou around the dancefloor and eventually called for the check – THANK GOD!'

Joe was an avuncular Japanese businessman in his sixties, generous and humorous who was universally popular with the Casablanca girls. He had taken a fancy to Lucie-san, so things were getting quite a lot better all round. Perhaps she wasn't so crap after all. And as a good modern hostess, just as she had been instructed, Lucie had given out her mobile number and was using her own e-mail account as a customer-catcher. She'd learned the cheesy come-on lines pretty well

155

too. On 21 June she messaged a new client she'd met a few days before, an eager salaryman called Hideo:

Hello, it is me Lucie here from Casablanca. I was the girl from London with long blonde hair who you got on so well with the other night.

I would like to apologise for not getting in touch sooner but over the weekend I had some family problems going on in the UK.

Let's meet up and have dinner and I can talk to my new special friend.

I hope you have a lovely day, I know I will as I will be talking to you.

Her message was sent at three in the morning. Hideo replied almost straight away:

How are you Lucie, a cute girl with long blonde hair? I always like girls with blonde hair and also with short skirt.

How about dinner – French, Japanese, Chinese . . . ?

Enjoy yourself your life in Tokyo anyway. See you maybe on Friday . . .

Lucie-san was well out of the Doggy Box. She e-mailed her sister to tell her she was earning the equivalent of £1500 a

week – and that was just for starters, as now she was being
asked for by name. The Roppongi nightlife was great, she
said, and she had been on a few real dates with someone
she fancied, as opposed to *dohans* with paying customers.
Her new friend was an American. She sent a postcard to
England addressed to her father and younger sister:

Dear Daddy and Sophie,
Everything has turned a rather large corner, wages
have finally arrived so few immediate pressures at the
mo. Customers are starting to roll in. I have a very loyal
customer who has been my lifesaver, he treats me like
a princess and makes me loads of money, not to
mention feeds me most nights!!!

All the weight I lost as the result of starvation in the
first few weeks has gone back on, but I've now joined
the gym!

I've met a wonderful guy. I met him last Friday in a
bar, he's blond, blue eyes, body to die for, American
(Texas), is a US Marine – my favourite things rolled
into one. Oh and his name is Scott.

The rainy season has started which is expensive as
it's too wet to ride bikes, so we have to take taxis
which are £25 each way – bollocks!

I have no idea when I am coming home or what I
am doing but I was no better off at S[ociété]

G[énérale] or BA so I'm just going to enjoy my adventure . . .

A friend of Lucie's from the Casablanca recalled: 'A couple of weeks later I met them again. This time Lucie was snogging a young, good-looking US Marine in the corner. They seemed really full-on together, although Louise told me they'd only met for the first time a few nights earlier. She said his name was Scott.'

So Lucie now had a proper boyfriend – Scott Fraser, who was stationed on the aircraft carrier the USS *Kittyhawk*, permanently homeported at the sprawling Yokosuka naval base, headquarters of the US Seventh Fleet, on the Miura peninsula south of Tokyo. She also had a paying customer who appeared especially interested in her, taking her on *dohans*. She didn't mention Joe's name in her calls or messages to Sophie, but she did record it in her diary: 'I got up at 4 [p.m.] and went to take dinner with Joe. Scott went to Roppongi with Lou,' she wrote in her entry for 8 June. 'I had a beautiful dinner with Joe', she wrote the next day. 'He is really starting to like me a lot.'

But after the 'beautiful dinner', the evening progressed into the usual bar crawl. As her diary entry recorded:

I left after dinner and went to the Internet café. Then I went to Geronimo's to wait for Lou. Finally she arrived with Hannah, Angie and Shannon. We had a load of tequilas. Lou was plastered and did another.

We then went down to Wall Street where the night started to go really wrong.

A fight ensued. Lucie and Lousie picked up their bags and ran home.

Lucie, however, was not superwoman. Her constitution – she'd had pneumonia and pleurisy as a teenager – was unravelling with the six-days-a-week routine of drinking, recreational drugs and hyperactive partying in the club and outside. Her diary entries for the second part of June featured less self-loathing and more old-fashioned moaning:

Woke up early feeling like death. I ached from head to toe . . . today was the day we were going to go to Disneyland. It was absolutely pissing and we both felt like shit.

On arriving home, I decided there was no WAY I was working and called in sick. Crashed out at 9 p.m. first normal night sleep since landing . . .

Hell *dohan* Joe. Cold sore massive, really painful, feeling so ugly – so gutted . . . so cancelled my date with Scott.

The fact that Lucie was getting better at hostessing brought its own problems. Club life was becoming real life.

As an American girl who'd gone through a similar trajectory from gawky newbie to seasoned pro in the course of a few weeks explained:

> Gradually I became embroiled in a drama that I created through my various customers and the other girls. The world of the club was both safe and thrilling. It was addictive. The better I became at my job, however, the more I lost touch with myself, and while my sham 'loves' with my customers deepened into something like real affection and compassion, the 'real' relationship in my life floundered.
>
> I didn't do it solely for the money. I wish I had. I did it for reasons far more dangerous: I needed adoration and approval and I, like so many victims of typically arid American upbringings, was addicted to the rush of adrenaline that love and praise, however insincere and deluded, can bring. After a few months in Japan's floating world, real life was, for a while, too slow for me.

Lucie's relationship with Scott Fraser was real enough. And the pace of it was just about right – not too slow and not too fast. In one of her last diary entries, she expressed her joy at discovering how the man she had thought of as 'Mr Confident' had confessed his fear that 'he was really just so AVERAGE': 'I felt my legs buckle and I really cried,' she wrote. 'Out of his mouth had come my words, my most deep rooted feelings.' She really had found the one.

In the space of just a few weeks, some full-on hostessing had trashed Lucie's self-esteem, then put it back together again. It was about competition. It was about long-ago school discos transported to this Tokyo theatre of the absurd. Each night in the club, Louise Phillips might have cruised to the winner's enclosure, but maybe she hadn't pulled a real guy like Scott. And now Lucie was winning on all fronts. She had her cute US Marine and she had real customers offering her real money. The 'rush of adrenaline that love, however insincere' might provide had indeed become addictive. What was it that Louise Phillips said later? 'Although Lucie was so beautiful, she didn't have much confidence, so she fell for flattery.'

There was a guy at the club, not Joe this time and not Hideo; a guy who seemed really interested in her. He came alone, not with big parties of drunken salarymen. He spoke English. He said he was a company director, some sort of property developer. He had a house in the Tokyo suburbs, a big place with a garden, plus an apartment downtown and one out by the sea. He had a boat.

Lucie's thoughts are easy to imagine. This one was too good to lose. She'd better keep this one to herself. Perhaps even from Louise. He was offering all sorts of stuff, if she'd just come to his fabulous apartment out by the coast. It was a bit risky. But it was a risk worth taking. It would bounce her right up the *dohan* charts. How could she say no?

On Thursday 29 June, Lucie called in sick with a head cold. She managed to send her mum an e-mail from the Sendagaya Internet café which began, 'I am still alive.' She asked for some very English cold-sore remedies to be sent out – Mum could get them from Boots in Sevenoaks. By the following night Lucie felt fixed-up enough to do a shift at the club and then go on to Hama's bar. Louise was there, so were Shannon and Mel. It was the usual stuff. The girlie party went on till after 3 a.m.

The first of July was a Saturday. The midsummer weather was humid, oppressively warm. There'd been some rain, but that hadn't cooled things down much. Lucie had gone to bed at the gaijin house some time in the early hours. So had Louise. Neither of them was going to work at the club that night. There was a kind of plan that they would go out that evening with Scott – Roppongi again; it was always Roppongi.

As she would recount the sequence of events soon afterwards to the Japanese police (as it was reported in a British newspaper), Louise Phillips left the gaijin house 'in the morning', leaving Lucie who was 'fine, happy and her usual bubbly self ... When I returned home [soon after midday] I was really surprised she wasn't there because she had no reason to go out and we had made arrangements to see each other.'

But Lucie clearly did have some reason to go out. As Louise was leaving, she was getting dressed, and not for some casual Saturday hanging round the house. She put on a black dress, a silver necklace – the one with hearts on it – and a square silver watch, and she packed a smart black handbag. She dressed as she would if she was going on a *dohan*.

In a later interview, Louise said she thought Lucie had said something about an arrangement with a customer from the club; going somewhere with him out of town to 'see the ocean' at a place called Kamakura. That made sense. As the summer heat of Tokyo rose, it would be much more bearable out by the sea.

Lucie was going to go to Sendagaya railway station not too far from the gaijin house where her customer had arranged to pick her up in his car. She would be back in plenty of time for them to go out that Saturday night. In their hurried morning conversation she had also mentioned a special gift, according to Louise Phillips. It was, apparently, a pre-paid, state-of-the-art, really flash mobile phone that this guy had promised to give her. The phone was quite a deal. That summer, the whole of electronics-obsessed Japan was transfixed by 'i-mode' mobiles that could connect to the Internet (even if the system did keep crashing). They were expensive and desirable. Lucie had left the rented mobile phone she and Louise shared behind at the house for her friend to use.

Two hours or so later the payphone in the hallway at Yoyogi House rang. Louise answered it. It was Lucie, saying that she had met her date and something about him buying her a mobile phone. No name was mentioned. She rang again around 2.30 p.m., this time calling the shared mobile phone to say: 'I'll be leaving here for Sendagaya in half an hour.' Where 'here' was wasn't clear.

At a little before 5 p.m. she rang Louise again and said, 'I'm being taken to the coast.' It seemed she was in a car; she must have been phoning from a mobile. Then, at 7.17 p.m., she called Louise again, saying 'I'll be back in half an hour.'

Lucie phoned Scott Fraser a few minutes later with the same message. They would all be going out together that night. To Roppongi. It was going to be fantastic.

She never showed up.

PART TWO

Only when he was with a girl who had been put to sleep could he feel himself alive.

Yasunari Kawabata, *Nemureru Bijo*
('House of the Sleeping Beauties')

That's the best thing a girl can be in this world, a beautiful little fool.

F. Scott Fitzgerald, *The Great Gatsby*

CHAPTER 14

Louise Phillips spent the rest of that Saturday night in a state of increasing anxiety. The number of the mobile Lucie had rung from had not registered in the memory of her mobile phone, nor in the payphone in the gaijin house. Scott Fraser hadn't a clue. Nor did anyone else. Perhaps Lucie would turn up later that night with a diamond necklace and an absolutely hilarious story. They'd all have a good laugh.

But she didn't show at the house in Sendagaya, Hama's, the Casablanca or anywhere else. Her friend Shannon recalled:

I saw Louise the night she came looking for me with another girl called Hannah. I'd just finished work and

167

was having a quiet drink in Hama's bar. Louise was distraught, saying Lucie hadn't returned from a date and she was terribly worried about her. I tried to reassure her, pointing out that Lucie had only been missing for a few hours. I advised the two girls [Louise and Hannah] to talk to Tahara first – as Nishi, the manager, was always too drunk to make any sense – and then to check out all the local bars. Then check the hospitals, just in case there'd been an accident.

But Louise continued to look very distressed. She kept repeating: 'You don't understand. This is so out of character. Lucie always calls me to let me know where she is. Something has definitely happened to her.'

Sunday passed in a blur of deepening anguish. That morning, Samantha, a girl who had worked at the Casablanca but who had left the club before Lucie went missing, rang Louise to find out the address of some café or other. Louise told her the news – that Lucie had not come back the night before. Samantha asked who she had been with and, as she would recall not too long afterwards: 'Louise wasn't sure, but thought that Lucie had gone to Kamakura where this man has a house and they were going to the coast there.' Kamakura was a good guess, a popular tourist place in Kanagawa Prefecture with temples and shrines. But that was not where Lucie had been heading.

There were more calls, the news was spreading. Could anyone remember anything more about Lucie's date? There had been some weirdos at the club off and on but nothing that anyone couldn't handle. How about that lawyer who started following people around in the daytime and had once dragged a girl into a taxi? What was his name – Hiroshi something? And there'd been a guy with a goatee hitting on Lucie. He'd bought Dom Perignon, the best. That had gone down well with the management. She'd seemed quite keen to get him on a *dohan*. Lucie had also seemed anxious to keep him to herself. What was his name – Kazu?

The next day, Monday 3 July, there was still no word. The heat was rising. At around three o'clock that afternoon Louise went to the British Embassy near the Imperial Palace to raise some kind of alarm. This was going to be difficult. She and Lucie had been working illegally – but so was everybody. The building was grave and imposing with stone Corinthian columns: a miniature version of an English country house. It had somehow survived earthquake and American-sown firestorm.

Breathless and distressed, Louise told the vice-consul, Iain Ferguson, what she knew. She had brought Lucie's passport with her from the gaijin house. It was stamped with the date of their arrival – 4 May 2000. Next of kin was her mother, Jane Blackman, of Argyle Road, Sevenoaks,

Kent. The Narita immigration admission stamp was for ninety days as a temporary visitor. Lucie was on a tourist visa, and so was Louise Phillips. But they'd been working as hostesses, Mr Ferguson noted. Earning money. He wasn't going to preach but, as he said in his report of the meeting, this would make an official investigation by the Tokyo police that much more difficult.

In fact, Louise had already been to the police that morning. She, and someone she called Kaz, 'a Filipino boss from the club' as the embassy transcript of her testimony recorded, had been to Azabu police station in Roppongi to file a missing-person report, so she told the vice-consul. She had been able to describe what Lucie had been wearing as she, Louise, had left the house on Saturday morning. Other girls at the club recalled later that she went to the police to make that first report accompanied by Tahara, the head waiter.

According to the transcript of her statement, Louise admitted to Iain Ferguson that she 'had not revealed that she and Lucie worked as hostesses at a club, nor that Lucie had been with a client when she went missing. Instead, she and the guy from the club had simply told the police that Lucie had gone for lunch with a Japanese man that she'd met and had phoned at 7 p.m. to say she'd be back within the hour [but] she had failed to appear.'

Louise was, however, much more frank in what she had

to say to the vice-consul than she had been with the police that morning. She told Iain Ferguson the story of the phone calls from Lucie on the afternoon of 1 July, when, again according to her statement to the vice-consul, she had told her she was 'with a nice man' and that she was 'having a lovely time'. Her client would drive her home, she had said.

Who was this client? Louise was asked, but she did not know. What was Lucie doing going out with a stranger on a Saturday? Louise explained something about *dohan* and how it worked. The embassy official was 'taken aback', as he put it in his report. He found it 'hard to believe . . . that girls within the club routinely and with the club's consent, hand out their own business cards [actually they were the Casablanca's, but with their own name and e-mail address handwritten on it] and that clients often make private appointments as a result.'

Louise Phillips explained to the perturbed diplomat that life at the Casablanca was a kind of constant competition to get the most *dohans*. Girls, however friendly, might choose to keep a big-spending client to themselves. Lucie had told her nothing of this man at the club – not his name, nor anything about any car (although she was clearly in one when she rang) or even where they had gone, other than to the coast.

As Iain Ferguson's report put it:

171

All of Louise's responses drew a consistent picture of a confident, worldly-wise, intelligent individual who had the experience and judgment not to have put herself in danger . . .

I asked then in that case why she would have gone off with a complete stranger in his car. Louise could not explain it, stating that such behaviour was out of character for Lucie.

And it was. This is what was so baffling – and alarming. Lucie always seemed to share confidences rather than try to hide anything. Just who this guy was, she had kept to herself, but she had called Louise four times during this mysterious date to tell her what she was going to do next. Then silence. Something really, really bad must have happened.

In spite of Louise's reluctance to report an illegal worker going missing, the embassy official stated his own intention of contacting Azabu police station to report 'an abduction rather than a missing person'.

'Is any of this going to be in the papers?' Louise asked. The vice-consul rather thought that it might be.

Louise Phillips was checking out through the embassy's security perimeter when her mobile rang. Thank God, it must be Lucie, she thought. But it was a man's voice, speaking in heavily accented English. What he had to say was menacing, bizarre and reassuring all at once. He said his name was Akira Takagi. He said he was calling at Lucie's request to say she was fine and had joined a 'newly rising religion' – a cult – and that she was 'safe and taking training in a hut in Chiba'.

Within minutes of taking the call, Louise was relaying to Iain Ferguson what the person on the end of the phone had told her. He'd said that Lucie and her client had got stuck in a traffic jam on the Saturday evening, driving back to Tokyo. Mindful of her promise to be back within the hour, Lucie had left her client to make her own way back by train. That was where she had met 'the disciple of this newly rising religion and had decided to change her life and move in with them'.

Lucie would not be able to 'leave the place for at least a week', according to the mysterious caller, who seemed to know a lot about her personal affairs. 'Her credit-card debt, around 1.1 million yen, could be returned much quicker if she stayed with the group rather than working at the Roppongi club,' he said. He almost seemed to be offering to pay it off himself somehow.

Louise had demanded to speak to Lucie, and to know how the caller had got her number. But he just answered that Lucie was studying and could not come to the phone. He said that he would have to ask his leader whether it might be possible, but he thought it would not be. The he added: 'This is it, this is goodbye . . . you will not see Lucie again.'

The vice-consul's advice was unequivocal. Louise must go back to the police and tell them everything. No half-truths about tourist visas or what it was they did for a living. Meanwhile, the consulate would do the same and tell the police exactly what Louise Phillips had told him.

Louise's next task was much more difficult than dealing with suspicious officialdom. She had to phone Lucie's family in England.

It was the mother, Jane, who picked up the phone. She was parcelling up some domestic comforts – the cold-sore cream from Boots that Lucie had asked for, and some pick'n'mix sweets from Woolworths. She remembered: 'I was just going out the door to the post office, and the phone rang, and it was Louise . . . she was hysterical. I could barely make out what she was saying, but I heard the words "Lucie" and "missing".' She recalled how she felt her knees buckle, followed by a rush of nausea. She broke off the call to be physically sick. She'd had premonitions of this moment ever since Lucie left, even if her daughter had done everything to reassure her she was safe. She called her younger daughter, Sophie, who was at work as a trainee cardiac technician at a hospital in Tunbridge Wells:

Mum called me at 3.20 p.m. My grandfather had been really ill, so I assumed it was about him. She said, 'It's Lucie.' That's all she said, so I said, 'What?' and she repeated, 'It's Lucie . . . she's been abducted.'

I called my best friend, Emma, and when I heard myself telling her what had happened I burst into tears. Talking about it made it real.

My colleagues made me sit down and drink tea and they offered to take me home. But all that was going through my mind was that I was going to go to Japan tomorrow and I couldn't leave my car at work so I had to drive myself home.

Sophie found the house in Argyle Road full of 'Mum's friends offering support'. As she told an interviewer a little later, 'Mum was silent and Dad was the same when we told him. I decided that afternoon to get on the next flight to Tokyo, and left the next morning . . . I borrowed the money from family and friends and the hospital gave me time off. Mum stayed at home to look after Rupert – there seemed no point in all of us going.'

But the Blackmans were not as silent as Sophie thought. According to Tim, his ex-wife ranted down the phone: 'Lucie's missing – what are you going to do about it?' According to Jane, she had to plead with her former husband to go with Sophie on her mission to Japan. 'I did not want her to go on her own. I had lost one daughter and I was worried what could happen to the other one,' she told an interviewer. 'I begged, but he said he couldn't go. We had a row and he asked me not to get in touch with him again.'

Sophie, meanwhile, had by now talked to Louise in Tokyo, who told her a garbled story about a weird phone call and Lucie 'running off to join a religious cult' in somewhere called Chiba. Sophie, in turn, relayed it all to her father in a desperate, tear-choked phone call. She also managed to talk to Iain Ferguson at the embassy in Tokyo who told her what he knew, which was no more than Louise Phillips had already outlined. Sophie told the consular official that she 'felt helpless in the UK' and would have to come out to Japan. He pointed out that 'she would feel equally helpless were she to come here'. He was right.

Nineteen-year-old Sophie left for Tokyo in the late afternoon of Tuesday 4 July. Jamie Gascoigne, who had been Lucie's teenage boyfriend in Sevenoaks and who had remained a friend of the family, went with her. Tim Blackman, meanwhile, was working the phones in England. As he explained:

I knew nothing about Japan at that time. So I immediately began making calls, to the Foreign Office, to the

British Embassy in Tokyo, as well as to anyone I could think of who knew the country. The first thing I discovered was that Chiba, far from being my fantasy of a tiny village with pretty-shaped roofs, had a population of two and a half million people.

Sophie told me later that her moment of realisation of the scale of the problem we had ahead of us was when her plane started to land at Narita Airport and she saw the massive size of Tokyo for the first time.

In his telephone conversation with the embassy in Tokyo, Lucie's father had been told the story of the 'newly rising religion'. He was also informed that the Tokyo police wanted details of the debts the strange caller seemed to know so much about. He had told them they were a bank loan, and store cards she had run up when she had started work in London, but she had been on top of it. The amount she owed would certainly not have driven her to do something so wildly out of character as to contrive her own disappearance.

Regarding the delicate matter of his relationship with his ex-wife, Tim had assured the consular section that Lucie's mother was being kept informed of developments via Sophie, although he himself 'hardly spoke to her'.

Asked whether he had had any communication from Lucie while she was in Tokyo, Tim told the vice-consul that there had been phone calls and a post card. The last call had been two weeks ago, and things had seemed to be going well. Lucie had mentioned someone she had met through the club, a 'Japanese friend' who had bought her gifts and taken her for meals. Meeting this friend had seemed to mark the change in her fortunes.

The vice-consul rang Louise Phillips in the early evening of Tuesday 4 July to ask her if she knew who this friend was. She had just arrived back at the gaijin house having spent, she said, all day at Azabu police station. It must be Joe, a regular at the club, she told him – 'a really nice guy known to all the girls'. In Louise's opinion he couldn't possibly be involved in Lucie's disappearance. The vice-consul asked if she had reported this to the police. She couldn't remember.

However, this time she *had* told the police much more about the events of 1 July, at least the bits she could recall, especially about the calls to the payphone at the gaijin house and to the mobile they shared. Much later, Louise would reconstruct more of the conversation for a Sunday tabloid newspaper:

I asked if she was all right and she said she was fine. She said she missed me because it was the first Saturday that we had been apart. And she said she would call again in a couple of hours. She also said [her *dohan* date]

178

Kabuki-cho, Tokyo's most full-on commercial sex district, offers services way beyond the drinks and flattery available in the hostess bars of Roppongi.

Time to relax: a tired salaryman gets the attention he has paid for in a hostess club. These Filipina girls operate a little down the exquisite hierarchy of the 'water trade' ...

... where gaijin girls have for years proved the most popular – pouring drinks, lighting cigarettes and laughing at the jokes of middle-aged Japanese executives.

Blonde-haired Lucie Blackman from Sevenoaks, Kent, who went from 'catching' customers in the streets of Roppongi to being a top hostess at the Casablanca club within six weeks. Then she went on a date from which she would never return.

Nineteen-year-old Sophie Blackman was the first on the scene in Tokyo's teeming streets when she heard her elder sister was missing. Tirelessly she sought answers throughout the summer of 2000, but Lucie seemed to have vanished into thin air.

The relations of Tim Blackman, Lucie's father, with the Tokyo police were brittle. He often had to press the detectives into action, while at the same time conducting his own intelligence-gathering operation in night-time Roppongi.

Right: Joji Obara as a young man, one of the few images to emerge of the son of Korean immigrants who had once led the life of a pampered playboy. He was arrested in October 2000 on suspicion of involvement in Lucie's disappearance.

Bottom: The sketches made through Joji Obara's multiple appearances in court showed a mild-looking middle-aged man with a straggling goatee, rather than the 'sex monster' of the British tabloids' imagination.

© Sutton Hibbert/Rex Features

Above: The Blue Sea apartment block close to Aburatsubo beach, an hour's drive from Tokyo. Obara's little-used apartment on the fourth floor was visited by local police a few days after the July night when Lucie went missing (following a complaint from the caretaker) but they failed to gain entry. After Obara's arrest in Tokyo, the Blue Sea's surroundings were searched but nothing found.

Left: Samantha Termini holds a picture of her sister Carita Ridgway on 24 April 2007, the day Joji Obara was found guilty of drugging and rape, leading to her death. In February 1992 a mystery man had dumped twenty-one-year-old Carita at a Tokyo hospital. She was suffering acute hepatitis which was due, the court would decide, to chloroform poisoning at the hands of Joji Obara.

Above: The beach at Aburatsubo, near Obara's apartment, was revisited by police in the first week of February 2001. This time, after five days of intense searching, the dismembered body of Lucie Blackman was found in a cave, buried under sand and stones.

Right: Tim Blackman saw the remains being brought out live on satellite television. He did not yet know for certain that it was his daughter.

Lindsay Hawker, the life sciences graduate from Warwickshire who sought experience and a little bit of extra cash teaching English in Japan.

Closed-circuit security camera images of Lindsay and her suspected killer, Tatsuya Ichihashi, in a Gyotoku café on 25 March 2007, the day she went missing.

Police tape and a blue tarpaulin screen off the back balcony of Ichihashi's apartment, where Lindsay Hawker's body was found half-buried in a sand-filled bathtub on 27 March.

Lindsay's father, Bill Hawker, addresses an extemporised press conference with an impassioned plea to find his daughter's killer.

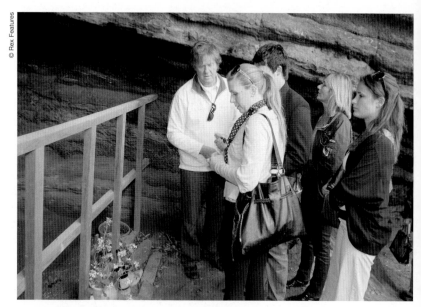

April 2007: Tim and Sophie Blackman pay tribute to Lucie at the Aburatsubo cave where her body had been discovered over six years earlier. They were joined by Jo Burr, soon to be Tim's second wife, and her children.

had surprised her by taking her to a restaurant at the coast and buying her champagne.

Sophie Blackman arrived at Narita on Wednesday 5 July at 11 a.m. local time and went straight to the British Embassy. She took the airport bus through the daunting sprawl of the city's suburbs. 'I looked in every window and field for Lucie's face,' she recalled, 'thinking she could be anywhere [then] I saw how built-up Tokyo is and the impossibility of the task ahead.'

The consular section led her as gently as they could through what she might be able to add to what was known already, then took her to Azabu police station in Roppongi for an interview with detectives. Time was of the essence. Lucie was alive – of course she was – it was just a question of finding out where she'd gone and putting her back in touch with the family.

The first encounter at Azabu was overwhelming for the nineteen-year-old. Just a few days before she had been pushing a crash cart down a hospital corridor in Tunbridge Wells. According to her father: 'Sophie got a terrible shock when she was told that, as far as the Japanese police were concerned, her sister was not yet even a missing person. As she did not have a work permit, the police appeared not to care what had happened to her.'

Sophie was overwhelmed by the sheer scale of the city –

the walls of humanity crossing the roads and crowding the pavements, the ant-hill department stores that blended into labyrinthine subway stations. And it was hot, becoming intolerably so as the neon lights blurred night into day while Tokyo worked all day and partied all night. The streets never seemed to empty of people.

Jamie Gascoigne described how he 'felt useless – the police didn't seem that bothered'. After a week he went home.

Sophie spent her first few nights in Tokyo at the gaijin house. There was not much of any practical use that anyone could do. As she would tell an interviewer: 'I met up with Louise and some of the girls who'd worked with Lucie but they weren't able to help a great deal. They were understandably very shaken and I found myself comforting them.' Mostly, everyone cried.

CHAPTER 15

As Sophie Blackman faced her questioners in Azabu police station on the afternoon of Wednesday 5 July, a Mercedes SLK two-seater convertible flitted down the twisting road that followed the craggy coast of the Miura peninsula. The air from the sea was warm and balmy but the hood was up. If anyone had chosen to peer inside they might have observed that the car seemed to be crammed with what looked like cardboard boxes under some kind of sheet or blanket. The driver was a middle-aged man with a straggly goatee.

The midsummer sun was setting, casting long shadows as the Mercedes turned quickly off the coast road down a long, potholed track that led to the sea. The nearest town was called Aburatsubo, one of several resorts on the Miura peninsula south of the capital that included Hayamara and Zushi, popular with holidaying families and as weekend refuges for wealthy Tokyoites. Glossy marinas with restaurants and shopping malls had arisen in the bubble years. But Aburatsubo had stayed more modest. With its neat blue-tiled villas and carefully tended gardens, it might have been the English seaside – but for the seaweed drying on racks and the tuna boats tied to a rickety jetty.

The inlet at Aburatsubo was a 'typhoon hole', a place of refuge for seafarers when the big summer storms blew in from the ocean (they were still about four weeks away). Mount Fuji rose ash-black across Sagami Bay. It was a beautiful and fearful place all at once.

At the end of the track was the stony beach where picnicking families came to clamber among the ancient lava flows worn smooth by the breakers. There were caves and crevices in the undercliff. Overlooking the beach was a white-painted, four-storey apartment building, a big concrete box with a screen of wind-blown palms around the entrance propped up by a shaky wooden lattice. It was called the Blue Sea. The new arrival had the lease on Apartment 401 on the top floor. He had had it for ages, but had hardly ever used it. As far as the people living here were concerned, he was a complete stranger.

The man had a little problem. The lock to his apartment was rusted up, so he had to call an emergency locksmith to get in. That's where a mobile phone could be so handy.

Mr Hasewaga from the K K key company in Miura City turned up at around nine o'clock that night. He met the apartment owner in the little car park as they had agreed over the phone. They went up in the lift to the fourth floor where the locksmith had to use a battery-powered Makita electric drill to open the door. The metallic screeching disturbed those few neighbours who were in residence, and especially the Blue Sea's caretaker Mr Nirokawa who had a flat on the ground floor, shared with his common-law wife, Ms Ayakao Abe. She noticed an unfamiliar car parked outside and took down its numberplate. It was a two-seater Mercedes.

It was Ms Abe who indignantly came up the stairs to see what was going on. The locksmith had done his work and departed having fitted a new lock. She saw lights on in Apartment 401 and heard thumping and banging, but she thought that number 402 was the top-floor flat that had been unoccupied for so long, and so she knocked on that door. When she did so, the lights in number 401 went out.

At 10.50 p.m. Ms Abe rang the local police to report that an apartment that had long lain empty was being burgled by an intruder. Four policemen turned up from Miura City station. By now it was close to midnight. Inspector Naoki Harada heard crashing and bumping noises coming from within Apartment 401. Several times he demanded to be let in but the door did not open.

When at last it did, the man inside was, according to the testimony the inspector would give later, 'half naked and wearing something like pyjamas, there were beads of sweat on his face and he was breathing heavily. He was covered in dust and dirt. He shut the door and opened it again five minutes later, this time wearing a black T-shirt.'

There were chips of what looked like concrete strewn around the hall and a large, grey linen bag in the living room 'with something inside it'. The man at the door claimed he was retiling his bathroom, even though it was so late in the evening. When the policeman asked to see inside it, he became agitated and refused to let anyone go any further. Letting anyone see his bathroom was like 'seeing his naked body', the outraged resident insisted. Anyway there was no intruder and no burglary. Check the records, he was the owner, or rather a company of which he was the director owned the lease. His name, he said, was Joji Obara.

Inspector Harada radioed for instructions. The reported burglar said he owned the flat. He was doing some sort of decorating at midnight and the caretaker had made a complaint. His superior told him to leave it and return to the station. But the inspector would not give up quite yet. He continued to insist that he be let in, until the indignant

Mr Obara made a big show of phoning his lawyer on a mobile phone (which clearly had a flat battery as the display failed to light up) and producing a pocket tape recorder to record their conversation. He was hectoring, defensive, flustered.

The policeman went back to Ms Abe in the caretaker's flat to take her statement when the man in Apartment 401 suddenly appeared outside the door and invited them back upstairs. He was more conciliatory this time.

'There is something I want to show you,' he said. 'There is nothing I want to see except the inside of your bathroom,' the policeman replied. He later said that

We went up with him and in front of room 401 I saw something wrapped up in paper. As if holding a baby, he cradled it then opened the parcel. I saw the head of a dog.

He said the dog he cared for had died. 'And if you saw the body of the dead dog I thought you might find it upsetting. That is why I didn't want to show you inside.'

I thought he was lying. I touched the body and it was hard. It was not something that had just died that day or indeed the day before. It was like it was stuffed. I gave up trying to see any further and, according to the instructions we had got from the station, we left him alone.

The dog's name, it would turn out, was Irene.

Lucie Blackman had not been reported missing, at least not to the snoozy out-of-town Miura police anyway. There was no reason for any suspicion over a noisy resident having a row with an apartment-block caretaker. Joji Obara, whoever he was, was allowed to get on with whatever he was doing in Apartment 401 with his bags of cement. Perhaps he really was retiling the bathroom.

CHAPTER 16

There was nothing about Lucie in the Tokyo papers – not yet. But on Saturday 8 July 2000 the police did brief some favoured crime correspondents that something was amiss with a foreign girl in the city. A short piece about an unnamed twenty-one-year-old female British 'tourist' missing in the city and her anxious family appeared in a Tokyo evening paper. The name Lucie Blackman, her disappearance and the story of her apparently running off with a cult as per the telephone call from the mysterious Akira Takagi were reported in papers on the morning of 9 July.

The reporters discovered that the information had come from a friend called Louise Phillips who, like the missing 'tourist' was also some sort of Roppongi hostess, they quickly assumed – but her testimony thus far had been 'vague and contradictory' according to the briefing that Azabu detectives gave to the Tokyo police press club.

The first English-language reports that Lucie Blackman was missing were running on the newswires later that day. Tim Blackman was found at home on the Isle of Wight by the *Daily Telegraph* which ran an admirably comprehensive news report on the morning of Monday the 10th.

The case of the 'kidnapped air hostess' grabbed the attention of British newsdesks on its own merits, but when it was discovered that she worked in some sort of sex club a stampede of reporters headed for Heathrow Airport.

Lucie already ticked every box of the missing white middle-class female syndrome – the kind of story that always boosted circulation. The fact her parents were divorced wasn't so terrific, but that could be got round. It might even make it more interesting. (And it did.)

'New fears for lost Brit,' declared the *Sun* the next morning as their man got the tale of the mysterious call to Louise. 'Fears are growing that former British Airways hostess Lucie Blackman is being held as a sex slave by an evil Japanese cult,' the red top claimed sensationally. 'Japanese cults have a record of using Western women as bait to lure men into their clutches. Recruits are offered unlimited sex, but are then forbidden to leave . . . Anyone caught escaping is murdered.'

Richard Lloyd Parry, the *Independent*'s correspondent in

Tokyo, got a long way forward with the facts when he reported: 'A hostess at the Casablanca [it was Louise Phillips] revealed yesterday [Monday 10 July] that on the day of her disappearance Ms Blackman agreed to go shopping with a Japanese man whom she had met for the first time two days earlier . . . She said: "He asked her to go shopping with him on Saturday, but the funny thing was it was two hours away, which I thought was a bit odd."'

The so-called 'pick-ups', the family photographs demanded by picture editors and now splashed all over front pages, showed a smiling young blonde woman. Lucie, the former flight attendant from suburban Sevenoaks, was now 'abducted Brit bargirl'.

Louise Phillips, meanwhile, was proving a bit more forthcoming. As she explained to the *Daily Mail* ten days after Lucie disappeared:

We were not into prostitution, I swear to God we were not . . . We were planning to make as much money as we could and then head off to Thailand and on to Australia and have a really good time.

We went to school together, we worked in the City together and we left our jobs with British Airways together because we couldn't stand being separated from each other with the different schedules we had to work to.

We decided we would see the world together while we were young and the plan was to come to Japan, where I have a Japanese aunt, and work in the club scene and make as much money as we could to finance the rest of our travels.

The facts speak for themselves. She had an American boyfriend she had met and was very much in love with and she hasn't contacted him.

And there's me, her best friend, and not a word have I heard from her since our last phone conversation a week and a half ago.

Of the mysterious customer Lucie had met 'two days before and she agreed to go shopping with' Louise could say nothing more.

Still there was no clue as to Lucie's fate and the press frenzy had heightened. Tim Blackman departed from Heathrow on the morning of Wednesday the 12th. A driver from the British Embassy was at Narita Airport to collect him from the limb-numbing flight. As he recalled: 'On the way in, the car phone rang with the news that the BA flight which followed mine was full of British journalists. By the time that Sophie and I were reunited and finally faced the press conference [held at the embassy on 13 July], it was triple the size that they had been expecting.' But it was the scale of the domestic media reaction that surprised the police and just about everyone else. Television crews descended on Azabu police station and the gaijin house at Sendagaya. British reporters scurried in their wake.

The media found a shabby-low rise block down an alley-way with 'handwritten signs scrawled in English inside a filthy lobby – clearly intended for foreign tenants – plead-ing for bicycles to be parked inside and noise to be kept down'.

'They paid their rent on time and never caused any trou-ble,' the startled manager told reporters. 'All I knew about her was that she was tall, slender and blonde.' Inside, taci-turn policemen were dusting the place for fingerprints and packing Lucie's possessions into evidence bags for removal. In the hall was a payphone with a pink plastic handset. That old-fashioned piece of equipment could reveal nothing. There was nothing to say; no news, no breakthrough.

Tim and Sophie Blackman's reunion could not have taken place under more stressful circumstances. There was so much for Sophie to tell her father, yet so much she herself did not know. Tomorrow they must face this horrible circus, but at least they would be together. Or would they? That night Tim Blackman was advised by the embassy that it was perhaps best that he be picked up from his hotel in an unmarked car and brought to the back gate to avoid 'running the gauntlet of the press'. Sophie should stay away as it was clear the media were hungry for shots of the 'emotional sister'. The embassy, meanwhile, set up a dedicated phone line for anyone with information to call in confidence.

Tim did as instructed. But he was going to be anything but shy once the press conference started (it had to be moved into an auditorium so great was the crush). 'When I walked into the room and saw the number of reporters and camera crews I knew that this was precisely what we needed if we were ever going to find Lucie,' he recalled.

News of their arrival spread. Expat well-wishers pressed in with offers of help, accommodation and general advice, such as this from a Tokyo-based Brit: 'Get as much publicity as soon as possible. Get the British community here involved, don't expect much of the embassy . . . make a major ruckus! Offer rewards for information . . . take pictures of the bar where Lucie was last seen . . . make this very personal and play hard on the embarrassment factor.' It ended with this hot tip: 'Consider approaching the yakuza. They know everything.'

Tim and Sophie Blackman were going down a path that others would follow, as reluctant ringmasters for a press circus in a foreign country in a bid to find the one they loved. Only the worst outcome, the very worst, could bring closure – the discovery of a body. But that was not in their minds. Not yet.

Tim resolved to stay as cheerful and as optimistic as pos-sible – at least in public. He urged Sophie to do the same. But they must unpick what Lucie had left behind, see if they could help with finding clues. And as they hung around Azabu police station by day and trawled the swel-tering streets of Roppongi by night, it was getting more and more difficult to stay hopeful.

On one especially grim morning, Lucie's possessions from the gaijin house were laid out for them to identify. He remembered 'a building like a church hall, Lucie's clothes laid out like a church jumble sale . . . inside every-thing was grey, grey lino, grey paint, grey walls . . . and all the policemen with what seemed like identical faces, identical white shirts and black trousers . . . I noticed her little British Airways crew label and popped it in my pocket.'

As he recalled: 'I kept up this bulldog front to such an extent that I felt the Japanese police were thinking, "What a bastard," and that I didn't care about my daughter at all . . . But then I recognised a pair of suede moccasin loafers Lucie had been so proud of buying just a few weeks earlier . . . I just started to weep straight away . . . after this the Japanese police were much nicer to me.'

It was the same for Sophie. 'A policeman opened Lucie's suitcases and pulled out all of her dresses, underwear, trousers and personal things,' she told a press interviewer a little later. 'I immediately recognised her scent and, perhaps because smell is so evocative, I started crying hysterically.'

The police found Lucie's diary of her stay thus far in the city. As Tim Blackman remembered, 'The police called us back for a separate interview . . . It was conducted much more formally. Sophie and I were asked to study the hand-writing to make certain it was 100 per cent genuine. It was. It was so hard for us to read, to feel Lucie's words coming off the page as if she was with us.'

In fact the diary didn't tell them much. She'd written about '*dohan* hell', whatever that was, and a lot of stuff about feeling fat, being average, hating her body, drinking way too much and being broke. Completely normal for a girl of twenty-one. There was some stuff about the guy named Joe, the American 'sailor' Scott Fraser (they already knew about him from the postcard home), a lot about par-tying with Louise and other girls and some oblique references to drugs. Her moods seemed to be swinging all over the place, crap one day, happy the next – but they knew that too from the calls and e-mails saying how home-sick she was. But there was nothing to say what had happened. There wasn't a clue in the diary as to where she might be now.

What could Tim and Sophie Blackman do? As far as they were concerned, Lucie had been abducted. She was being held against her will, and every hour that passed added to her jeopardy. The methods of the Tokyo police seemed opaque. It was all grindingly slow. Thus far, it seemed, all investigators had done was to question Louise Phillips a couple of times and interview Tetsuo Nishi, the Casablanca's manager, who either would not or could not reveal anything that would help them find her. Other than questioning him, they had paid no more attention to Lucie's place of work, its staff or its customers. They still seemed to think Lucie had gone off willingly with a boyfriend. Lots of girls went off like this and chose not to tell anyone about it. And anyway, she should not have been working as a bargirl. As *The Times* reported on 13 July: '"People like Lucie are the tip of a huge iceberg of illegal labour," said Toshihiko Mii, who is in charge of the Blackman case. "But of course the safety of Miss Blackman is our first priority."'

It was the police's apparent indifference to the Casablanca connection that seemed increasingly perverse. That's where she must have met the guy – the one who took her to the coast. It was surely the same guy who had made the weird phone call to Louise. Whatever the police at Azabu might assume, he was not a boyfriend.

Lucie's friend Shannon from the Casablanca, the one who had told Louise Phillips to try the usual bars in any search for their friend, remembered those first days when Lucie went missing with a mix of self-blame and anger at the police's lack of interest: 'I've often asked myself whether I gave Louise the right advice that night,' she said, 'and if there was any way we might have found Lucie any quicker. But what more could we have done? We were gaijin – working illegally. Who knew how long someone had to be missing for before it could be considered a serious incident? It's not how it is at home where if someone goes missing it's an immediate concern. There are over 120 million people here.'

Thus far, Sophie Blackman, overwhelmed by the heat and the sheer size and strangeness of the city, had been unable to add much to either the police inquiry or the slavering media's hunger for novelty. At first she refused to talk to newspapers at all and tried to make sure Louise Phillips did the same. (It was a little late for that.)

'Miss Blackman says that she cannot answer any of our questions without the permission of the British Embassy,' Deputy Superintendent Toshihiko Mii, the officer in charge of the investigation, was quoted as saying. 'It's very strange.' In fact the embassy knew that the British press (and not just the red tops) wanted images of Sophie looking traumatised and had advised her to lie low.

'The police are not making any inquiries other than of Ms Phillips,' said the Tokyo detective, who meanwhile had his own theory about Lucie's motivations and potential whereabouts. 'Speaking personally, it's possible she got to know someone, was attracted to him and ran away,' he told a British reporter. 'There are many possibilities and we don't rule anything out.' That would become a bit of a catchphrase.

The combination of bungling Japanese sleuths (the 'Lucie cops' as a section of the British press would have it) and a suburban English rose lost in a city of alien sex perverts could not have made a better story. Roppongi was trawled from end to end by seasoned sleaze-busters and plucky female reporters going undercover.

British newspapers had not, up to now, been that interested in Japan, not the non-financial press anyway. Reporting had been largely limited to technology (especially mobile phones and computers) or some resurrected wartime nip-bashing when they did anything nationalistic or showed a taste for whale meat. Japanese wackiness was always a staple for the UK media and television – but what the nation of over 120 million did for sex was a mystery.

Then a blonde girl from Sevenoaks disappeared in 'teeming Tokyo' and Japan's sex business in all its manifestations inspired an explosively lurid interest. 'Millions of Japanese men' were looking for 'the love of a young Western girl'.

'One Tokyo high-school girl in twenty has engaged in prostitution,' so British broadsheet readers were breathlessly informed. The *Observer* went as far as buying a copy of *The Stage* (published in London), which was evidently packed with 'adverts aimed at enticing out-of-work young models and actresses to have drinks with Japanese businessmen, who often offer their Western companions vast sums for sex'.

The broadsheet's investigation moved on to Brighton, where a girl in a lap-dancing club revealed she had three friends who had left Japan after being sexually assaulted. 'Hostessing is not something you want to do for a long time. You end up doing drugs to stay awake and to stay as happy and cheery as you are expected to be and that is just the slippery slope,' she said.

The paper did much better a week later, in getting 'Jo' to tell her story – she'd been a hostess at the Casablanca a few months before Lucie worked there. She'd been taken on by Tetsuo Nishi in spite of being over six feet tall, 'something Japanese men found intimidating'. Her experiences were certainly eventful. As she wrote:

I was offered incredible sums to 'go outside' (sleep with) customers. One elderly customer said I was the reincarnation of Boadicea. He took pictures of me which he would bring in a beautifully presented album on his next visit. I was invited to lunch one day with his wife. Customers often pestered girls for dates outside club hours, but the idea of spending time with these men for free seemed insane, so this lunch date was the only one I ever accepted.

His wife had no problem with him lavishing gifts and hours of his time on me. The afternoon took on a surreal twist when he got drunk and made his wife sing patriotic war songs.

Another customer insisted I follow him in his aerobics routine to 'Fantasy Island' . . . Others thought only of sex. One told of how he enjoyed raping his wife and mistress. Another insisted I watch his holiday video. After a few seconds the footage changed to hard porn. He said, 'I thought you would like the joke.'

But there were compensations. The money for a start, and the 'camaraderie between girls is incredible, a fiercely protective sisterhood from which lifelong friendships are forged and travelling partners found,' said Jo. 'It was frequently bloody good fun – your mates, free alcohol, nights of partying until dawn. And more money than you knew what to do with, all of it illegally earned.' Jo ended up spending three and a half weeks in prison for visa violations.

The sensational press reaction was not surprising. Hostess-bar culture of the Japanese variety simply did not exist in Britain – or anywhere else for that matter. There had to be loads of sex and drugs in it somewhere. So what had Lucie Blackman been up to?

Exploring Roppongi, 'the steamy, neon-lit heart of Tokyo's booming, twenty-four-hour sex-and-sushi industry', British reporters strove to find out. In the 'sleazy executive fleshpots of Tokyo' and 'smoke-fugged hostess clubs', they noted 'empty glasses were instantly refilled; cigarettes instantly lit; steaming towels were proffered after a visit to the bathroom'; and (handily for expense claims) 'all charges were meticulously logged on a clipboard kept on the table'.

The *Sun* found that 'Lucie's bar, the Casablanca, on the sixth floor of a block of debauchery, is relatively respectable [but] several around it are dens of iniquity. Directly opposite is a gay hangout, which caters for transvestites and other weirdos. And a couple of floors below . . . is Seventh Heaven, which boasts nude live sex shows and bondage acts.'

A Roppongi hostess – Alice – told the *News of the World*: 'This is very hard work, you live rough and hardly get any sleep. You quickly discover you are basically working for the local mafia . . . We were taught three things when we started: how to light our client's cigarettes, how to pour his drinks, and not to put our elbows on the table . . .You meet all kinds of weird people and you have to go out with them for dinner as part of the job. This could easily have happened to any of us, you don't really know who you're going out with.'

So what was this debauched world of steaming towels, going out for dinner and no elbows on the table? In a set-piece feature article Professor Anne Allison, a Chicago academic who had worked as a Tokyo hostess in the eighties, was able to inform *Times* readers two weeks after Lucie went missing that:

Japanese sex, like Japanese society, is ordered and orderly. Japanese men like to know exactly what is expected of them and how they are meant to behave before entering any situation. And in the hostess clubs, they know that the only thing on offer is titillation. Price determines what's on offer. The more you pay, the less sex or bodily contact there will be.

You tell him you wish he was your lover. He tells you he would like to take you home. You say that would be lovely, but my sister is in town and I have to show her the sights. It is the answer he was expecting; he might well have been frightened at any other . . .

Japanese men certainly fantasise about sleeping with Western women, but the reality of having one as a real wife or mistress frightens them. We might intrigue them, and there is certainly kudos in having a Western woman on your arm, but Western women are known to have opinions, to be neither obedient nor subservient. The men are much happier to keep their fantasies in the safe world of the hostess bars, where they can pretend it is true for an evening.

Japanese wives aren't threatened by hostesses for that very reason. They resent their husbands going to the clubs as much as English women resent their husbands going to pubs. Their real rivals are their husbands' female work colleagues . . .

There is so much sex available in Japan, particularly in Tokyo, that there is simply no need to bully hostesses into sleeping with clients. It is much simpler to find a willing woman and pay her. There is no shortage of Western women who would be willing, and there would be no need for such a woman to disappear. What has happened to Lucie Blackman is, so far, a mystery.

It was as if all the sexual predilections of the whole of Japan were under the spotlight. Homely bedrooms were being burst into, the tender office love affairs of salarymen spied upon, the whole theatre of romantic illusion held up for global mockery. Japanese men had to pay for the company of attractive women and they didn't even get sex! What chumps! What had Professor Allison said in *The Times*? 'If that same man went to a disco, he would probably fail to pick up a woman and go home feeling deflated and rejected. The hostess clubs remove the risk of failure.'

The Japanese reaction to foreign scrutiny was an overall

sense of revulsion. In the same way that gaijin customers were banned from Kabuki-cho's wilder shores, and indeed the highest-end hostess clubs, the idea of mocking foreigners trampling through the nation's erotic psyche was loathsome. And the media's assumption that Japanese men were somehow bewitched by goddess-like gaijin girls who they could only get to look at by paying them a fortune was crudely racist. As the *Independent*'s Richard Lloyd Parry later commented, 'The notion that Japanese men are "obsessed" with Western women is a lazy cliché – from my perch in Tokyo, cocky, skirt-chasing foreign men with an appetite for Japanese women are far more obvious . . . [and] anyone who believes that this is a sexually repressed country should spend a Friday night in a district such as Roppongi, where young Japanese women feed on foreign men with equal enthusiasm and ferocity.'

Hence, perhaps, the unforgiving tone of some letters to editors of Japanese-language newspapers about Lucie's apparent fate. One reader declared that Lucie 'just got what was coming to her' for working without proper papers in a place such as the Casablanca. Another wrote that if she purposefully took such a job without a visa, 'she should have expected what she got'.

The international interest in Japan's sex life was becoming a diplomatic embarrassment. When the *New York Times*' Tokyo correspondent wrote in the context of the hunt for

Lucie: 'For Japanese men, paying for sex and other entertainment by women is common, and carries no stigma,' the
Ministry of Foreign Affairs was moved to make a formal
reply:

> The article claims that it is a very common practice for
> Japanese males to pay for sex without bearing much
> sense of guilt. Without any factual basis, [the author]
> alleges that 'thousands of Asian and European women
> are smuggled into the country as virtual slaves'. He fur-
> ther asserts that this 'is a feature that sets Japanese
> society apart from much of the West'. This view is an
> extreme over-generalisation, based on a stereotype of
> Japanese society.

Perhaps the best stereotype-free reporting came from
Richard Lloyd Parry. He always seemed to be a day ahead
of the pack. On Tuesday 11 July he filed a reflective, well-
informed story on the Casablanca club (which was now
barring its doors to even the most forceful reporters) and its
place – or otherwise – in the water trade as a whole. He
explained that '[a]t one extreme, it includes the geisha,
female entertainers of exceptional skill who are only to be
found in the most refined parts of Kyoto and Tokyo. At the
other are the Korean and Chinese prostitutes who provide
hurried relief in massage parlours ... And somewhere in

the middle are the Roppongi hostesses, girls such as Lucie Blackman, a twenty-one-year-old British woman who worked at Casablanca until she disappeared without a trace eleven days ago.'

The thirty-one-year old reporter did very well, cruising Roppongi, 'where the foreign hostesses gather after work', to find in the small hours of the sweltering Tokyo summer night that 'the talk is all about Lucie. There is little else but talk, for the facts are so sketchy.'

He found girls who knew Lucie. 'Helena' (not her real name), for example, who worked at the Casablanca told him 'It was always *dohan*, *dohan*, *dohan*. Girls who didn't get any *dohan* were asked to leave. But the ones who got a lot were the top girls. Lucie was a top girl . . . Her customers were very nice, no weirdos that I could see.'

'Maybe this is a warning,' Deputy Superintendent Mii told the *Independent*'s correspondent. 'If I compare my policewomen who go on patrol and the hostesses in the bars, the hostesses are in more danger. But the fact is that there are so many of these hostesses and they keep coming.'

He was right, of course. Girls working clubs on a tourist visa – illegals in the water trade – were always coming and going. Why should there be such a fuss about this one?

Deputy Superintendent Mii seemed nostalgic for the Roppongi of old. 'It used to be very high class,' he told

Japan Today. 'These days, people from more than thirty different countries roam the streets. More and more people are being arrested for drug trafficking, violence, pick-pocketing and prostitution.'

The global interest in missing Lucie, the prurient fascination in just what it was she had been doing, and the fact that the political leaders of the industrialised nations (the G8) would be in conclave on the island of Okinawa the following week, all served to concentrate minds. Robin Cook, the British Foreign Secretary was already in Tokyo on a warm-up visit to the capital before the G8 summit, and Tony Blair, the Prime Minister was due to join him on the 21st. Cook was reported to have been assured by Yohei Kono, Japan's foreign minister, that the search for Lucie was a top priority and that the investigation has been placed in the hands of Superintendent Akira Mitsuzane, the Metropolitan Police Department's chief homicide officer.

But still it was all agonisingly slow. Why was the management of the Casablanca unable to tell police anything at all about the man Lucie had gone off with on 1 July? It was clear she must have met him at the club. Was it a cover-up, a code of silence because Lucie was a gaijin? Was having a dead English girl on your hands bad for business?

One of Lucie's hostess friends, the one Louise had

called on the night Lucie failed to come home, remembered how the Casablanca manager

> warned us under threat of dismissal not to talk to any journalists, although there were plenty around. Tim and Sophie Blackman came to the club. Like any father would be, Tim seemed desperate for information. I felt terribly sorry for them and could see the anguish in their faces . . . I didn't get seen by the police until quite a lot later, but the questions they asked me were all very superficial, like what I was doing on the night Lucie disappeared, and whether we had seen her go off with any particular man. You got the impression they weren't really interested.

As Tim Blackman recalled: 'The club may well have known who Lucie went off with. But if they did, they certainly wouldn't admit it. While I was in Roppongi, I quickly realised that a successful hostess business depended on absolute discretion . . . Any whiff that club owners would be willing to reveal names and details of their clients would have put them instantly out of business . . . I guess word would get round quickly too.'

The Tokyo police insisted that they had got all they could out of the Casablanca. Had they impounded its computers, Tim Blackman wanted to know. They had not, but they would need special authority to do so. And what about a membership list? There wasn't one. But surely there were business cards and records of credit-card transactions. Indeed there were, but so far they had revealed nothing relevant.

In a drawn-out interview with the police held at Azabu, Tim Blackman was told that Tetsuo Nishi had been sacked, but that had nothing to do with Lucie. The meeting was prickly, the interchange minuted by a translator:

'Has [Nishi] been found, has he been questioned?' asked Tim Blackman.

'Of course we are talking to him,' replied the Tokyo detective. 'He knew a lot about the club and the hostesses and has been questioned many times. He has given information about customers who may have been close to Lucie . . . we have several names but cannot yet draw conclusions as to who might be of special interest.'

'What about this man Joe? He seems to have occupied eighty per cent of Lucie's time. Why has he shown no interest or tried to contact Sophie or me? He should be very concerned.'

'Are you suggesting a meeting with him?' asked the detective.

'Not necessarily.'

'We will consider it.'

Joe was quickly ruled out of the inquiry – even if Tim Blackman, according to his notes, entertained the idea for a few days that he was the 'go between', who 'arranges and gets paid'.

It was Tim who brought Scott Fraser to the detectives' attention, but they at first seemed uninterested. They hadn't listened to Louise Phillips either when she'd told them about an American boyfriend in one of her first, tearful interrogations at Azabu. 'We don't know who he is or where he is,' said Deputy Superintendent Mii in response to a press question. In fact, they would get round to interviewing him pretty soon after that, but he had clearly had no involvement in her disappearance. Nor could he add anything to what Louise or anyone else had said. His name, if not the fact of his existence, would be kept out of press reports for a little while yet.

The revelation that Lucie had a real boyfriend when she went off on her mysterious trip to the coast at last persuaded some of the more cynical Azabu detectives that she had not just simply gone off for a long weekend with her lover. Anyway, far too much time had now passed for that.

Meanwhile, Tim Blackman tried another tack, to see if there was something he and Sophie could identify in Lucie's personality, habits and preferences that might provide a clue. 'She would only be attracted by a well-groomed, "designer" man,' he told detectives. 'He would have to be very attractive and/or wealthy. This man in turn would have had to work hard to gain her confidence, keeping his profile low over days and weeks, then made her an offer of some kind . . . When she was a child, if she wanted something she would get it, but she would only tell half the story to do so if necessary. This is what she did to Louise.'

Ah yes, Louise. If Lucie had been telling her friend only half the story of what she was up to, how could Louise Phillips tell the authorities or Tim Blackman? Was she holding anything back, as she clearly had been when she had first gone to the police to report Lucie missing? According to Tim Blackman's notes he thought she 'was frightened, threatened, scared for her own safety'. In public he defended her as 'confused and traumatised, and doing her best to recall everything'.

In that first frantic week, Louise had been at Azabu police station more or less every day – on one occasion for eleven hours. She was not in trouble she was assured; she was free to leave Japan at any time. 'The police told me that if I go home they have got nothing to go on. When I heard that, I was determined to stay,' she told a British newspaper reporter on 13 July. But whatever she had told anyone thus far was desperately sketchy.

She had called her mother back home in Bromley and

told her about the weird call she had received as she was leaving the embassy. Maureen Phillips, in turn, relayed to the *Daily Telegraph* what her daughter had said:

'Lucie is going on to a better life,' this man said. He wanted her address because he claimed Lucie couldn't remember it, which Louise found very hard to believe. He claimed Lucie was going to write a letter as a final goodbye before she joined the cult.

Louise kept begging to speak to Lucie but he said she was not well enough . . . He said he knew Lucie was six thousand pounds in debt, which she had picked up buying a car and other things . . .

'I knew the girls were doing hostessing, but loads of foreign girls do it and it is by no means prostitution,' said Mrs Phillips. 'Lucie is very, very reliable with Louise. She would never, ever let her down by not turning up as arranged. So when she failed to show up, Louise knew something was wrong. They have been best friends since they were thirteen.'

As far as Tim now understood it, Louise and Lucie had been working at the club together on the crucial date, which, so he thought, was Wednesday 28 June. Lucie had been dancing and doing karaoke with an unknown man. She had later told Louise that this man had offered to give her a mobile phone. 'There is a high probability this is the same man,' he said in an interview at Azabu police station.

'The club must know who this man is . . . but if he is a big spender, the mama-san will not talk,' said Tim.

There was a further indication, from what Tim himself had been able to put together, that this man had been in the Casablanca before 28 June. He had frequented the club on several occasions, including on the previous Friday when he had been buying champagne. During the week that followed, Lucie decided she would have to go out at the weekend with this guy if she was going to be any good at *dohan*. She had lost her last *dohan* customer due to turning down a weekend invitation.

But there was a glaringly obvious way of unlocking the puzzle – the phone calls that Louise Phillips had received on the afternoon of 1 July, relaying Lucie's progress to the coast. Tim Blackman asked pointedly what the police inquiry had thus far discovered on their origin.

'We have obtained records of the mobile phone they shared at Yoyogi House and sorted out which calls are Lucie's and which are Louise's,' said the detective. Well that was something. The Azabu police had already briefed the press on the sequence of calls – the one at about 2 p.m. on 1 July when Lucie had rung Louise Phillips on the 'pink plastic public telephone at the boarding house' and the ones which followed on the shared mobile that Louise had

had in her possession that day. The number had been provided to clients at the Casablanca, according to the police. It was to that phone that Lucie had made her second and third calls through the afternoon and early evening.

'So what was the number of the phone Lucie used to make those calls and who was it registered to?' asked Tim Blackman.

'Unfortunately we cannot obtain the number due to technical reasons,' the detective replied.

'Somebody will have been billed for that call. That information is sitting in a computer somewhere,' said Tim Blackman.

'In the Japanese telephone system we can get a record of calls made, but not received.'

Tim seemed beaten. The Japanese privacy laws and telephone companies' ways of operating blocked off that line of investigation. At least that was what he was being told. Tim Blackman was coming close to despair.

Yet there was more to crush his spirits. The way Lucie had been living was clearly not conducive to her general welfare or anyone else's. There were drugs around, lots of drugs, as he had quickly discovered in his trawl of Roppongi. Some girls were coy about it, others more forthcoming. Some seemed to be smashed out of their heads all the time. An Iranian called Powen, with a 'dominant personality', seemed to be the chief dealer – in Lucie's circle anyway. He supplied Envy (Hama's bar) and a club called Quest.

Like any parent, Tim Blackman was keen to believe that his daughter was only at the margins of any real wrongdoing, that others must have led her 'astray'. But just how far astray would you have to go to have disappeared from a hostess bar in Roppongi?

It is clear from Tim's handwritten notes made in those anguished and exhausting early days of looking for Lucie that a terrible conspiracy theory gripped him. Was the answer 'closer to home'? Was all that stuff about Lucie being summoned to the coast on a date, then being abducted by a cult, a cover-up? Were the phone calls real? What if the police could not – or would not – find traces of them because they had never existed? 'Motive fear, panic. To cover an accidental overdose. Where is body?' Tim Blackman scribbled on a notepad, among myriad contact numbers and scraps of garbled facts. '70 per cent [of murders] committed by people close . . . ice [crystal meth] $100 a bag . . . Powen is trader.'

One particular incident shook the ground beneath Tim Blackman's feet as surely as an earthquake. Nothing could be certain. As he recalled it:

One night I was just wandering distractedly round Roppongi. It was very late, and I was feeling so desperate

I did not even really know what I was doing. I found the whole place deeply intimidating. Suddenly I was approached by a man working as a tout outside One Eyed Jack. He seemed to recognise who I was, whispering in my ear as I walked past, and suggesting I come back in ten minutes and come into the club like a normal customer.

Hoping he might know something about Lucie, I did as he told me. Once in the club he drew me into a side room and produced a large book of double-sided A4 pages containing the names of all the girls he had approached to work as hostesses in the last two years. He pointed to two names – Louise and Lucie. To my amazement the entry was dated 1999, over a year before Lucie ever went to Japan. Or so I thought.

Afterwards I asked Louise about this. But she flatly denied it, and has continued to do so ever since. But I cannot help thinking that this was more than coincidence. The spelling of Lucie's name was unusual . . .

However bizarre the now multiplying theories were, Tim Blackman had to keep believing that his daughter really had been abducted, and that she was still alive.

Everybody had a theory. 'Cult rescue' specialists waded in with all sorts of strange advice. She had been kidnapped by gangsters or inducted into an S&M fetish ring to be held as a sex slave. The girls from Casablanca and other Roppongi clubs themselves had views, but they weren't terribly helpful. She was in Bangkok; she was in Singapore; she was hiding somewhere in the city. She wasn't the first to disappear.

In Britain, meanwhile, Lucie's mother was also beginning to have doubts about what everyone was saying. Desperate to do what she could to aid the search for her daughter, she began by consulting mediums. Both likeminded friends and total strangers were anxious to help in any way possible.

Back on the ground in Tokyo, Tim and Sophie Blackman were making as much noise as they could. They had brought videos of home movies with them to give to TV stations. Sophie organised a 'Have you seen Lucie?' poster campaign. She had already set up an information line with 'the help of a technological whizzkid called Michael from Virgin's Tokyo office' as Tim put it. They printed thousands of posters and flyers to hand out on the street. Huw Shakeshaft, an expat British businessman with an office in Roppongi, encountered Tim and Sophie in a restaurant and offered the use of his facilities for their campaign. Virgin boss Richard Branson fronted a television appeal.

Updates on the search were running each night on the evening news. Lucie's face was everywhere – on magazines, in the subway, on posters stuck on powerline posts.

Lucie Blackman, British female. Lucie Blackman, confidential hotline. Lucie Blackman, missing, Missing, MISSING!

All those reporters and film crews scouring Roppongi represented a little army of investigators who might blaze a trail for the Blackmans as they tried to get their own resolution on what had really happened. They just had to find out who she had gone off with on that last date. Surely the police must soon discover who that was? And if they were too dozy, then the London hacks would light the way.

But by now the first wave of British journalists were being ordered home. Tim had just about resisted the 'buy-up' offers that had come with the arrival of the British tabloids in Tokyo. But they had gone through the streets of red-light Roppongi in search of talkative bargirls. One of them – 'Claire, 25, from Brighton' – spoke to the *Mail on Sunday*. What she said had a ring of truth:

> It was devastating to all the girls and the club owners that Lucie had been abducted, particularly when the police suspect it may have been one of our clients.
>
> I hate to say it, but I think Lucie is not coming back. I didn't like her at first but once she got to know me, we became good friends. I have to say that Lucie did appear to be on the lookout for a rich guy to spend money on her.

She had her eye on the main chance. There are bars here that give the girls money for bringing men in and persuading them to buy them drinks. You can make thousands of yen a night doing that and Lucie was a good drinks hustler.

Like most of the girls, me included, she liked to go out and party. We are out to have a good time and make a good bit of money in a short space of time.

There is no sex on offer at the Casablanca; the men who come here are happy just to drink, sing a few karaoke songs and enjoy the company of beautiful Western girls.

Reporters found sex and sensation galore – but not a single clue as to where Lucie might really be.

By far the most effective thing Tim and Sophie had done so far was to set up a dedicated telephone line, with an additional e-mail reporting system to supplement the British Embassy operation. They hoped that it might attract more calls from the marginal and the visa-less than its 'official' counterpart. The volunteers who were pressing themselves on Tim and Sophie with offers of help could take calls, in confidence, round the clock. In fact both operations would run in parallel and share information. The overwhelming majority of calls to the embassy were in Japanese. The Azabu police had made their own dispositions. Just as well, as it would turn out.

With the sudden explosion in domestic press interest in missing Lucie, the hotlines were ringing pretty much all the time with sightings, theories, cranks, friends, expressions of goodwill or otherwise. She was seen getting into an expensive car in Chiba with a middle-aged driver. A caller saw her in a pink dress on a road crossing in Ginza. She had been seen in a launderette in Sendagaya on the afternoon of 1 July. She was seen at a road crossing in Roppongi with an 'Indian-looking girl', who was overheard saying to her, 'Let's go – you don't want to be found.'

Lucie was spotted holding hands with a man in the Just Co. store in Nagoya. She was at a party given by 'Mexicans' at Fujisaw Beach. She was seen at Mount Fuji. She had been abducted in Roppongi by a yakuza organisation called Super Production which made pornographic movies. A dry-cleaning shop assistant claimed that she saw Lucie with a 'surly' oriental man less than twenty-four hours before she vanished; she said that she remembered thinking them a 'weird couple' because the man said nothing, not even offering to help when 'Miss Blackman' – who spoke no Japanese – scrambled in vain to find the receipt for a pair of trousers.

There were scores of such reported sightings made during those crucial first few days around or after 1 July. Not one proved positive. Not one delivered anything to provide a lead to whoever had picked Lucie up at

219

Sendagaya station to drive her to the coast. She had, so it seemed, vanished into thin air.

In the meantime, something had happened to raise the stakes dramatically. On 20 July, a typewritten letter post-marked Chiba arrived at the Azabu station purporting to come from Lucie. It was written in clumsy English telling police to 'leave me alone' and included a passage seemingly addressed to her father: 'Don't worry about me. I'm fine,' it said. And 'I want you to return to England.'

With the letter was enclosed 1187 million yen (£6800) in cash. The careless language might have been produced by computer translation software. It was clearly a fake. But was it from a kidnapper or was it a cruel hoax? And why send money?

The next day, 21 July, Tim was summoned to the embassy to meet Tony Blair, who seemed profoundly concerned. He had already made an appeal to the Japanese people to help in the hunt for Lucie in an interview the day before: 'It's obviously an appalling, heartbreaking story, and every parent's nightmare is to have their child working abroad and then disappear,' he had said.

The Prime Minister promised to raise the case with his Japanese counterpart, Yoshiro Mori. 'I know the Japanese authorities are trying very hard. We are obviously going to work very closely with them,' said Mr Blair. Actually that would turn out to be true. And, under discreet but high-level pressure, things began to move.

At the end of July, Lucie's face was on the front pages of Japan's newspapers almost daily. TV reporters followed every move the Blackmans made. The blondeness of the victim and the assumed Japaneseness of the murderer gave social commentators and pundits an excuse to wallow in national navel-examination. After the great panic over teenage cash-for-dates, what did all this say about Japan's moral state?

The speculation and reported sightings grew ever more frenzied. Lucie was spotted in Hong Kong, to where, having been dosed with heroin, she had been taken with a bunch of other Western girls on a merchant ship that had sailed from Osaka. She was seen in Qatar. She was sighted in Korea. It was all nonsense.

And it got weirder. The sensational weekly tabloid, *Shukan Hoseki*, reported that a fifty-two-year-old Japanese man had been found hanged in a 'suburban Tokyo apartment three days after being questioned by police in the disappearance of Lucie Blackman investigation'. An unidentified source revealed that 'several police posters concerning Lucie's possible abduction were found in the flat with the body of the dead man. Police refused to comment or to speculate on a connection,' according to the story.

*

In the UK, Jane Blackman's spiritual search was also producing results. A medium in southwest London had clear indications that other girls had gone missing. One was an Australian student called Katrina or Katherine. 'If they could find one they could find them all,' according to the seer. (The message about an Australian called Katrina was spookily close to what was. at this stage, a totally unlooked-for truth.)

Lucie, she said, was alive and being held in a boarded-up house in a run-down street near a sewage outlet, about a mile or so away from where she was originally staying. Jane e-mailed her daughter Sophie in Tokyo on 26 July with the news: 'The police are looking in the wrong place . . . surely we can get Louise hypnotised.' She thought that Louise Phillips might subconsciously have more information, and suggested that Sophie pass the information on to the presumably sceptical police, saying it came from the hotline. Otherwise they might not take action.

The next day Jane Blackman relayed news from another medium that Lucie was being groomed as some sort of pamphleteering 'slave' by 'fanatics' who kept her against her will in a big house surrounded by candles and incense. The police, she said, were not doing a great deal; one policeman was corrupt and was not to be trusted – and nor was an 'evil' Japanese woman aged thirty-five to forty-two with a single plait of hair and a mole on her face. She was both a police informer and some sort of go-between to the yakuza. 'She is lethal.'

The letter of 20 July, supposedly from Lucie, had not gone unremarked on the spirit plane. It was revealed that another, genuine letter was on its way to the police, better written this time, which would refer to her (Jane Blackman) and contain a picture of Lucie that would prove shocking – it would show that her hair had been hacked off and what remained was dyed dark.

The next day Jane sent information from another seer who discovered by dowsing over a map of Japan that Lucie was being held on 'a heavily guarded island off Yokohama', and was being used as a prostitute by wealthy men who have government connections. She was transported to this island on a 'gin-palace' yacht which was 'big, white with blue on it'.

'My medium mentioned a Georgian house and when I reread Lucie's e-mails she said that Joe took her to a lovely Italian restaurant that was in a Georgian building,' she told her daughter Sophie. 'Also we have hacked into Lucie's e-mails and [I] am very concerned about the ones from Sam[antha] who is a friend of Emma Phillips – they are really weird and strange. We need to hack into Emma's e-mails, Louise's and Joe's and then I think we will find the missing link.'

Jane Blackman had clearly sought and believed in these spirit revelations with the utmost sincerity. Any parent would hope and pray that their missing daughter was still alive and be as positive as they might be about messages that reinforced that belief. But how they were supposed to help at the Tokyo end was not clear.

A private investigator engaged by Lucie's mother – an ex-Metropolitan Police detective called Dai Davies – prowled around Roppongi, only to become very alarmed by the quantity of drugs that hostess girls seemed to be doing. British newspaper reporters inevitably caught up with him and, equally inevitably, he regaled them with a view of what he had seen. Even for a veteran copper it was all pretty shocking.

Davies told Richard Lloyd Parry that Lucie had somehow got mixed up in the crystal methamphetamine business and that was the reason for her disappearance. 'It's important to emphasise that Lucie is not the kind of girl who would have taken this stuff herself,' he added. 'But some of her fellow hostesses do not have the same morals and she may have become inadvertently involved.' More usefully, he was able, from the testimony of one Casablanca hostess, to get a description of someone Lucie had been with in the club in the days before she disappeared. His name was a mystery. He wasn't a regular and he had always come alone. He never gave out business cards. The ex-detective put together a photo-fit with the help of former Metropolitan Police colleagues and toured the clubs with it (it was pretty crude). Still no one had a clue.

Every second person in Roppongi, it seemed now, was an investigative reporter stalking the sticky streets of the new Babylon. The *Washington Post* reported excitedly: 'By day, Roppongi is a busy commercial section. At night, it becomes a bazaar of titillation. The streets are lined with touts trying to lure customers into the clubs with sugges-tive promises and brochures of busty models. They peddle a lusty smorgasbord of strip joints, hostess clubs and dim bars offering private sessions with women in back rooms.'

After shutting its doors to reporters, the Casablanca shut its doors altogether (if only temporarily). Other clubs stayed open, of course they did. People had to make a living, after all. Girls still went to work and the customers still came just as eagerly. Although the conversation could get a little stilted.

Meanwhile, the big girlie party was in ruins. Emma Phillips flew to Tokyo from England to comfort her younger sister Louise, who was 'practically living down the police station', as she told a friend. 'I'm losing hope and losing my mind. The police want me to stay as long as pos-sible, so I've no idea when I'll be going home, but hopefully soon, meaning we'll find her,' she e-mailed

Shannon whose visa had expired and who had had to leave the country to go back to Canada.

Mel had moved into the gaijin house at Sendagaya to provide a little solidarity, but, as she told a friend a little later, 'Things got really weird and scary when I stayed with [Louise] and the police were putting a lot of stress on her.' Louise was now keener that ever to get out and, in fact, she did go back to England at the end of August, but with the police proviso that she return if summoned back to Tokyo.

The summer was passing in a sweaty miasma. It was too hot and humid even for the water trade to operate. Tim knew that he too must go home, with the idea that Sophie (who had gone back to England for a break after the first frantic weeks of searching) would fly back out to supplant him in Tokyo and keep their end of the find-Lucie operation alive. He was running out of ideas. He told an interviewer:

I call on the Azabu police regularly, but they have nothing to tell me. The embassy has nothing to tell me. I've got to find some way to learn something. I'm trying to get in touch with someone associated with the yakuza. I figure the organisations might have fingers into the underworld that might have a clue where my daughter is. I've heard horror stories about girls who've gone missing similar to

Lucie. I've heard of girls being drugged, taken away, photographed, abused, then returned [alive].

But there was still a flicker of hope and a reward for information was offered by an anonymous sympathiser: 150 million yen.

Sophie arrived back in Tokyo at the beginning of September and played her elder sister in a reconstruction of blonde Lucie in a black dress getting into a car, staged at Sendagaya station. Still, there was no breakthrough. As Tim Blackman recalled:

With the combined pressure of the British and Japanese press now mounting, by the time we had been there nine weeks, they had put one hundred and fifty police on to the case . . .

The police did not like our relationship with the media. They told us this was because it would damage their investigations. But I believe it was because it would highlight their shortcomings . . . From then on the Japanese police refused to tell us anything at all.

Tim, now back in the UK, was close to utter despair. Richard Lloyd Parry described him in a piece published in the *Independent* on 20 September 2000: 'He looks tired, it is true, but so would anyone who has been making this flight as often as he has. Since the middle of July, Mr Blackman has made this thirteen-hour journey six times. The police have, according to Mr Blackman, thoroughly interviewed and eliminated from suspicion everyone connected to the club where Lucie worked plus her boyfriend, a sailor [Scott Parry, the US Marine].'

Lucie's mother now flew out to take up the search, 'knowing I wasn't going to find her. I just wanted to be on the same soil as she was,' as Jane Blackman told a reporter afterwards. In contrast to Tim's high-profile performances, the trip was as discreet as she could make it, other than giving one press conference. She appealed 'to the women of Japan: the mothers, the daughters, the sisters, the aunts and the grandmothers – anyone who can give either us or the police those vital clues needed to solve this dreadful mystery. We believe there is someone out there who knows who did this and we desperately want this witness to come forward.'

'The police have been marvellous,' she said on her return to England. 'I believe they are doing everything they can. But I couldn't stop crying. I was crying for the whole four days I was there. I don't think I'll go back, not unless they've found her.'

In the meantime, Shingo Takahashi, a criminal profiler and a director of the Japan Cult Recovery Council, had dramatically declared that 'a serial killer who preys on attractive Western women may be on the loose in Tokyo'.

Dr Takahashi was, among other things, an expert in *kit-sunetsuki* or 'fox possession'. This was a common diagnosis for mental illness until the early twentieth century. The victim was typically a young woman, whom the fox spirit entered for some reason beneath her fingernails. Stories of fox possession still appeared in the popular Japanese media. He profiled the man who apparently had kidnapped Lucie.

He probably acted alone, said Takahashi, was obsessed with Western women and most likely did not have a steady job, although he would be well dressed and would have enough money to cruise the hostess bars of Roppongi. 'He would have been around Lucie before . . . He was possibly a customer or part of her surroundings . . . He probably has past convictions for offences against women.' The psychopathologist added this chilling line: 'I believe the same man may be responsible for the disappearance of as many as seven other Western women in the past five years.'

More missing hostesses? A serial killer preying on gaijin girls? But it was all meant to be safe; there were no monsters on the loose in Tokyo, unless they were in a manga comic book.

Superintendent Mii was asked for his reaction. He tacitly admitted his team was 'looking into the possibility that they were hunting a serial killer', and conceded that the figure of seven disappearances was plausible. But apart from the Blackman case there was only one relevant investigation still open. It concerned a Canadian girl who had left a Roppongi bar in September 1997 and had never been seen since. She was a hostess.

It had happened before.

CHAPTER 17

She was called Tiffanny Rain Fordham, from Calgary, Alberta, and she disappeared on 29 September 1997 after getting into a seventh-floor lift at a Roppongi hostess club. She was the thirty-one-year-old daughter of the well-known Canadian rock musician Kelly Jay.

The police had got nowhere, and a web campaign – 'Find-Tiff' – ran out of steam. The story of her disappearance had not had anything like the same media impact as Lucie's and it had fizzled out into a cold case. After almost three years, poor, vanished Tiffanny was a half-forgotten ghost in the karaoke machine.

Lucie's story revived her memory, if only briefly. A friend from Alberta came forward to state that on the night she vanished, Tiffanny had been accompanied to a club 'by a known member of the yakuza'. Her fiancé had gone there with her, but they had argued and she had left to go down in the lift to the lobby. Tiffanny Fordham was never seen again.

In her friend's supposition, the yakuza guy had abducted Tiffanny as some sort of 'sex-slave' and Tiffanny had 'probably been sold on four or five times by now. She has turned thirty, her looks will be fading. Maybe she is not worth so much to him . . .' so she would tell a reporter from the *Daily Telegraph*. 'Since Tiffanny disappeared, we have learned of seven white women who disappeared in Tokyo over the past five years. It's happening all the time,' she said.

Well that is not what the Tokyo Metropolitan Police thought. At least not up until now. And a Roppongi club owner called Kazuo Iizuka came forward with a story which demonstrated their indifference. On a Saturday night in early October 1997 one of his employees, a young British hostess, had come into his club clearly seriously unwell. She was so weak that he'd called for an ambulance to take her from the Club Cadeau to a hospital, he told an investigative reporter for *Time* magazine who was following the story of Lucie's disappearance.

This girl had been on a *dohan* to 'the seaside'. She had been drugged and, she suspected, sexually assaulted. Medical tests revealed her liver function was badly compromised, but did not show why. Mr Iizuka said that he had taken the young woman to the Azabu police station and urged her to file rape charges, but they had been met by a wall of indifference. She was foreign, she was a hostess and she was almost certainly working illegally. The police hadn't wanted to know then.

Well now they did.

The Blackmans' hotline had been set up with the intention of finding Lucie. By September the reported sightings of a blonde gaijin woman had begun to tail off. The embassy still got alerts from oddballs, including someone who wanted to go out with Sophie, who he thought was 'cool'.

Still, the volunteers and Japanese-language speakers who took down information from callers (most of whom wanted to stay anonymous) *had* gathered some strange but, as it would turn out, vital intelligence. Sophie Blackman typed up their statements, which were passed to the police at Azabu.

One woman had said that she was English and working as a Roppongi hostess. Four years earlier, a club customer had kept insisting that he take her out, to 'Kamakura and then Zushi on the coast,' she thought – some sort of marina apartment where he promised he would cook her dinner. They had duly gone. He had pressed more and more drinks on her and she had passed out.

'He probably took pictures of me,' she said. 'I woke up the next day; he had washed my clothes. He said that I was sick and that I should stay in bed for a few days.' The caller mentioned GHB – the date-rape drug. She clearly was in no doubt about what had happened, but she had been too ashamed or too frightened to tell the authorities. Nor would she even admit to the hotline volunteers that she had been sexually assaulted, but she thought 'he had done the same' to other girls.

There was another lead – a description of a 'small man about five foot seven inches, who wore too much cologne. The restaurants and clubs all know him.' The information was passed to the police. Not much happened.

Then, in the first days of October, a Canadian girl contacted the Azabu police station direct. She wanted to be known simply as 'Donna'. 'It is not clear why she took so long before she came forward,' commented the *Asahi Shimbun* newspaper, which reported the approach. However late she may have been in doing something, Donna had lots to say (although her questioners insisted she say none of it to the press). Inevitably, though, it would all come out via leaks to the police press club.

In March 1996, she said, a man calling himself Kazu had moved in on her in a Roppongi club where she was working as a hostess. 'Let's go and see the ocean,' he had suggested and she agreed to go on a *dohan*, ending up, she thought, in the town of Zushi, south of Tokyo, where he had taken her in his Ferrari. They had gone to his apartment in the luxurious marina complex with its sprinkler-watered lawns and soaring palm trees. He gave her a drink which he had described as 'a very rare herb wine from the Philippines'.

Blackness followed. When she had come to, feeling nauseous and lethargic, Kazu told her that she had passed out after drinking a bottle of vodka.

Two more young women contacted the police with very similar stories about a well-dressed businessman who had taken them on *dohans* to some seaside restaurant. He called himself variously Yuji or Koji. Each of the them reported going back to an apartment – out by the sea somewhere – then blacking out and waking up, they didn't know how many hours later. One witness spoke of being persuaded into 'making a good-luck toast' that required her 'to down an entire glass in a single gulp'. If she didn't drink it all, he warned, her luck would be bad.

One girl remembered seeing a red light blinking on a video camera before she fell into blackness. When she at last came to, he told her a story about a gas leak and having woken up himself with a mysterious headache.

At last they were asked to give full statements and were told, meanwhile, not to say anything more to anyone else (especially the Blackman operation) about their experiences.

A pattern was emerging, a seaside apartment, girls taken there on Saturdays, expensive sports cars, a Ferrari, a two-seater Mercedes SLK, the victims – if that is what they were – complaining of feeling drowsy and vomiting after being given a glass of 'special wine'. This was some sort of date rape. The girls had survived to tell their grisly stories. But where was Lucie in all of this?

There was the matter of the phone calls, those from Lucie to Louise Phillips at the gaijin house on the afternoon and early evening of Saturday 1 July, and those to Louise again from Akira Takagi as she was leaving the British Embassy on Monday 3 July. Lucie had also called Scott Fraser. Of all the leads, those calls should have been the most traceable. But there was still a thumping fault on the line to finding out.

There had been a police leak to the press, saying that the second batch of calls in which it was said that Lucie had joined a cult turned out to have been made from a public phonebox in Chiba, so the *Asahi Shimbun* reported on 9 August. They were, it seemed, untraceable to any individual.

'I'd been asking the police since the beginning to trace all the mobile calls,' Tim Blackman recalled. 'They claimed this was not possible, firstly because they did not have the technology and secondly because it was an invasion of personal privacy.'

'The British Lord Chancellor, Derry Irvine, was on some kind of global tour when I met him in Tokyo,' said Tim Blackman. 'He asked me if there was anything in particular I needed help with . . . Lord Irvine pointed out a criminal or murder investigation overrode any quibbles. He said he would say something and miraculously, a few days later, the police announced that they could and would, after all, trace the calls.'

The British politician's high-level intervention came in mid-September. The Japanese police later denied the move had anything to do with Derry Irvine. But whatever the degree of political pressure and the reaction to it, if the phone was of the pre-paid variety, tracing who bought it was going to be fraught with difficulty. Mr Hasawaga of the telephone company NTT DoCoMo personally explained to Tim Blackman how the system worked: 'A user can choose whether or not to show their number to the one they are calling,' he said. 'If the number is displayed, the phone will keep it in its memory until it is bumped by a new one, up to ten and no more. After that, it is lost for ever.'

In this case, the caller had evidently not shown their number when they had phoned Louise Phillips. Either that or more incoming calls had deleted it from the phone

at the gaijin house. So it was going to be a more complicated hunt.

'There are three main phone companies and the first
block of four digits after the 090 show which one the
number in question is subscribed to,' Mr Hasawaga went
on. 'In theory, a private company might buy a block of
phones then rent them on, which makes things more difficult. Until a few weeks ago, mid-July 2000 in fact, one
could buy a pre-paid phone without proof of identity, when
it became clear that just such phones were being used for
criminal activity and the rules changed. Now the owner
must register.'

So Lucie could have been using an unregistered mobile
when she made those calls, since she disappeared before
the change in regulations. But there was another way.
According to Mr Hasawaga:

It is possible to trace a call by looking at entire national
network. If they are given a definite time when the call
was received such as 11.35 a.m., the company can look at
the calls that went through their thousands of radio ter-
minals at that time and find the one that called our
phone. This is a very difficult and lengthy process. But
it can be done if given the right timescale.

It can also show roughly where I was when I made the
call by looking at the terminal the signal went through. In

fact, as long as my phone is switched on, I don't even
have to make a call to register with the beacons.

Things began to move. Whether the name of a suspect
emerged by ascertaining where the phone was bought, or
by tracing the contract for the number or by a mix of the
two, was never fully brought out in the judicial process
that followed. Nor was it ever really made clear whether it
was the calls that Lucie herself made to Louise on 1 July or
those made two days later by Akira Takagi that led to the
identification of a prime suspect. Both avenues were
reported by newspapers as being the route to the breakthrough. But in trial evidence it was stated simply that the
accused had bought pre-paid phones in discount electrical
stores under false names. He bought lots of them.

Still, the matter of the mobile phone that Lucie used to
phone Louise Phillips was clearly pretty important in
delivering a name and address (in fact, multiple addresses)
even if it could not be used directly in bringing its owner
to justice. That Tokyo Metropolitan Police detectives
were watching an individual whose real name they had
pinned down with the co-operation of a telephone company, was also not immediately revealed. Nor was how
long they were watching for, and by what methods. It
would also seem from a statement made by the suspect
after his arrest that one of his previous sexual partners had

239

direct information on where he lived and had gone to the police with it.

Things were drawing to a climax. It may have been that the police were trying to bounce their mark into doing something that would be immediately incriminating (if that was the plan, it failed) using their operating method of choice – leaking unattributable snippets to favoured tabloid newspaper reporters.

The Azabu police were investigating the disappearance of two other foreign women who vanished in Tokyo at around the same time as Lucie Blackman, the *Sankei Shimbun* reported on Monday 9 October. The two women were living 'in similar circumstances to Miss Blackman, who was working as a hostess in the Casablanca nightclub in Tokyo's Roppongi district when she disappeared'. The police were questioning a male customer of the Casablanca who behaved 'suspiciously at around the time of her disappearance', according to the cryptic story.

On the evening of Tuesday the 10th, the *Yukan Fuji* reported that a man in his mid-thirties, 'an S & M enthusiast with a taste for radical play', was 'under suspicion in the Lucie Blackman case'. He had made a connection with the foreign hostess at 'Club C' where she worked:

From the beginning there was a rumour that when Lucie Blackman worked at Club C she used to visit

Club M in Roppongi which has S&M shows, in the company of a male customer of Club C, according to someone connected to the sex industry. The owner of the company that owns Club M has been questioned by police . . . but no connection has been established.

The story got stranger. Apparently Lucie had registered herself at the office but, according to a dominatrix, 'it was rather a tame kind of club compared to the harder places like Ebisu and Gotanda'.

The *Yukan Gendai* evening tabloid got a lot closer to it when it reported a 'businessman under suspicion, a man of means and a good customer of the club in Roppongi, a man of property who was very enthusiastic about Lucie, who visited the club quite often and exchanged lots of e-mail just about the time she disappeared.' The paper wondered whether this really was the solution to the case or 'just a show put on for the British Embassy'.

The *Yomiuri Shimbun* got a tip that the police were about to make an arrest, not in the matter of Lucie Blackman but in connection with something else. In Japan a suspect could be arrested and held for questioning for up to twenty-three days, the report noted.

The waiting was over. The British Embassy was told very early on the morning of 12 October that 'the police would be arresting a man in connection with Lucie Blackman's dis-appearance'.

Just after dawn on Thursday 12 October detectives from Azabu hit four addresses across the Tokyo region. At one of them, an apartment in Moto-Akasaka Towers, a soaring early eighties-built block in swanky Minato Ward south-west of the Imperial Palace, they found a slightly built middle-aged man dressed in a towelling robe. The apartment was expensively furnished but shabby and unkempt. Boxes of old papers were piled high in the cor-ridor. A laptop computer was sealed in an evidence bag and the man was taken in an unmarked car to Azabu police station and put in the cells. The police surgeon who examined him was baffled by a livid rash on his arms and upper body.

This was it, the big breakthrough. The Tokyo evening papers all put out a similar story, based on the police brief-ing to the press club. Jake Edelstein, Tim Blackman's journalist friend on the *Japan Times*, faxed him a transla-tion of what the *Yomiuri Shimbun* evening edition was going to say when it hit the streets:

The Metropolitan Police today arrested the president of a real estate developer/holding company on charge of sexual assault. In March of 1996 he invited a twenty-three-year-old Canadian woman employed in a hostess club to go with him to the ocean and took her to a mansion he owned in Zushi. He then fed her drugs and alcohol and took advantage of her while she was incapacitated.

The police also believe he may have been involved in the disappearance of the English girl, Lucie Blackman. They are searching a former house in Setagaya Ward, Den-en-Chofu and other buildings he owns.

The police, through an analysis of the phone records have been able to prove that the mysterious phone calls made to Lucie's roommate on the day she disappeared came from a portable phone that had been contracted under his name.

It was Joji Obara.

He was arrested on suspicion of abducting and drugging the Canadian girl, 'Donna'. More police leaks appeared in the press very soon afterwards, claiming that he had allegedly sexually assaulted at least three foreign bar hostesses, drugging them after bringing them to the apartment at Zushi. The women, who were working illegally on tourist visas, had been too afraid to go to the police, it was said.

The British Embassy had been told, however, that this arrest was all about Lucie, as was Tim Blackman at home in England. In his words he had got 'a brusque, early-morning call' to tell him of the arrest of a suspect in the matter of his daughter's disappearance. The next morning, Japanese television and newspapers were full of stories about the mysterious Mr Obara, although there was not much yet to go on. He was a 'property developer' and a 'playboy'. His father on his death had left him rental properties and restaurants across Japan, it seemed. He had moved from house to house, so it was reported, 'to stay one step ahead of creditors'. There was an apartment at Zushi and a house at Den-en-Chofu, locations which Tokyo newspaper readers would immediately associate with wealth and exclusivity.

The next day and the next, more details emerged. 'As well as the Zushi and Den-en-Chofu homes, he has an apartment in the expensive central Tokyo district of Akasaka, from where police were also removing cardboard boxes yesterday,' said the Kyodo news agency. There were several more properties linked to him or his companies in his native Osaka, it later emerged. There was another residence by the ocean, investigators discovered, at a place called Aburatsubo on the Miura peninsula in Kanagawa Prefecture, about an hour's drive along the narrow coast road from Zushi marina. It was in a block called the Blue Sea, Apartment 401. It was the kind of place well-off city-dwellers had as a holiday home or weekend retreat.

The various properties were sealed off and searched. In the end, twenty separate locations would be accounted for. The garden of the Den-en-Chofu house was dug up, it would be difficult to hide a body, if that is what they were looking for, at the Zushi marina with its gated entrance, security cameras and manicured lawns. If a boat was involved, that was a different matter.

But the apartment block at Aburatsubo was itself isolated from other buildings, and down a potholed lane leading to the sea. The white-rendered building abutted on to a pebble beach overlooked by shrub-covered cliffs with shallow caves at the bottom worn by the waves into the volcanic rock. One cave was loosely filled with rubbish, an old bath, driftwood, bits of masonry. There were poisonous mamushi snakes in the undergrowth. It would be a good place to hide something.

A thirty-strong team of forensic investigators moved into the Blue Sea building. Apartment 401 was taken apart. The sweep using sniffer dogs moved on to the beach. Television crews in helicopters buzzed overhead. Nothing was found.

CHAPTER 18

Just who was Joji Obara became a hot topic for the British
and Japanese press. To the relief and comfort of a consid-
erable number, he turned out not to be Japanese at all. He
was ethnic Korean. To the London media Joji Obara was
simply the sex beast of Tokyo. The *Observer* newspaper
dubbed him the 'Tokyo Ripper'. The writers of that story
spared no cliché in their description of the 'suave, successful businessman' (at least, he looked like one) with an
allegedly murderous secret:

> He wore an Armani suit and expensive cologne and
> oozed sophistication . . . Standing at the bar in the
> Casablanca Club, he studied the pretty blonde British
> hostess as she moved among the wealthy customers,

taking their orders for cocktails and indulging in friendly chit-chat.

Lucie Blackman had certainly noticed him. The twenty-one-year-old was impressed by Obara's perfect English and polite manners. She was told his name was Kaz and it was his first time in the bar, situated in Tokyo's entertainment district of Rappongi [sic].

The forty-eight-year-old looked different too – he had had cosmetic surgery on his eyes to change their natural slant. According to the owner of the Casablanca, Blackman joined him for a few glasses of brandy. The pair talked for more than an hour . . .

Who was he really? He was born Kim Sung Jong in 1952 in Osaka. His father was a Korean immigrant who built a fortune in taxis, property and pachinko, the pinball arcade game.

At fifteen, he was accepted by a preparatory school affiliated with Keio University. His father had bought the mansion in Den-en-Chofu and sent the boy to live there with a maid. He started visiting downtown Tokyo clubs as a teenager.

At Keio he studied politics and law. He had had, or so it was said, surgery on his eyes to make them less oriental. He himself said that it was the result of a car crash which had shattered his dark glasses and driven his face into the windscreen.

In his late teens had adopted a new Japanese name, Seisho Hoshiyama, and spent some time in America. His father died in Hong Kong in 1969 and Seisho shared the inheritance with his two brothers. At the age of twenty-one he underwent another identity change – this time to Joji Obara, under which name he became a naturalised Japanese citizen.

He was rich, he was spendthrift, but he was prepared to play the part of the thrusting Japanese, bubble-era businessman. The Zushi apartment, for example, he had acquired in 1982, when the swanky marina with its pastiche Côte d'Azur-style apartment blocks was being built. He formed an investment company called Plant in 1988, relatively late in the bubble cycle. He was linked to eight more companies, all in the property or asset management business. There was real estate and parcels of land all over the place. When the Japanese economy collapsed, nearly taking all of Obara's assets with it, his mother, who still controlled the family pachinko parlours, helped bail him out, or so it was reported.

There were press stories that the yakuza had kept him afloat in return for money-laundering operations. He liked to tour Roppongi at night in a Bentley or Rolls-Royce, according to the more sensational papers, with a yakuza member as his chauffeur, identifiable by a missing finger. These stories were all denied by Obara.

One intrepid reporter found a local court report on someone called Obara who had been arrested in a women's lavatory in a seaside town called Shirahama in Wakayama Prefecture. He was wearing women's clothes and attempting to videotape a woman using the toilets. He had been charged with a misdemeanour and fined the equivalent of fifty pounds.

No Obara snippet was overlooked. For example, he had 'ordered the most expensive dishes for two for home delivery about once a month for the last three or four years,' a sushi restaurant manager in Zushi told the Japan Times. And as the police searches continued, concentrating now on the Zushi apartment and at the second address by the sea at Aburatsubo, tidbits of progress were fed to the hungry press.

It was at Aburatsubo that a neighbour recalled how Obara had started using the apartment over that summer after an absence of almost five years. The Blue Sea's caretaker was reported to have seen him returning from the direction of the nearby beach with a shovel or hoe a little after the time that Lucie disappeared. There had been argument over Obara changing the locks to his apartment without consultation. The apartment owner was later seen with cement or mud on his hands. The matter of the police turning up at the Blue Sea close to midnight on 5 July and what they might or might not have seen in Apartment 401 was not reported, however. Not yet, at least. Perhaps that was all a bit too embarrassing to leak to the Tokyo Metropolitan Police press club. It would soon come out anyway.

But there were plenty of other leaks. 'I wish we had had a month more to follow him secretly,' a police source told the Kyodo news agency. The implication was that Obara had been under covert surveillance for some time as police looked for a cast-iron link to Lucie Blackman's disappearance, at least until the political pressure to make an arrest became too great and they had to act. Tim Blackman joined the conspiracy theorists. He told a reporter: 'My personal belief is that they always knew about Obara. People had gone to the police and made claims about him, club managers had reported him . . . Maybe there was some agenda which prevented him being hauled in. I imagine the police agonised for a number of weeks about whether to pull him in.'

And there were more twists. The manager of a motor-boat dealership in the city of Yokohama, south of Tokyo was reported to have told police that this man Obara had bought a boat on 1 October 'in a state of agitated haste . . . Not only did he choose one of the first boats he saw on display, he asked for the customary two-week delivery time to be reduced to one.' It did not seem that he had done so to go fishing. According to the reports he 'pointedly refused to allow the dealer to keep a copy of his boat licence and the photograph it bore. He asked in detail about the best way of sailing to the Izu chain, a series of volcanic islands seventy miles to the south. He also asked repeatedly about how to identify Japanese coastguard vessels.'

The arrest of a suspect was, of course, to be applauded – but Tim Blackman's belief that Lucie was somehow still alive was profoundly shaken. A man with a spade, cement, a beach, a motorboat. From his home on the Isle of Wight he told reporters in Tokyo by telephone: 'I think we're realistically preparing ourselves for the worst.' He felt that he must return to Japan. Speaking to reporters at Heathrow, he said: 'Maybe without actually finding a body yet, I suppose there is a little part of us that hopes that she's still around somewhere.' But even that last scrap of hope that Lucie might indeed be alive was fading.

The Japanese national reaction to the arrest of Joji Obara was a mix of relief that he was Korean, self-criticism and dark humour. There were plenty of phone calls to the British Embassy from Japanese who wanted to express their 'shame'. A certain Mr A. Suzuki wrote to 'Miss Lucie's Father c/o the foreign ministry of Great Britain . . . The other day, North Korea accused Japan in connection with your daughter. However the suspect is a Korean Japanese who acquired Japanese nationality some years ago (according to the TV). Anyway, please accept our deepest sympathy . . . on behalf of the Japanese people.'

At the same time hostesses and snack girls reported a rash of male customers introducing themselves as 'Joji Obara'.

Leaked stories of progress in the police investigation continued to appear. It was all about getting closer to Lucie. A photographic negative was found in the Zushi apartment with the digitised date, 1 July, so police sources revealed. It showed someone identifiable as Lucie with the sea in the background. The shadows were long. It was evidently taken in the evening, around the time she was phoning Louise Phillips to tell her she would be home in half an hour. She was wearing a black dress.

And there was this little nugget: a man who looked like Obara bought dry ice from a store in Miura City in early July, and was quoted as telling the shopkeeper it was 'to preserve my dead dog', according to 'sources'. When asked by the shopkeeper how big the dog was, the man said, 'It's large,' and bought ten kilograms of dry ice and cardboard boxes for four thousand yen. Around 5 July, Obara's 'imported car' was seen near his apartment containing piles of luggage and cardboard boxes.

Neighbours were quizzed, and their stories duly appeared in the press following police leaks. At Zushi a woman named Yumiko Saito recalled being out with her young children the previous summer, and seeing a couple near the marina. She described a 'foreign' woman, who was much taller than 'a man in a white polo shirt', who she was walking slightly behind. She did not seem to be enjoying herself especially. The woman 'was about 175 centimetres tall, thin but not model-thin and had blonde hair'.

It was a sign of the times, she'd told her husband, that this strange couple should be out together, but were not holding hands or talking – and certainly did not seem to be romantically involved. She had thought nothing more of it until later when, as she said, 'Police put up a notice in the Zushi apartment block about looking for information on a possible incident.' There was a similar reported sighting in a nearby restaurant called the Captain's Café, of a girl with a man that fitted a description of Obara. The date was on or around 1 July.

Then there was the phone evidence – the matter that Tim Blackman had pressed the Tokyo police to take forward from almost the minute after his arrival in the city. Multiple phones were found in Obara's various residences, both used and still in unopened boxes (the prosecution would account for eighty-three in total). Many had pre-paid call tariffs that had been acquired in a number of false names. He seemed to favour buying them over the counter in a discount electronics retailer in Shinjuku, where he had bought no fewer than thirty in one go just before registration of the owner's name became a legal requirement.

On the laptop retrieved from the Moto-Akasaka Towers

apartment, an investigation of its owner's Internet use disclosed that early on the morning of 3 July it had been used to search for information on a bizarre range of topics including how to obtain quantities of hydrochloric and vitriolic acid.

And there was hair – 'hundreds of loose strands in his [Zushi] apartment, most of which are believed to be from non-Japanese women' – as well as 'easily moveable floor boards with large spaces beneath them,' according to a news agency report. The *Asahi Shimbun* reported the discovery of a fingerprint in the kitchen at Zushi. Jane Blackman was urgently contacted in England and asked to provide fingerprints from Lucie's bedroom, plus her own hair samples for a DNA-matching exercise.

A little later it would be reported: 'Tokyo police obtained a DNA sequence believed to be that of Blackman by analysing hair collected in a Tokyo apartment she lived in and samples of fingernails provided by members of her family in Britain . . . Several of the roughly twenty strands of hair found in the Zushi condominium cannot be ruled out as belonging to Blackman, investigative sources said.'

And there was the news from within the investigation that a tape recording of a phone conversation between a man and the Zushi Fire Department had been found during a search of Obara's apartment. The call was placed at 9 p.m. on 1 July, when a man urgently asked for information on hospitals still open at that hour of the night and which hospital had ambulances to collect a patient at that time. The recording was made, so the sources speculated, so that Obara would have proof that he'd sought medical intervention in the case of Lucie Blackman suffering an accident.

And still there was more: bottles of chloroform – the old-fashioned anaesthetic – mountains of sleeping pills and sedatives of Japanese and foreign origin, and unlabelled plastic bottles containing a clear liquid that turned out to be GHB, or gammahydroxybutrate, the so-called 'date-rape' drug. Police also found Japanese–English translation software and drafts of letters that matched the rambling notes sent to the police on 20 July, which were supposed to have come from Lucie.

The strangest thing was the way this man had hoarded scraps of documentation – bills, tickets, receipts – stretching back for years. The prosecution would eventually account for 2884 individual items. He had also, police found, systematically recorded in journals and spoken-word cassette tapes his own weird life and times for almost three decades. Police leaked some of it to favoured weekly news magazines. *Shukan Shincho*, for example, published this snippet: 'Women are only good for sex. I will lie to them. I will seek revenge. Revenge on the world.'

From 1983 onwards his journals began to mention something he called 'conquest play'. What he referred to as his *purei nohto*, or 'play notebooks', listed the names of 209 women, beside many of which Obara wrote cryptic code words like 'CROCO' or 'GMY'. These, according to investigators, stood for the different kinds of drugs with which he had dosed them.

There was also something called 'The Great Plan', written up in ten separate notebooks (he seemed to have begun it in his late teens) which, as its author would one day explain to a court, 'describes the means by which I would stimulate myself, conquering the world, establishing companies . . . I wrote things I dreamed of . . .'

But as *Shukan Shincho* reported, 'If there were any doubts about his main interest, these were dispelled by an entry in his journal in which he stated, "I cannot do women who are conscious".'

And there was direct evidence of just what he meant. The VHS videotapes – hundreds of them – neatly labelled with names and dates. It was also on Super 8 film stock, movies dating back three decades. 'Conquest play' consisted of him lugging unconscious women on to his bed. Police leaked details of how he tied some of the women down, penetrating their vaginas and anuses with various objects. He would assault most victims for twelve hours or more. But who were they?

The names and timings in his creepy log books linked with at least two complainants, who were there, right then, in Tokyo, and who were prepared to do something about it. There was also a third woman, an Australian, the police were in touch with. Their identities were all carefully screened. 'Donna' had given her deposition before Obara's arrest. The British woman (who had first come forward to talk to the Blackmans' own unofficial investigation) filed her official complaint after police showed her a videotape of a woman being assaulted in the Zushi rape chamber. It was clearly her. The 'play notebook' gave her name and the date: 10 October 1997.

On 28 October 2000 Obara was charged on suspicion of the drugging and rape of Donna and rearrested in his cell for the rape of the second woman. Still he would admit nothing. Cynics pointed out that his legal training had fore-warned him of the Japanese criminal justice system's reliance on confessions. In almost all cases prosecutors brought charges only when they had a signed admission of guilt. Investigators were allowed to interrogate suspects with no filing of formal charges for twenty-three days and without a lawyer present. Suspects were legally obliged to answer questions. Interrogations were 'rigorous'. Almost all of those accused ultimately confessed. It was an honour thing.

Obara and his lawyers could see what the police were up

to. They would keep their prime suspect in police custody the better to continue their high-pressure interrogation. Arrest warrant would follow arrest warrant as each twenty-three-day term elapsed. It was all about getting a confession.

Meanwhile press leaks would bring the investigation ever closer to the fate of a blonde bar hostess whose case had flooded Roppongi with probing journalists and TV crews and invited the attention of prime ministers. Politics demanded a conviction in the Blackman case. The defence team accused the police and prosecution authorities of abuse of power and demanded – unsuccessfully (for now) – that Obara be transferred to the Tokyo Detention Centre under the control of the Ministry of Justice.

The remand centre was part of the notorious Kosuge prison in Katsushika-ku. They executed people there. Kosuge was where Japan's most notorious murderer Tsutomu Miyazaki, convicted of abducting and killing four girls aged four to seven between 1988 and 1989, had been on death row since his eventual sentencing to death in 1997 after an eight-year trial.

That was long, but not the longest: one famous criminal trial lasted twelve years. The trial process in Japan did not run from start to finish. Instead, juryless courts sat in short sessions of one to three hours, convening only every month or so. Police and prosecuting authorities routinely leaked details of investigations to favoured newspapers through the *kisha* (press club) system, which published them with a bravado that would be instantly judged prejudicial to a jury trial in any other country.

Criminal trials would typically turn into marathons in which the circumstances of how a confession was extracted were picked over endlessly. Otherwise the defence was in the business of showing their client's contrition, the chances of his being rehabilitated and the low risk he posed to society – factors that affected the sentence and not the inevitable (99 per cent of the time) guilty verdict. A criminal trial in Japan was aptly described as a 'formal ceremony on the road to conviction'.

In the child-murderer Tsutomu Miyazaki's case the road was straight, but had been wearisomely long. He had been caught in 1989 shortly after having committed his last gruesome murder having attempted to insert a camera lens into the vagina of a schoolgirl in a park. He'd been attacked by the girl's father. Miyazaki fled on foot, but returned to retrieve his car, whereupon he was arrested.

A police search of his residence turned up thousands of manga and anime with pornographic and violent contents. The case transfixed Japan with the same kind of moral panic that had surrounded assisted dating. He was dubbed the '*otaku* murderer', *otaku* meaning an enthusiast or fan – especially those who were manga obsessives or comic

nerds. A team of psychiatrists from Tokyo University diag-
nosed Miyazaki as psychotic (with dissociative identity
disorder and/or schizophrenia), but the court judged him
to be aware of the consequences of his actions and therefore accountable. And there was a confession. He was
sentenced to death in 1997. His lawyers appealed, arguing – unsurprisingly – that the confession was inadmissible
because it was made under duress. It was turned down.
After multiple stays of execution, Miyazaki went to the
gallows in June 2008.

Capital punishment (by long-drop hanging) was
enshrined in Japanese criminal justice and enjoyed broad
popular and political support. 'Why do you think Japan is
so safe?' went the argument. But Joji Obara was not facing
the death sentence. Thus far, the most serious charge was
rape, for which the minimum sentence might be two years
and the maximum a theoretical fifteen.

The days were passing and there was still no confession
from Joji Obara. Then came a kind of admission. Yes, he
had been with these women. And yes, he had met Lucie –
once. He said this in an odd public statement made
through his lawyer on 10 November 2000, as allowed in
Japanese law. Some, but only a small portion of it, was
reported in Japanese and British newspapers. It was
bizarre, rambling, conspiratorial, but as a glimpse into the
workings of his mind, absolutely fascinating.

These ladies who are supposed to be victims are all foreign hostesses or sex-club girls. Many took cocaine or other drugs in front of my very own eyes, and all of them agreed to have sex for money. I am being held for the crime of paying money to prostitutes [who I paid to participate in] what I like to call *seifuku* – conquering play, sexual activity in which the female wears elaborate costumes.

Obara hit a nerve when he said that. What he freely confessed to doing was just a variation on what many thousands of Japanese men did routinely – indulge in sexual role playing, real or virtual through the medium of image clubs, 'cosplay', pornography, manga, anime, adult videos and computer games. His strange statement continued, becoming very detailed:

Police tell me they have received official complaints from girls listed below:

1 CM (formerly FCA) Though press reports say she is Caucasian, she has Philippine father and looks like a Philippine girl. Her nationality is Canadian.
2 DMK On her complaint I was rearrested.
3 TM I met her five or six years ago, but since then I have not met her. She is the one who reported on me

to the police directly this time, informing them of the way to get in touch with me as well. This woman is playing a sort of leader's role among foreign hostesses working here. She was a lover of Mr Sagawa, notorious for his cannibal case.

Foreign hostesses in Tokyo are usually moving from one place to another but form a closely connected small society of their own.

When I first met her she claimed she was running away from Mr Sagawa and begged for help. I secured a room at Shinjuku Washington hotel for about a month, there she stayed with her girlfriend (perhaps with initial R) under a false name until she returned to Australia, her home country. I have not made a single sexual play with her. She is a habitual user of drugs and the police now have the photographs of herself taking cocaine, etc. Her nude photo appeared in a letter from Mr Sagawa in a book written by him.

He offered no further explanation. Japanese citizens needed little reminding of the story of Issei Sagawa, born two years before Joji Obara, the son of wealthy parents in Kobe. As a young man he became obsessed with tall Western women. There was an incident at Wako University where he had crept up *yobai*-style on a sleeping

German woman (she was his English teacher) apparently with the intention of killing her. She had woken just in time. While studying for an English literature degree at the Sorbonne, Paris, he had more success, shooting dead, raping the dead body of, then over the next two days eating substantial amounts of a Dutch fellow student called Renée Hartevelt.

Five days later, he was arrested by French police after he was seen dumping Hartevelt's remains in a park. Psychologists found him legally insane and unfit to stand trial. Instead, he was eventually deported back to Japan, where he was put in a mental institution. But the deportation order did not specify for how long he should remain there, and Sagawa was freed on 12 August 1986, having been judicially contained for just five years. He emerged as the world's first celebrity cannibal – who somehow got away with it – not to mention a best-selling author. He appeared on TV chat shows, on the covers of gourmet cookery magazines and gathered a group of intellectual admirers to his cause who supported his 'artistic insanity'. As well as his cameo acting performance in the film *The Bedroom*, Sagawa really did go on to produce a sequence of books and manga comics about himself and his unusual crime.

Joji Obara perhaps did not share the same literary (or culinary) ambitions, but his account continued with a strange mix of moral indignation against the loose morals of 'foreign' hostesses and a wider conspiracy theory:

> The police have rounded up every foreign woman that I have ever had sex with and are making them lodge complaints. And until they can make me confess involvement in the vanishing of Lucie Blackman they intend to keep arresting me and hold me prisoner. On the other hand the police are completely closing their eyes to drug use, the illegal employment and acts of prostitution committed by these foreign hostesses and telling the girls as much. They intend to make me the scapegoat of everything.

On Lucie Blackman:

> I met Miss Lucie Blackman at a foreign club only once attending me and later, through her introduction I came to know a certain man. After that many strange things happened one after another.

Obara suggested that a mysterious Englishman had arrived in Tokyo after his arrest (so two veteran detectives had told him in his cell, he said) who, he implied, was a 'professional sniper' sent to assassinate him. 'I feel as if I have been drawn into a massive plot but I am not involved in Lucie's disappearance,' he insisted.

He also referred to a report on morning TV that he had cut up and frozen his dog. 'With the improvement of cloning technology, and in the hope of resurrecting my beloved dog, I laid him to rest inside a large freezer,' he said. 'I also included roses and some of his favourite treats.' That he had, it was reported, acquired a quantity of dry ice from a supplier near one of his homes in the first days of July was part of this cryogenic tribute, Obara explained.

As for the newspaper accounts published thus far on the strength of police leaks about his unusual lifestyle – he had detailed answers for each allegation. On the matter of being spotted with cement on his hands at the Blue Sea apartment block one night in early July: 'I was retiling my bathroom; the caretaker was out for the night – Wednesday was his night off – so I called a locksmith.' Of the purchase of a motorboat a few days before his arrest he said: 'It was to go fishing. The boatyard man, Mr Itoah, sailed it from Yokohama to Aburatsubo Marina.' Of the drugs and potions reported to have been found in his various properties: 'The human growth serum is mainly used to help dwarfs. I used it when I was in my twenties to enlarge my bone structure . . . phenobarbital, chloral, ether, etc. I have used it to enhance meditation since my time as a student. The pyschotropics I need for insomnia, without them I cannot sleep . . . I have never used these anaesthetics in my sexual plays,' so he insisted.

Obara threatened to sue newspapers for inaccurate and libellous reporting of the sort of which there had been plenty thus far. Of the alleged earlier arrest of someone called Joji Obara in a seaside public toilet, he said: 'I never disguise myself as a woman and I am not a transvestite.' Of his supposed connection with Korean nationals: 'I have numerous Chinese friends but none among Koreans nationals in Japan; I suspect someone is intentionally setting me up.' Of the fingerless yakuza member driving him around Roppongi in a Bentley or Rolls-Royce – that was 'rubbish': 'I haven't used the Rolls for four years and the Bentley for eight. The automobile inspection validity [MOT] for both vehicles had long expired. Incidentally my Bentley is a Continental with a Park Ward body, a novelty of museum class.'

As for more yakuza friends: 'If I have any, please tell me who they are.'

Obara was involved in a company that had developed the most modern detection devices including wire tapping and clandestine video surveillance, so he claimed. 'Through all these experiences I now fully realise that the mass media would gladly carry articles that disclose the hidden, secret part of a human being even though they know it's not the truth and all made up.' Not the English-language media, surely. He continued in this conspiratorial vein:

The Keishicho [Tokyo Metropolitan Police] are telling me they fear international pressure. If they cannot solve the disappearance of one girl that it will affect negotiations regarding Japanese citizens believed to have been kidnapped by North Korea.

Japan is becoming a police state.

They say that they will keep arresting me on the charge of forcing sexual abuse on hostesses so that they can hold me in custody perpetually.

Police tell me that Miss Lucie Blackman is already dead. They are starting a big-scale search using helicopters. They tell me they are thoroughly checking all possible places where I might have visited since July. They tell me I have not much time left.

The rambling statement, or extracts from it, was the lead on national TV news that night, although presenters were keen to point out that parts of it contradicted the facts as already known and this might be a sign of Obara's increasing uneasiness. They also reported a senior police source staying they were confident the Lucie case would be solved soon. They were wrong.

Bloggers – Japanese and gaijin alike – picked up the conspiracy aspects of Obara's case with glee. Since his arrest, his Korean origin was stressed over again (although he *was* born in Japan). It was eagerly pointed out how *burakumin* (Japanese descendants of historic outcasts) and ethnic Koreans dominated the yakuza – and how the pachinko connection (a very Korean business) underpinned the family fortune. This kind of hysteria would be added to two years later when a senior US State Department official told Congress that Japanese organised crime was funding North Korea's nuclear weapons programme.

Obara's reference to kidnapping also hit a nerve. Mysterious disappearances of young adult Japanese had been reported since the early eighties. By the time that Lucie vanished it was a burning political and media issue. (In September 2002 the Prime Minister, Junichiro Koizumi, would visit North Korea to meet its leader Kim Jong-il, who admitted that the country had abducted thirteen Japanese citizens over many years by various means for some weird spy purpose. He gave an oral apology and attributed the kidnappings to 'some people who wanted to show their heroism and adventurism'. There were rumours that many more disappearances could be explained this way.)

Obara's first formal hearing at Tokyo District Court was set for 14 December. There were long queues for the public gallery comprising, in the main, fashionably dressed young women. Charged with two alleged rapes, Obara, who gave his profession as company executive, pleaded not guilty. He told his accusers indignantly that these women had 'used drugs' and that 'they had come to the country to be prostitutes'. They asked for money in return for their company, he said, and had 'agreed to sexual play' when they visited Zushi. He had paid them a hundred thousand yen (around £500) in advance, so he insisted, but according to the prosecution he gave Donna sixty thousand yen and the second woman twenty thousand on leaving his apartment and paid for their cab fares back to Tokyo.

The details of what allegedly happened in between were bizarre. According to the prosecution both women had said that 'he put on a Mariah Carey video', and asked them to sing karaoke. At the same hearing, one of Obara's lawyers argued that police had served his client with the multiple arrest warrants so as to keep him detained over the still officially unrelated Blackman case. He was right about that.

Meanwhile, more of Obara's alleged victims had given depositions to the Azabu detectives. It was clearly a sensitive business. The invitation for girls to come forward after Lucie's disappearance and talk to police had produced a limited response in the semi-legal twilight of the foreign hostess world. But what about Japanese women? A number of them were in contact with the police. They gave names, dates and times when they might have been with this man.

Three young women were willing to file formal complaints after police told them they had evidence from Obara's videotapes and notebooks of them being drugged and sexually assaulted.

Obara had already been charged on 18 November 2000 with having raped a Japanese woman in May of the same year. On 28 December he was charged with drugging and raping another in early June, just a few weeks before he had encountered Lucie. On 4 January the drugging and raping of a third Japanese woman (it had allegedly happened in January 2000) was added to the list of charges.

On 24 January 2001 Obara was led into the Tokyo District Court in handcuffs to confront the prosecutors again – and, this time, to face at least two of his alleged victims in person. The public and reporters were strictly barred. The court went into closed session to hear the evidence.

But some details emerged. Describing one alleged rape, the prosecution claimed that: 'He ordered a sushi delivery for her and asked her to drink sparkling wine to which he secretly added a sleeping drug. Shortly after drinking it, she lost consciousness. The accused removed her clothes and made her inhale a narcotic chemical. He then raped her while filming their sex.'

As Obara told the court: 'I met these [Japanese] women through a telephone-dating service for the purpose of fun or assisted dating (*enjo-kosai*).' It was by the system known as a 'two-shot dial'.

The 'foreign women' he had seemed to have met at random in bars (although he would claim later it was via a mysterious American woman who made the introductions). They had told broadly similar stories, which the police began to leak to favoured tabloids. This man had met them in hostess clubs, invited them on *dohans*, driven them to the sea and lured them into his condominium using a variety of methods. It seemed very domestic. He invited one woman over offering to cook her dinner. He asked another to go with him to a party later in the evening. Another, he simply drove to the apartment block at Zushi and asked to help him carry up some boxes from his car.

A week after the closed court hearing, a British newspaper found a foreign hostess who said she was prepared to add to the testimony against the accused. Her name was 'Anna', an Israeli. According to her story, in 1995 she was invited by a club customer to go for a drive to the beach. She had then been aged twenty-one. She was picked up at the Hilton Hotel, Shinjuku, in a silver Mercedes two-seater.

'From the moment I met him, he behaved like he was under pressure,' she said. They had arrived at an apartment complex separated from the ocean by a small breakwater but the man refused to tell her where they were. He took two big shopping bags out of the car and led the way up to his apartment, telling her that he was going to cook them a meal.

'The first thing he did was put on a video of Mariah Carey and asked me to sing,' she said.

While he prepared the meal, Anna was given champagne and caviar, she said. He put more and more food and drink on the table. Anna suddenly felt very ill. Then she passed out. When she woke up she tried to call a friend in Tokyo but she did not know where she was. The man came out of the shower and grabbed the phone.

'I felt that was it, he was going to kill me,' she said. 'He kept screaming and I kept begging him to take me back to Tokyo. I threw up and he became even more aggressive.' Eventually he put Anna into the car and drove to the outskirts of the city, threatening that he would kill her if she was sick again. He then flagged down a taxi and paid the driver to take her home.

'After that, I never saw him again or heard from him,' she said. 'A few days later I tried to call him after a friend offered to try to find him and go to the police, but his mobile phone was dead.'

The police and prosecution now had lots of testimony like this. And they had the suspect's 'play' notebooks to collate and cross-reference. But there was no record of Lucie. There was no note of her name, no written or any other sort of evidence about her whatsoever.

The Tokyo-based journalist Jake Edelstein thought he might know why and urgently contacted his friend Tim Blackman with this suggestion: 'Girls use hostess names like "Passion" or "Tatiya". Did Lucie use an alias? There are only three people who will know, Obara, that sono-fabitch Nishi and Louise. Ask Scotland Yard to ask her – she's back in UK.' But there was no name that might conceivably be Lucie using an alias to match any relevant date.

Obara's peculiar utterances served to keep the story of Lucie's disappearance in the news even if the chances of finding her alive had become vanishingly small. And Obara himself was an object of perverse fascination. He was a monster certainly, a figure from Japanese demonology. But he was also comic – a mother's boy who never married, someone who not only could not get sex without paying for it, but could only do it to a partner who was comatose. Obara claimed to have had sex with over two hundred women. During his trial it was revealed that it was his goal to have sex with five hundred by the time he was fifty years old. In his mind it was not even rape. It was image play.

But had he actually killed anyone? Was he capable of

killing? It must be assumed by now that Lucie Blackman was a victim of more than abduction. There was a mountain of freakish, circumstantial evidence, but no proof. There was no confession. Above all, there was no body.

CHAPTER 19

The Casablanca had barred its doors to reporters; then it shut its doors altogether. A closed-for-repairs sign (briefly) joined the credit card logos at the door. Then, in September 2000, it reopened as the 'Greengrass', named thus because, according to one of the girls, Tetsuo Nishi and Mama-san both liked to play golf.

Things were different now, but not everything had changed. Girls were given a written code in English on how they should behave which, following Lucie's disappearance, now gave some advice for the first-timer on how to handle *dohan* and what it coyly called other 'activities outside the workplace'. It said:

Be absolutely sure to leave contact info (name of person you are escorting and a phone or e-mail address) with a member of the staff before you go.

You should leave contact info with the staff when going to have a drink with a given customer for the first time or accompanying them somewhere as a matter of course.

Do not agree to join the person you are accompanying anywhere in which you will be alone with them (such as private room, car, etc.). Also be aware that there do exist persons with perverted intentions as well as members of organised crime groups who will try to take advantage of you by posing first as ordinary customers. You should observe the same precautions when taking long or short trips or taking a drive etc. on your own time (your days off).

All that good advice was a little late for Lucie. That month, her friend Shannon went back to work at the renamed Casablanca after a brief return home to Canada. Apart for the name of the club, and the new guidelines on how to handle *dohan*, not much had changed. 'It seems OK,' she told a friend, 'it's getting busier, old customers are returning.'

One of those old customers had e-mailed her, meanwhile. In light of what had apparently happened to Lucie Blackman, it expressed the eternal up-for-itness of the Japanese male:

A lady in the Casablanca has been killed and reported many times on TV, etc . . .

One morning I watched TV news and I saw a photo,

it was a big astonishment of me. But I couldn't tell the story to my wife, though I wanted to tell someone.

Please be optimistic about above. I don't care what happened around there. Let's do *dohan* soon and let me know how you are. I could be promoted to *kacho-san* [boss] and I hope I can use more congress fee (expenses for entertaining clients, etc).

The same day Shannon messaged Mel (who had followed Louise Phillips back to London) with the latest news:

Nishi is still the same. He wants it to all go away so they can still be greedy with the club getting busier, now it's like an infamous club whatever.

There are many new girls at the club, it's a sea of peroxide at the moment . . .

It's so strange . . . like I never left all the same. Yesterday the police interviewed me for the first time. I gave them the pictures I took from Envy [Hama's] one evening, remember we went? They are the last ones of her alive . . . They were OK and nice to talk to. They told me they are still building a case against this man they arrested but lack enough evidence.

That was absolutely correct. DNA retrieved from hair found in the Zushi apartment at first looked as if it would

277

provide a match, but in the end proved inconclusive. Police went through the gruesome diaries over and over again. Still there was no mention of Lucie.

But the 'play' notebooks were beginning to yield up something. One note had been scrawled down a page alongside the name of another young woman – who from her name was obviously not Japanese. It dated from February 1992. It read: 'Carita Ridgway. Too much chloroform.'

To the police the name was meaningless. There were so many of them – off limits to the hungry news weeklies (although they were fed plenty of background from the diaries for publication). But in autumn 2000 a thirty-five-year-old Liverpool-born lawyer was following the reports in the Australian press about the Blackman case and the arrest of a businessman in Tokyo. Robert Finnigan took a special interest – and not just because he was now a successful civil litigation specialist based in Sydney. The unfolding drama of a missing gaijin girl and a distraught family's trawl through Roppongi's nightlife in search of an answer, rekindled a memory from years before. It was of a girl he had met while backpacking round the world and fallen in love with. Carita Ridgway.

This man Obara had kept notebooks detailing names and had even videotaped comatose women who had been unfortunate enough to cross his path, so it was reported.

Could there be a connection between him and the mysterious 'Nishida' – the creepy guy who had dumped Carita at a hospital emergency department eight years before, claiming she was suffering from food poisoning?

Robert Finnigan contacted the federal police in Sydney, as he said, 'to get the Japanese police to investigate whether Carita was one of the victims found in Obara's video and diary evidence'. It was the coldest of cold cases.

Meanwhile, Samantha Ridgway, Carita's older sister, was living in America. She was reading the same press reports. All the questions about Carita's death she had tried to bury were jumping off the pages. But she had not been able to forget. After her sister's death she had broken up with her boyfriend and left Japan. Returning home to Perth, she developed problems eating and sleeping. Realising she was becoming obsessed by her sister's death, she struggled to make sense of her bereavement, and to try to forget the whole grisly episode with 'Nishida', whoever he might have been. But something inside her, a restless need to discover the truth, made her resolve to return to Japan. As she told it:

A year later I went back to Tokyo, and picked up my teaching job again. Convinced that the clue to my sister's death remained linked to Nishida, I started compiling a notebook, detailing everything I could remember about him and what he had said about his relationship with Carita.

Looking back on my behaviour now I think that, distracted by intense grief, I started to go slightly mad. At night I roamed the streets of Roppongi vainly searching for Nishida. Each time I was accosted by a Japanese man, I would turn on him in fury, scratching and punching a complete stranger, projecting my feelings of hatred for Nishida on to the nearest available predatory man.

Samantha's search went unrewarded. As she trawled Roppongi and its bars and fetish clubs, asking questions, the twenty-five-year-old Australian girl was getting noticed. She had to get out of Tokyo, get away from Japan altogether. She describes what happened next simply enough:

I took a job in 1996 as an air hostess with United Airlines and went to live in the US. During all this time I continued to feel rootless and grief-stricken, unable to move on with my own life until I knew the truth about what had happened to my sister. Only after meeting my husband Richard, a musician, in New York in 1999 did I begin to feel that I might ever be happy again.

Both of us wanted children. We might just be ordinary people, a little happy family.

Which is what she and Richard Termini – an Italian-
American musician – became, setting up home in the
sheltering woods of Stroudsberg, Pennsylvania, a couple of
hours' drive from New York. They married in 2002. Her
own childhood family memories, letters and photographs
were packed away. Her parents had long ago divorced – it
had happened when she and her sister were in their early
teens. Her mother Annette, a one-time model, had remar-
ried. Memories of Carita would never fade, but
recollections of the horrible way in which she had died just
might.

Then, quite suddenly, there was all this stuff from
Tokyo about a vanished nightclub hostess and a business-
man under arrest. What should she do? She contacted
Robert Finnigan and asked him 'to find out from the
Japanese authorities if the man we had known as
"Nishida" could possibly be Joji Obara'.

He was already on the case, and the Australian Embassy
in Tokyo was making noises with the interior ministry. But
the Japanese authorities seemed to be doing nothing. Like
Tim Blackman, Robert Finnigan felt he must act himself.
He flew to Tokyo in January 2001, back into the nightmare from which he thought he had awoken years before.

The Japanese police regarded Finnigan's intervention with the utmost suspicion. Yes, there had been a case of a foreign woman dying of apparent liver failure in early 1992. Yes, her family had requested some sort of investigation and records showed detectives had been assigned, but they had found nothing untoward and anyway they had long since retired from the police department. Their where-abouts were now unknown.

'Well, that's incredible, because they're two of your former officers,' said Robert Finnigan. 'You're the Tokyo Metropolitan Police and if you can't find them, who can? They got very angry about that line of questioning,' he said. 'And then I asked them whether Obara had been interviewed by the police in 1992. They said no . . . and that was the first time I realised that the police had not properly investigated Carita's death at all.'

In fairness to the Tokyo police, any connection between millionaire property developer Joji Obara and the mysteri-ous Nishida would have been unfathomable at the time or afterwards. But now they would have to take the death of the young Australian girl a lot more seriously than they had done in 1992. There were immediate connections once you began to look for them – the cryptic entry for a start in Obara's 'play' notebooks: 'too much chloroform'. Although that gruesome snippet was not yet in the public domain it soon would be. Then there were the videotapes.

One was worthy of special attention. It was apparently recorded by the suspect showing him naked, but for a Zorro mask, in the act of sexually molesting an inert woman while intermittently holding some sort of cloth up to her face.

The notebooks indicated it had to have been taken on either 15 or 16 February 1992, although there was no imbedded date stamp on the tapes to say so. Could the body on the bed be positively identified as Carita? Was there anything else that could make a link? There was.

The forensic trawl of Obara's sedimentary layers of old papers had thrown up a receipt for a payment to a hospital – Hideshima in Musashino, Tokyo, where, so Samantha Ridgway insisted, her very sick sister had been left by a mysterious stranger over eight years before. The date matched. They were getting very close. But there was nothing more to tell what had happened. Obara would say nothing.

As Robert Finnigan recalled:

From what we could piece together, when Club Ayakoji [where Carita worked] was near to closing, Obara, a customer there, invited the other customers and all the hostesses, to a Korean barbecue. Several customers and some of the hostesses, including Carita, decided to accept his invitation. The events of that night are unclear, but it seems that Obara offered to give Carita a lift home in his car at the end of the evening, which she accepted. No one, except Obara, knows exactly what happened after they left the company of the others.

This time the police had to take action. On 26 January 2001 the Tokyo prosecutors added the drugging and raping of Carita Ridgway to the charges against Obara – actions 'resulting in her death'. On 2 February the Ridgway family consented to her being named in public. It was the first time police had charged Obara in a case in which the victim died. But it was not quite murder. Sexual assault resulting in death was the equivalent of manslaughter.

Obara reacted with his by now characteristic outraged innocence. 'I feel unspeakable indignation toward the allegation imposed on me of raping and killing her, as I had a romantic relationship with her then and even took her to the hospital out of concern,' he said through his lawyer. It was a matter of record that this woman, Carita Ridgway, had suffered hepatitis in southeast Asia where she stayed before coming to Japan, so he insinuated. It was the fault of the medical staff at Hideshima Hospital. He still refused to admit the use of drugs or sedatives with any of his 'partners'.

Not once in any of his interrogations would Obara allude to whether Lucie Blackman might be alive or dead. If she was indeed dead, whoever was responsible for killing her would know the fate of her body. And that was not him. Without a body there was nothing to progress the case – nothing to accuse him of.

Then they found her.

CHAPTER 20

The body of Lucie Blackman was found in a seaside cave worn by the winter Pacific breakers into the foot of a lava-flow cliff on the Miura peninsula south of Tokyo. It did not take long to half-walk, half-clamber from the front lobby of the Blue Sea apartment block down a narrow path leading across boulders and broken cement pilings to the spot where Lucie's remains were discovered.

The police had come looking here in October 2000 soon after Obara's initial arrest – but they had found nothing. Now they were back. They had moved in on 4 February to begin poking the tidal shoreline with sticks, using sniffer dogs and ground-imaging radar. After five days they came again to the cave in the undercliff still with driftwood, stones and bits of rubbish piled inside. This time the search was more thorough.

The first body parts were found at around 9.15 a.m., with the discovery of a plastic bag buried in sand in the floor of the cave only 32 centimetres below the surface. It contained an arm and two feet and ankles. A pair of cotton gloves was buried with it. There was another bag, and another.

A marquee of blue tarpaulins was erected over the site as investigators in rubber boots and face masks continued the grisly work. A flock of crows gathered on the beach sensing carrion. News of the find reached an equally hungry media in Tokyo. By midday, TV satellite vans were pressing against extemporised police barriers, camera crews buzzed the shoreline in helicopters and press photographers scrambled aboard fishermen's boats to get close enough for a shot. Tim Blackman, at home in England, saw events unfold on live TV. It was the middle of the night. As he recalled:

We were watching twenty-four-hour news ... the ghastly sight of those blue tarpaulins on the beach ... and then seeing police carrying something out that looked like a body and knowing it could be my child inside ...

Then the phone's ringing and I've got the guy from

the *Japan Times* saying 'Tim, we're here now on the beach watching them. I've just spoken to one of the officers who confirms they've found something.'

The same American journalist called Jane from Tokyo minutes later. She was at home in Sevenoaks with Sophie. It was her daughter who managed to give reporters her reaction the next morning.

My mother and I have been up all night trying to comfort each other. In our hearts, none of us has really given up hope of seeing her again. Because of this, we are treating this news cautiously and are anxiously waiting for the Japanese police to confirm it either way.

We have become used to calls from Japan in the middle of the night since Lucie disappeared. It has become part of our life.

My immediate thought was that another rumour had broken in Japan and someone was calling us to see what we thought. We have had false alarms. We've been woken when rumours that Lucie has been found have broken.

But this time the call was from a journalist who we have got to know quite well.

This time it was no rumour. The body had been cut into bits, crudely sliced up by something like a chainsaw. What appeared to be the head was encased in concrete. On first inspection the gender of the remains was indeterminable, but it was too tall to be a Japanese woman.

After a few hours, detectives carried the summation of their discovery, wrapped in a blue plastic body bag, past the throng of craning reporters and TV crews. Inspector Hayashi could give no explanation as to why it had taken so long for police to search the area properly. The body bag was loaded into a police van heading for Azabu police station – thence to Tokyo University Medical School for further examination.

The autopsy was performed on Saturday morning. The first task was to confirm that it was Lucie. When the concrete was broken open, a partially mummified head inside a vinyl bag was found inside, the blonde gaijin hair shaved or burned off. Lucie's dental records were already on hand. They were a conclusive match with the skull as retrieved from its miniature cement tomb. They had found her.

'We have determined through an autopsy,' announced Akira Hiromitsu, head of the first investigative section of Tokyo's Metropolitan Police the next day, 'that the body we discovered yesterday was that of Lucie Blackman. The time and cause of death have not yet been determined.'

'A Tokyo property developer named Joji Obara – already charged with raping five foreign and Japanese women –

will be charged with abandoning a body,' the detective told reporters.

DNA tests on the fragmentary remains confirmed the identification from dental records. There was absolutely no doubt it was Lucie. 'I got a call from a journalist in Tokyo to tell me a formal ID had been made,' Tim Blackman recalled. 'It was Lucie, my daughter.' Jane received a call at home in Kent from a police family liaison officer to tell her the same thing. 'And that was it really, the end of hope,' she would tell an interviewer.

At the same time, Obara in his cell was told by his lawyer about the formal identification of the body in the cave. 'The police must have buried her there,' was his reply.

Dr Masahiko Kobayashi of Tokyo University Medical School and two colleagues, Dr Koichi Sakaruda and Dr Keinici Yoshida had performed the autopsy. Enough soft tissue had survived from the liver and upper stomach for further more specific tests to be carried out. The key points would be presented at the eventual trial.

The body had been dismembered and was in ten separate parts, which had been placed in four plastic bags, except the torso. They were generally 'adiposed' – a condition typical when a body is kept in a moist environment, thus itself retaining some moisture.

Other parts were dried out, which reflected the conditions in a seaside cave, as water came in and out onto a bed of fast-draining sand. An inspection of the burial site by the autopsy team confirmed these conclusions.

The patterns on the severed bones gave further information. Some surfaces were smooth, others jagged, there were cuts on some bones which did not go all the way through – suggesting that the bones might have been partially sawn through, then crudely broken off. The width of these incisions, six millimetres, the jagged pattern and the fact that most of the bones had been cut in a single motion by an instrument with small teeth suggested the use of a powered chainsaw.

A part of the head that was visible outside its horrible cement carapace was damaged. The surviving soft tissue (including samples from the liver) was tested for traces of chemicals and drugs. There was no trace of amphetamines, nor any evidence of chloroform, but that would have dispersed readily. It was not possible to determine whether the anaesthetic had been present before death. Traces of flunitrazepam (the 'date-rape' drug otherwise known as Rohypnol) were however detected, using a testing technique developed by Scotland Yard pathologists – but it was unclear in what quantities and how long before death it was taken.

No test for semen or other evidence relating to rape was retrievable. There was no actual forensic indication whether the brutal dismemberment had been inflicted before or after death. It was, so the autopsy team would conclude, 'not possible to determine the actual cause of death'.

There were more judicious leaks to the Japanese press from the investigation. The *Asahi Shimbun* quoted police as saying that they had explored the area around the beach last year but that 'the site was so grassy and littered with rubbish, and in addition there might be snakes'. Furthermore, having up to now publicly denied being able to trace the final call made to Louise Phillips about Lucie joining a cult, the police chose this moment to reveal to the press club that 'they had known for some time' that it came from a mobile phone linked to Obara.

Everything pointed to the suspect toiling on some gruesome task in the short, humid nights of early July. On the evening of 1 July he'd made that call to the Zushi Fire Department asking for information on local hospitals with emergency departments. Some time on the second he had called medical services (by telephone from Tokyo) asking how to treat a victim of a drug overdose. The following day he had gone to a shop in the city to buy camping equipment, a small tent, two large bags of quick-drying concrete, mixing equipment, a cooler box, plastic bags, cutters, scissors, hammers and saws (including a battery-powered electric chainsaw). He had kept the receipts. There was a closed-circuit videotape of him buying some of the equipment from the ruggedly American L. L. Bean store in Shinjuku.

Records for 4 July, the day before he turned up at the Blue Sea, showed that Obara was treated at a hospital for extensive dermatitis.

The skin rash thing was strange. He'd still had it when he was arrested in October.

'When Obara was first arrested on suspicion of sexual assault of a Canadian woman last October, we noticed a peculiar rash on his arms,' a police source had revealed. 'We asked an expert what he thought it might be, and he told us it looked like a rash caused by contact with *chadoku-ga* [literally 'brown poison moth'].' The insect produces a toxin that protects it from predators. Contact with human skin can produce a severe rash that lingers for three months.

According to an expert consulted by the *Shukan Bunshun* weekly: 'The moth feeds on camellias and tea plants. It often appears among camellia trees from June through August. As it sheds its hairs, some people can develop an itch just by walking past.'

But there were no *chadoku-ga* present near Obara's condominium in Zushi, although there were plenty of camellias around the Blue Sea and, sure enough, signs of the disagreeable insects as well.

There were rumblings in the media that the police had

somehow massively tripped up in taking so long to find the body. There were counter rumours that the cunning cops had known the location of Lucie's remains for months and had kept watch over the site in order to somehow trap Obara. The sensational weekly tabloid *Shukan Asahi* ran a story to this effect. 'They were waiting for Obara to confess. His leading them to the place where she was buried would have given them an ironclad case,' so a former policeman told the paper.

But the October search had failed to find the body – at least in the official version of events. Maybe it actually had been retrieved by the police and reburied, or put there later by a confederate of Obara, it was widely suggested. The grisly speculation in the press did not help at the time, nor did it help later during Obara's trial when the mystery of why the police did not find the body in their October 2000 search gave credence to Obara's claim that somebody else had indeed put it there when he was first taken into custody.

So the investigators now had a body. But a fresh warrant for Obara's arrest in the Lucie case was compromised by the autopsy. No cause of death was retrievable. And there was no confession, the turning point of virtually every criminal prosecution in Japan.

But a supposition about the sequence of events *could* be made: Lucie had died at the Zushi apartment some time early on 2 July. The cause of death was an overdose of sedatives administered without her knowledge or consent. Her body had been transported by car to the Miura peninsula some time thereafter. Her body had been 'destroyed' using an electric chainsaw on the night of 5–6 July, either in a remote spot on the road between Zushi and Aburatsubo or in the Blue Sea apartment itself, before being buried in plastic bags in its under-cliff grave.

It was just a question of proving it.

What had happened in the apartment at Zushi was more or less beyond reconstruction. The strands of blonde hair, the fingerprint, the photograph, the witness testimony, the mobile phone – what did they prove? Anyway the accused admitted that Lucie had been at his Zushi condo, but claimed she 'had been fine when she left'. But what about events in Apartment 401 of the Blue Sea at Aburatsubo down the coast? Could Obara really have dismembered a body and there be no trace of blood or human tissue in the apartment? The blunders of the July before when local police from Miura had confronted Obara on the very night, it might now seem, that he was cutting up Lucie's body, had in some way to be expunged. Investigators had found purchase receipts for a vinyl mat, a folding table, a tent and chainsaw (although this crucial piece of evidence could not be physically found).

In a gruesome simulation, police used a tent and chainsaw – identical to those for which they had found receipts – to carve up a pig's carcass (both frozen and at a natural temperature) inside it, set up at Tokyo University's forensic medicine department. Blood and fluids were retained within the tent. All of them, no leakage whatsoever. But it proved nothing conclusive. The experiment only showed that it could have happened that way.

Poor Lucie's body had by now given up whatever clues it might. It was released to the family for cremation. On 24 February Jane Blackman flew to Tokyo to retrieve it, in what was her fourth such journey across the globe. She was met by consular officials who took her to the British Embassy. She was followed three days later by Tim, Sophie and Rupert. The parents did not meet. Lucie's mother told reporters: 'I have to sign documents to enable the body of my beloved daughter Lucie to be taken home and arrange for her funeral to be conducted with the dignity she deserves . . . There are no words to describe my grief. If you have a child, you will know exactly how I feel.'

Then she added this: 'What has upset me is the way some people still see Lucie as some kind of prostitute who had it coming to her . . . This is extremely hurtful. There was no sex involved with what Lucie was doing. I have been to the club where she worked and it is nothing more than an expensive karaoke bar . . . She was just the tragic victim of a perverted psychopath, a lunatic who preyed on her trusting nature.'

The occasion was an excuse for reporters to make a return to Roppongi where, in the space of seven months since Lucie first went missing, two entire holiday-visa generations of nice suburban girls had come, gone and been forgotten. 'You feel sorry for her,' said one. 'But in the end, she shouldn't have got in his car.' And: 'His family were Koreans, you know,' said another. 'Japanese customers always tell you that. "Don't worry," they say. "He came from Korea."'

Jane and Sophie accompanied Lucie's remains on their doleful flight back to England in the cargo hold of a Virgin Atlantic 747. Questioned by the media in Tokyo, Jane Blackman had refused to comment on Obara. Anyway, he had yet to be charged with anything to do with the death of Lucie. For the Tokyo police that was getting a little embarrassing.

On Friday 6 April 2001, Japanese prosecutors at last felt confident enough to formally rearrest Joji Obara in his cell. As Tadao Sugawara, chief of the serious crimes division of the Tokyo Metropolitan Police told a press conference later that day: 'We arrested Joji Obara on charges of kidnap, assault resulting in death, and mutilating and abandoning a body in relation to Lucie Jane Blackman. Circumstantial evidence has built up and we believe we have conducted thorough investigations which resulted in the arrest at this time.'

The accused had asked Ms Blackman out for 'a lunch' in July the previous year and took her to his condominium in Zushi City in Kanagawa Prefecture, he said. 'He plied her with drinks laced with drugs and made her lose control of her body and mind and assaulted her . . . That resulted in her dying of drug intoxication . . . The suspect mutilated her body and left it in Miura City, Kanagawa Prefecture.' He would not say where, in the investigation's opinion, Lucie Blackman had died, nor where Obara had allegedly mutilated her body – or if the two events occurred in the same place.

Two days later, police formally turned the Blackman case over to the Tokyo Public Prosecutor's Office. Police 'sources' told favoured press outlets that weekend that searches of Obara's properties conducted since October had secured about five thousand videotapes, 'several hundred of which depicted him having sex with or raping women, including the six cases he has [thus far] been indicted in'. But they could not find any footage showing Lucie Blackman, so the police sources said. As the Kyodo news agency reported on 7 April:

Investigators believe he destroyed the Blackman tape as well as a shovel and electric saw he is believed to have bought on July 3, two days after her disappearance.

Police have discovered that Obara rented a car,

298

despite the fact he owned one, in mid-July when media started reporting Blackman's disappearance. They also think he bought a motorboat in early October, immediately before his first arrest on a rape charge.

They believe the purchases were related to the destruction of evidence in the Blackman case, the sources said.

Her hair and a photo of her he is thought to have taken were found at the Zushi condo, the sources said, adding mobile phone records indicate he was in Zushi with her when she went missing.

On her mournful trip to Tokyo to collect her daughter's ruined body, Jane Blackman had predicted the funeral would be 'another dysfunctional family occasion'. Actually, when it was held in the Anglican church of St Nicholas in Chislehurst, Kent, on 29 March 2001, it was appropriate and dignified enough. It was where Lucie's parents had married all those years before, when Jane had been twenty-two – just a year older than Lucie.

Both Tim and Jane were at the funeral. They sat separately. The church was packed with two hundred mourners, including twenty of Lucie's former colleagues, wearing their BA uniforms.

A bouquet sent by the British Embassy in Tokyo was laid next to one from the Japanese ambassador in London.

The Azabu police sent sticks of incense which burned next to a portrait of Lucie. The Prime Minister, Tony Blair sent a personal note of condolence. A letter was read from a Japanese family who had lost a daughter in Europe. It said: 'Our hearts were praying for Lucie to be found safe and sound. We are so ashamed of ourselves as a nation.'

But the wave of national shame was not universal. A Japanese newspaper editorialised:

Miss Blackman's death ... raises ... delicate issues. Chief among these is the whole context of the work she did and the kinds of people it brought her into contact with, some of them disturbed or violent or both. The truth is, Blackman, like many other foreign hostesses in Japan's nightclub districts, ventured into a world where even many Japanese would hesitate to go ...

Some will protest that even to mention such things in the context of Blackman's [alleged] murder is to impute blame to the victim. It is not. But it is to suggest that her death was avoidable. Bar owners are neither parents nor policemen to these girls. If Lucie's fellow hostesses learn even this much, then perhaps some good may come from her sad, senseless death.

A memorial mass was held at the Catholic church of St Francis Xavier in Chiyoda Ward, Tokyo, on Sunday 29

May. Father Hiroyuki Arakawa expressed his concern over 'the plight of foreign women in Japan who have been subjected to violence by men, and the nameless women who had died under such circumstances'. Lucie's death had also caused deep grief and suffering for her family, made worse by 'the prejudices and rumours that had swirled around her disappearance,' he said.

It was further noted how cases involving foreign victims were often 'forgotten and shelved', unlike those involving Japanese victims – and how Lucie had come to 'represent various sectors of society in Japan, such as women and foreigners, who have fallen prey to suffering and injustice'. That was a nod to the sex-workers of Kabuki-cho as well as the partygoers of Roppongi.

The arraignment of Joji Obara was set to begin at Tokyo in midsummer 2001. The multiple charges would mean a hugely time-consuming effort by the prosecution to collate information. It was painfully slow. It had been clear since his arrest in the Lucie case on charges of kidnap, assault resulting in death, and mutilating and abandoning a body that, without a confession, proving intent to murder was going to be impossible.

After his formal arrest, his interrogation and the overall investigation had continued. There were more leaks to the press – notes 'apparently written by Lucie Blackman' were found in Obara's Tokyo apartment, it was reported. 'The notes show handwritten figures and names that appear to be jottings detailing from whom and how much money someone had borrowed.'

On 3 July 2001 came a sort of admission, or so police sources had it. On the day before the first hearing of the case at Tokyo District Court, the Kyodo news agency, citing 'sources', quoted Obara as having told investigators: 'When I was entertained by Lucie at the club, I told her: "I have a cool drug and I will give you some soon." I took her to the Zushi condo and gave her the drug. She took it.' The 'cool' drug was the date-rape sedative GHB, so 'sources close to the investigation' were keen to reveal.

That Lucie had taken narcotics willingly would be the foundation of Obara's defence – that she was an eager drug user who had come with him to the apartment at Zushi marina with her full consent. She had taken too much, stuff she herself had brought with her, and he had left her there 'tripping', in his description, while he had gone back to the city late on the night of 1–2 July.

More of what had gone on in Apartment 4914, Building No. 4 of Zushi marina on that allegedly fatal evening (at least Joji Obara's version of it) would emerge later in his trial testimony. It was bizarre and in places distressingly intimate. Some of it might be considered to be deranged fantasy. Some of it was terribly believable.

But less believable, perhaps, was the narrative that
Obara and his defence lawyers would weave around who
had actually committed the crime. This was the summation of it. When he had gone back to Tokyo that night of
1–2 July, Obara had, in his kindness, contacted a professional 'fixer' – a character known in Japanese culture as a
nandemo-ya. This certain 'Mr A' was to go to the Zushi
apartment, collect Lucie and take her home to Sendagaya.
He had further hired Mr A to bury the frozen remains of
Irene the dog in a specially constructed tomb at a place
called Emerald Town, where he owned yet more land.
This, he said, explained his purchase of shovels, cement,
tools and sheeting. The dog, however, seemed to have
ended up back in Tokyo.

The trial began on 4 July 2001 at Tokyo District Court
before a panel of three judges, Judge Tsutomu Tochigi
presiding. The juryless tribunal heard the full story – as far
as it was known – for the first time. In the matter of Miss
Lucie Jane Blackman, the ten-page indictment relayed
how Obara and Lucie had driven together to Zushi, the
phone calls to her flatmate and boyfriend – and the allegation that between that time and dawn on 2 July 2000, Joji
Obara gave her a drink containing sleeping drugs and
administered chloroform, leading to her death either from
failure of her heart or respiratory system.

The judges heard how the next day, Obara drove back to

Tokyo and made a telephone call to Louise Phillips claiming that Lucie had joined a cult. They heard how he visited a series of shops buying camping equipment, two large bags of quick-drying concrete, mixing equipment, a cooler box, plastic bags, cutters, scissors, hammers and saws (including a chainsaw). They heard the story of the locksmith being called to Apartment 401 at Aburatsubo, the caretaker's excitement, the policeman's visit and the dead dog, and how the accused had, in the meantime, sought treatment for a skin rash.

They heard an outline of the phone evidence links to Obara, about the caches of videos and sleeping pills and chemicals discovered at his various residences. It was all circumstantial, full of gaps and assertions. But for the first time in open court the accused admitted that Lucie was with him on the day she disappeared. Speaking 'clearly and calmly', dressed in a dark suit and open-necked shirt, Obara gave his version of events:

'She told me she wanted to go somewhere where the scenery was nice. We drank alcohol and watched videos at my mansion in Zushi,' Obara said. 'She seemed fine when we parted.' He insisted that although he had previously had consensual 'play' with Miss Blackman (he did not say where or when) after meeting her in the Tokyo hostess bar where she worked, 'I did not make her consume drinks that included sleeping pills or other drugs.'

'Though I am responsible for what has happened, I did not take any action which led to her death,' he said.

There was no DNA evidence to prove rape, no video, no bloodied weapon, not even a cause of death. They had found Lucie, but still had no way of proving how she had died.

CHAPTER 21

Samantha Ridgway had been formally informed in early January 2001 by the Australian police that the investigation into her sister Carita's death was to be reopened. It was both a relief and the beginning of a terrible new ordeal. Robert Finnigan was already in Tokyo trying to get the police to do something. Then they had made the connection between the play notebook entry, the video and the receipt for Hideshima Hospital. They had indicted Obara a week before the discovery of Lucie Blackman's mutilated remains. As Samantha said:

At last after nine years we knew the truth – that Carita had been drugged, raped and left to die. I felt nauseated, realising too that if only Obara had told the hospital that Carita had been given chloroform she might have survived.

Now Robert discovered that a biopsy sample of Carita's liver had, after all, been kept by the hospital.

The police refused to show us the full video of Carita's ordeal to spare us unnecessary trauma. But my mother witnessed a short clip showing my unconscious sister with a masked Obara.

That biopsy sample was vital. Joji Obara had his own answer when the prosecution came to open its case in the matter of the dead hostess from Sydney. In his statement to the court in September 2001 he insisted she was killed either by an injection she received in hospital from incompetent doctors or from poisoned seafood. 'She ate a raw oyster and afterwards she said that her stomach hurt,' he told the court. 'Before she had the injection she looked fine, talking and walking around the room, but after the shot, she became lethargic and fell unconscious.'

However, a police pathologist examined the preserved liver sample and concluded, as the court would eventually be told, that 'it was highly likely hepatitis was induced by drugs to which she had been exposed fourteen days before the tissue sample was taken.' An expert also examined the Carita 'rape' video. He concluded that a bottle of chloroform could be seen in the background as an inert, naked female suffered repeated indignities under an unblinking floodlight. A naked male figure in a Zorro mask cavorted around the bed.

Joji Obara had become a national embarrassment (even if – although it was politically incorrect to say it – he was really a Korean). Nevertheless, for a while his trial was a fashionable place to visit: 'You always see several dating couples in the spectator seats. I guess young women get a thrill out of watching,' the *Shukan Jitsuwa* newspaper reported.

The evidence presented was certainly stimulating – if you liked that sort of thing. In a statement put out later by his defenders, it was explained how the accused got his own kind of excitement. It was a reiteration of the strange statement he had made soon after his arrest with some new twists. Everything was consensual, everything was paid for; and anyway, the women were drug-takers. A bizarre statement in clumsy English was later posted on the Internet as 'The Truth Of Lucie's Case':

None of the partners Obara, the accused, 'played' with was an amateur. All of the non-Japanese bar hostesses received some money from Obara, when they 'played' with him.

Before his 'play' the accused pours into a small shot

glass, a nasty liquid with a burning smell, commonly known as 'Philippine liquor'. Then he and his female 'partner' drink from the glass in turn. The accused drinks two glasses of the liquid. As made clear at court, Obara loses the last bit of his sense of shame after drinking two glasses of the liquid. Then, the accused alone takes a great quantity of a stimulant. His 'partner', as she continues to drink the 'Philippine liquor', loses consciousness.

Then the accused puts on a mask and begins the 'play'. This mask makes him turn into someone else, a person outside the ordinary. Then he gets into his nasty 'play'.

To 'play' with, the accused preferred non-Japanese bar hostesses who were drug-addicted, punk women (with a mean personality) known as 'bitches'. Sue, a non-Japanese woman [identified separately in courtroom testimony as 'an American'] of misbehaviours, introduced to the accused such women for him to play with. He also chose his 'play partners' from those women searching for some male company over the phone. In such a case, the accused preferred waist-less, plump women who were often compared to a pig or a hippopotamus. Under a mask, Obara had his nasty 'play' with such ugly women.

The world's attention moved on after 9/11. Sex-slayers stalking Tokyo looking for foreign girls had, for the time being, lost some of their salacious appeal for the British and American media.

The Japanese were keen to forget such things. To begin with, however, the unmasking of Joji Obara as the beast of Roppongi chimed with a national mood to clean up the nation's sex act. The moral panic about compensated dating and underage sex had already led to new laws banning child prostitution and pornography, and further attempts followed to shut down websites, phone clubs and two-shot dial set-ups where young people offered themselves or where someone offered money for sex with a minor.

All this was given new urgency by a shocking case in July 2003 when four junior high school students vanished from the Shibuya area of Tokyo. The girls, who it turned out had gone there looking to sell their underwear, were sexually assaulted before the assailant killed himself in his apartment and one of the girls managed to escape.

The rescue of the four girls and the circumstances that had brought them into danger, all of which was sensationally reported in the Japanese press, led directly to the enforcement of the Revised Youth Protection Ordinance that effectively imposed a curfew on under-eighteens, banned scouts from trying to recruit young people for indecent activities and obliged clubs and bars to check IDs, 'a sight almost unseen before'.

Most girls were accessing the sex websites through their mobile phones, it unsurprisingly turned out. A Tokyo banker was arrested after meeting a girl through a telephone dating club. The girl turned out to be fifteen but he thought she was eighteen. A police officer arrested on the basis of the same law for meeting a seventeen-year-old was released because the business told her to lie about her age. Another man posing as a policeman was given a life sentence for molesting twelve elementary school students in his car. A fireman was arrested under the anti-child prostitution and pornography law when he ran off and failed to pay his fifteen-year-old victim. A fourteen-year-old girl was arrested for pimping her high-school classmates using a mobile phone. It went on.

All those schoolgirls behaving badly (and the men who bought their favours) represented sex in the suburbs, hidden encounters brokered through new technology. It was an all-Japanese affair. But old-fashioned, Kabuki-cho sex was also in trouble, especially after the Super Loose fire where the dancers posing as Japanese schoolgirls turned out to have come from Taiwan. Outside attention on the water trade's wilder shores continued, as did an unwelcome high-level diplomatic focus on Japan's apparent appetite for imported female flesh. At this end of business, the young hands and tongues for hire were not Japanese, nor did they come from Sevenoaks or Bromley.

In June 2004 a US State Department report demoted Japan to a 'Tier 2 Watch List' of governments (the same ranking as Laos and Russia) who were culpably slack on human trafficking. It declared that Japan had 'a huge problem with slavery, particularly sex slavery', and that there was a 'tremendous gap' between the size of the problem and the resources devoted to addressing it. At the centre of it all was a legal fraud – the so called 'entertainer visa'.

Girls like Lucie and the others working as hostesses on tourist visas were illegals anyway – it was a matter of the police's willingness to enforce the existing law and the compliance, or not, of employers. The entertainer visa went back to an archaic provision for live musicians to tinkle away in hotel lobbies. Some gaijin would-be hostesses had worked out you could pick one up in the Japanese consulate in Thailand.

But the entertainer visa loophole masked a much bigger 'scandal' – which became the special target of American campaigners. In 2004, the peak year, Japan issued more than 130,000 such visas of which over 60 per cent went to women from the Philippines. Where were they doing so much singing and dancing? In fact these young women (a big proportion of them were minors with forged dates of birth in their passports) were to be employed as anything but musicians or dancers. They were bound for fuck-shacks and soaplands.

Legislation that year made trafficking in persons a new category of crime, and the next year the number fell dramatically. But still, according to the US government's extensive report on human rights in Japan in its audit of 2005,

> Trafficking of women and girls into the country was a problem. Women and girls, primarily from Thailand, the Philippines, and Eastern Europe, were trafficked into the country for sexual exploitation and forced labor . . . In previous years many women trafficked into the country entered legally on entertainer visas. Entertainers are not covered by the labor standards law and have no minimum wage protections . . .
>
> Women trafficked to the country generally were employed as prostitutes under coercive conditions in businesses licensed to provide commercial sex services. Sex entertainment businesses are classified as 'store form' businesses, such as strip clubs, sex shops, hostess bars, and private video rooms, and as 'nonstore form' businesses, such as escort services and mail-order video services, which arrange for sexual services to be conducted elsewhere.
>
> According to credible sources, most women who were trafficked to the country for the purpose of sexual

313

exploitation were employed as hostesses in 'snack' bars and were required to provide sexual services off-premises.

'Instore' or 'nonstore', all the so-called sexual exploitation was just all too visible in Kabuki-cho. It had long been time for something to be done. In 2003 the Governor of Tokyo had already established the 'Emergency Office for Public Safety' to, as it was said, 'prevent the capital turning into the city of crime New York once was'. It was headed by Vice-Governor Yutaka Takehana, formerly of the National Police Agency, who embarked on a series of nocturnal inspections.

'One of the biggest tasks in restoring public safety in Tokyo is to control crimes by non-Japanese residents,' the public safety committee said in its mission statement. 'Some foreigners who have entered Japan illegally or overstayed their visas are setting up crime organisations and engaging in violent crimes, creating a major social threat.' Vice-Governor Takehana was referring to, although he did not say it, criminal gangs from mainland China and Taiwan, the Iranians who dominated drug distribution and the Nigerian touts who were such a high-visibility feature of the sex-trade. He seemed to have a special thing about the Nigerians.

The Prime Minister, Junichiro Koizumi, gave his full support, saying: 'I want to make Kabuki-cho a place where

I can go have a couple of drinks.' The Hoanka, the division of the national police tasked with maintaining public order, found a new urgency in their otherwise sleepy routine while an Organised Crime Control Department was established to crack down on trafficking.

And manga porn was in for a kicking. The new sobriety was signalled in January 2004 when, to general astonishment, Monotori Kishi, a fifty-four-year-old publisher, was given a one-year prison sentence suspended for three years for violating Japan's by-now rarely used *waisetsu* laws on the sale and distribution of obscene literature. His manga production, *Misshitsu* (*Honey Room*) featured 'bodies . . . drawn in a lifelike manner with little attention to concealment (of genitalia), making for sexually explicit expression and deeming the book pornographic matter', according to the presiding judge who heard the case. There was a mix of public incredulity and outrage. *Misshitsu* was tame compared with many other offerings. Kishi appealed, pleading an unconstitutional violation of freedom of expression. He lost (although the accompanying fine was reduced).

The crackdown on the streets of Tokyo began in earnest in mid-2004. Mr Takehana ordered the shutting down of adult shops and massage parlours with Kabuki-cho getting most of it. A little later, a revision to the six-decades-old *fuzoku* laws made aggressive 'catching' of women in the street illegal. It also required sex establishments to disclose detailed information on their lease agreements and limited the hours when drink was available. A sex-shop owner complained: 'Customers are coming in during the daytime and they are all sober and therefore unwilling to pay high prices. They complain if the girl's face is not exactly what they want. They will also have done extensive research beforehand, often arriving with discount coupons.' It was all very Japanese.

There was a raid on the notorious quickie joints under Koganecho station in Yokohama. A US women's rescue charity reported: 'As usual, there was only a cursory investigation and none of the organised crime involved was investigated. This is typical of the Japanese enforcement of anti-trafficking laws – close the clubs, arrest the low-level manager, do no follow up investigation, and while announcing that organised crime is behind the operations, fail to arrest any organised crime members.'

The crackdown reached out to Roppongi. Mr Takehana made a set-piece visit to its night-time streets accompanied by television crews. The touts and *massaji* girls behaved as usual. The Vice-Governor was not pleased, and a series of busts followed: G. Martini's, Excel and One Eyed Jack were raided; at Don Carlo's club all the foreign hostesses were arrested for visa violations. A Chinese massage parlour twenty feet away from the

Roppongi Crossing police box was closed down. A number of American and Australian investment bankers caught in the trawl were arrested on drug charges and held up to the light of publicity. It was foreigners, gaijin causing all this trouble.

An American visitor who witnessed the raid on One Eyed Jack thought the strip club was 'clearly nostalgic for the heady bubble days of expense accounts and cocaine. It opened on to a strip bar called Private Eyes across the hallway . . . The passing of the golden years was underlined by the cavernous disco beyond, now vacant of hostesses except for those clutching, of all things, marriage visas.' Marrying a Japanese citizen was one way for a working girl to get round the crackdown on 'entertainers'.

Roppongi's loss of immunity was very much *not* a result of the Lucie Blackman case. With alarming frankness, an anonymous senior policeman from Azabu put it like this:

> It used to be that crimes against foreigners by other for-
> eigners or by Japanese [against foreigners] didn't
> concern us. It was not worth the trouble and paperwork
> to arrest them. Crimes against Japanese by foreigners –
> that is an issue, of course. Other than that, this is an area
> where we always looked the other way. For most

Japanese, Roppongi isn't part of Japan and Japanese standards don't apply. It's like that area in Saudi Arabia where all the foreigners live and ignore the Saudi rules.

But all that was changing. And if Lucie's fate had not been the trigger for the crackdown, it had served to make the idea of a little light hostessing in Tokyo rather less attractive for gaijin girls from the suburbs. It was better left to the professionals – to the Japanese themselves – or to those young women perhaps who really, really needed the money.

The place was changing anyway. At the time Lucie disappeared, Roppongi had already long been targeted by the legendary property tycoon Minoro Mori with a bubble-echoing plan to raise a glittering city of towers ('Roppongi Hills') out of the modest urban landscape where foreign hostess bars and strip clubs tackily clustered. The huge development was well on its way to completion by 2003. Some of the lower-rent sex operations were squeezed out, while the competition to profit from the remaining space got greater. A tougher breed of Roppongi club manager realised that strip joints and hostess clubs with added private-room services had better margins than the more staid variety where karaoke and a *dohan* or two were the height of revenue-earning decadence. It was like the arrival of the strip clubs at the end of the twentieth century, touting harder, coarser sex on a production-line basis with girls from Russia, Hungary and Romania doing the business.

How could the illusion of the fantasy love affair survive this new challenge? It was struggling to do so already.

Tim and Sophie Blackman met Tetsuo Nishi, the Casablanca's one-time manager, in Tokyo in November 2003. They were in Japan for the formal opening of the trial of Joji Obara. Nishi, now working as barman in Geronimo's (one of Lucie's haunts), expressed to a British reporter his regret at the passing of the old ways:

> Within a few years, there will not be any hostesses left. It may have been a job that occasionally led to other things, but basically a good hostess should be like a geisha – it is all part of the ethos that a good night out should involve a bit of refinement and a bit of class.
>
> But the girls don't want to take the risk any more and the customers have different ideas about how they want to spend their money. All the girls that would have become hostesses five years ago are now becoming strippers – the same sort of money but half the risk and half the effort.

'These are not even the twilight days of that kind of pour-the-drinks, laugh-at-their-jokes hostessing,' an American girl told a British newspaper reporter in Roppongi. 'Unless you're going to take your clothes off, the party is over.'

But the Roppongi party was never over.

CHAPTER 22

The trial of Joji Obara opened, at last, in the Tokyo District Court on 27 November 2003. It was already more than two years since he had first appeared in court to formally plead not guilty. Things had ground to a halt in December 2001 when the entire seven-man defence team resigned because: 'Obara refused to heed his attorney's suggestions and during the main questioning spoke only the things he wanted to say.' Ten months later the leader of his new legal team, Kimio Iwamoto, announced that he had taken on the case 'out of a sense of duty' after three Japanese bar associations were unable to find anyone else.

The judicial process was already very complicated, embracing multiple indictments, but it was the cases that had allegedly resulted in fatalities, those of Carita Ridgway and Lucie Blackman, that invited the most interest and the most contentious testimony in the juryless court.

A British Embassy official attended each full trial day with an interpreter. The Blackmans in England were kept informed via this route, as well as by sympathetic English-language newspaper reporters and by Scotland Yard liaison officers. It was a drip, drip of testimony and allegation, sometimes unbearably gruesome, at others comically bizarre.

As the drawn-out process unfolded, Lucie's parents each rebuilt their lives with new partners, Tim with Josephine Barr and Jane with Roger Steare, a 'corporate philosopher' and visiting professor of organisational ethics at the Cass Business School at City University in London whom she married in 2003.

The prosecution sought to make the closest possible link between the defendant and the fate of Lucie Blackman. She was identified as being at Zushi marina on the evening of 1 July 2000. That was not in contention. But what sequence of events had brought her there?

The most interesting testimony (for lovers of detective fiction, if no one else) concerned the hours when Lucie was last reported alive and the defendant's explanation of what had happened on the night and early morning of 1–2 July and in the days thereafter.

Prosecution witnesses were called, including Mrs Yumiko Saito from Zushi who had seen someone she could identify as Obara with a tall foreign woman walking behind him, and the caretaker from the Blue Sea who reprised the story about seeing Obara with cement on his hands at Aburatsubo.

One witness was Toru Aoyma of the Tokyo Gas Company, Kamakura branch. Logbooks showed that Obara had called that office at 4.20 p.m. on 1 July asking for an emergency repair at Zushi. The repairman, Mr Aoyma, had called at 7.14 p.m. and finished the job at 7.31. He told the court he could not recall whether it was Obara who had let him in – it was two years ago. He had seen no sign of Lucie Blackman or anyone else.

Inspector Harada of the Miura police gave his story about being barred from Apartment 401 by its sweating, dust-covered resident and his appearance later with the frozen dog wrapped in some sort of parcel.

None of the gaijin house inmates or girls from the Casablanca was called on to give more testimony other than that they had already given to the police.

The prosecution advanced its evidence about the receipts for hardware and cement, the videos and Super 8 movies (4880 of them, of which more than two hundred showed women being sexually abused), the 'play' note-books and the closed-session testimony of those women who had encountered the defendant in his various incar-nations as 'Jazu' or 'Koji' and survived to tell the tale.

Most of this was already in the public domain from police leaks to reporters after the arrest and arraignment of the defendant. But Obara's defence, when its turn came, revealed intimate details of his version of what had happened in those hours and days which had so vexed Lucie's friends and then her family following her disappearance.

The defendant's version emerged bit by bit over months of courtroom appearances, yet it retained a certain continuity. Some of it was clearly what had actually happened, confirmed by bit-player walk-ons like gas repairmen and locksmiths. Joji had met Lucie in the Casablanca club on 24 June. She had agreed to go to his flat near the coast the following weekend. In fact, it was her suggestion – she was keen to see some 'nice scenery'. He proposed that they meet in front of Sendagaya station where he would pick her up in his Mercedes convertible. Which is seemingly what happened on the early afternoon of 1 July 2000.

On the way out of the city she had talked about a planned trip to Australia that August to see relatives and her desire to visit a particular prizewinning vineyard – the Montana winery. After that, she thought she would go to New Zealand.

They bought a bottle of beer in Zushi before going up to the apartment at around 5.30 p.m., where they started to drink champagne. A man from the gas company had come to fix the hot water and while he, Joji, was dealing with

that, Lucie had telephoned her friend Louise and then
Scott Fraser, the American, on a mobile phone he had
given her. The fact that he had given her the phone
showed that he had no intention of drugging her – even
less of killing her, he said.

They talked. Lucie was excited, voluble, getting drunk
on the champagne. The Zushi catering service brought up
some snacks. She told him that 'her sister was very clever
and her brother was very cute, her mother was very lovely
and she was her good friend.' However, 'her father gave
great pains to her mother and he had many girlfriends.'

Lucie had offered to massage his shoulders to ease the
pain caused by a car accident sustained a month before.
Obara said he had asked Lucie whether she would stop
working as a hostess if he gave her enough cash to pay her
debts – and she had said yes. He also said that he had
made such a proposal to every foreign woman and it was
just a game.

Lucie, so he claimed, had then offered him drugs which
she had brought with her, which he declined to take,
although he did drink alcohol. This is where Obara's defence
turned on the character of Lucie Blackman. She was a drug-
user, like the other girls (he did not, however, brand her
directly as being a prostitute who did what she did simply for
money), and it was flaws in her character that had embroiled
him in this tragic sequence of accidental events.

In the apartment he had shown her a photo of the girl TM (the one he claimed to have rescued from the celebrity cannibal Issei Sagawa) taking heroin, and Lucie said she wanted some of it. In the absence of heroin she proceeded to take pills and smoke cannabis, both of which she had with her.

On the morning of 2 July Lucie was alive, according to Obara. He went back to the city, to Shibuya, by taxi to buy some earrings for her, he claimed. He phoned the Zushi apartment but Lucie was clearly still intoxicated – 'tripping', in his words. That's why he had phoned a hospital with an urgent inquiry about how to treat an overdose.

He went back to the coast by train, he said. He got to Zushi at around 11.30 p.m. on 2 July, Lucie was conscious and, he suggested, she had taken an overdose of tablets that had been in the apartment. She said she wanted more. 'I can't give you any more because they belong to TM,' he'd replied. 'Anyway, you need to go to a hospital.'

'I can't. They will find drugs in my body and deport me,' Lucie had said. 'She said she had a brain problem, she said she was desperate,' claimed Obara. He knew all about her search for love and was not afraid to reveal it to the court. 'She met her American boyfriend, Scott, in June 2000 but she left her boyfriend, Alex, behind in England; she was not happy with her life,' he told his judges.

This was the cruellest and, at the same time, the most poignant component of the defence case. By the rules of the court, Obara's team had been given access to e-mails home from Lucie to Sophie and her mother, as well as to Lucie's diary – the one found in the gaijin house and given to Tim and Sophie in Tokyo during those desperate mid-summer days of July 2000 to see if it might provide them with a clue to her disappearance. It had not.

But in Obara's eyes it did just that – or at least her writings exposed her disturbed state of mind. He knew more than enough English to interpret them as them as the out-pourings of a decadent, mentally unstable young woman playing a dangerous game of drugs and sex. At the same time, he was emotionally literate enough to realise just how vulnerable Lucie was in her family relationships and her search for love outside them. The diary gave him a prurient insight into her hopes and fears, her relationships with boyfriends and indeed those of the other gaijin girls as they bounced around Roppongi bars looking for whatever it was they were looking for.

In its innocence and honesty, Lucie's journal was the absolute opposite of Obara's horrible conquest 'play' note-books, although if he saw the irony, Obara did not say so.

'To tell the truth about Lucie's character will shame her family and make them depressed,' he told the court. 'I haven't changed in my wish to avoid revealing her charac-ter. But it was because of that that I became embroiled in this terrible incident,' he said. So it was her fault.

On 24 April 2005, Obara, under cross-examination by his own defence counsel, read extracts of Lucie's diary out in court in his own cell-made, Japanese translation (the police had made their version almost five years earlier). Tim and Sophie Blackman were there to hear him. They could not understand what was being said, only the word 'Lucie' punctuating the droning delivery. There was nothing they could do to stop the extracts from being made public. Indeed, when a little later 'friends' of Obara posted them on a website, a UK police liaison officer told Tim: 'Defamation [and the diaries in their references to drug-taking might be construed as such in some instances] of a deceased person was not illegal unless a lie was involved and, as everyone accepted the diaries were genuine, that was not the case.'

In a rambling delivery, Obara stressed how a psychiatrist consulted by the defence had described the diary entries as the work of 'manic depressive'. He pointed out Lucie's anxiety over her credit card debt. There was stuff about disgust at her own appearance and her 'ordinariness'. She had written of buying drugs and of 'tokes'. A dictionary was produced to check the word after Obara said the police translation had missed that it was 'a reference to the use of marijuana'. He seemed especially keen to present Lucie and everyone around her as deep-dyed drug users – at least that was the view of the translator from the British Embassy in her report produced for the consulate (and sent to the Blackmans) on Obara's court-room performance.

Obara's extended, halting translations provoked several complaints from Tsutomu Tochigi, the chief judge. 'This is torture,' he said. 'What does this have to do with the trial?'

Tim Blackman confessed to being quite upset by the episode. There was Obara across the courtroom who was 'looking at Lucie's personal diaries and trying to make a picture of her as a mentally unstable, drug-taking young woman, which was obviously not the case,' as he put it. And Sophie said: 'Hearing him take Lucie's diary entries out of context and put his own interpretation on them, I thought I might have to leave the room.' But it was their authenticity that was so haunting, the real voice of Lucie in her search for love, so full of self-doubt in an overwhelming city, now being expressed in the wheedling voice of the man who, it was alleged, was responsible for her death.

Obara's explanation of how that had come about did nothing to alleviate the Blackmans' anguish. 'Mr A' – who Obara had hired to take Lucie back to Sendagaya – had given her more drugs, causing her death by overdose, and it was he who had disposed of her body. Mr A had himself died in hospital of liver failure in December 2001 as a result of abuse of stimulants and sleeping pills. His drug of choice – according to Obara – was Halcion.

Mr A, meanwhile, was also going to build the tomb for Irene at Emerald Town, according to Obara. He himself had taken the frozen canine from the freezer at Den-en-Chofu on 5 July (that explained the dry ice and the vinyl sheeting) and driven it to the coast. He had waited for Mr A near the expressway exit, but at 11 a.m. Mr A phoned to say he could not make it, so he drove to his apartment near the cave. He had to replace the lock.

He took a room in a *ryokan*, a traditional country inn, called Seikanso on the night of 5–6 July and checked out on the morning of the seventh, having eaten heartily (he had twice emptied a fridge in his room) and been generally cheerful. The manager of the inn, Ms Yumi Kimura, could attest to that. He had, he admitted, used a false name to register. It was 'Mr Takada'.

It may have all sounded pretty implausible, and the story of Mr A triggered smirks and giggles in the public gallery. But the prosecution still had its own gaps in reconstructing what had happened beyond reasonable doubt.

How had Obara transported the body, as it was alleged, from Zushi marina to the Blue Sea without anyone noticing? There was no blood in Apartment 401 – nothing that luminol testing (the chemical used by forensic investigators to detect trace elements of blood) could discover. And there was no DNA trace of Obara – blood, hair, semen – on Lucie's remains.

The post mortem evidence was the most problematic of all. Dr Masahiko Kobayashi, the pathologist who had led the three-man team who performed it back in February 2001 (he was now at the University of Texas) told the packed courtroom four years later how Lucie's body had been cut into ten pieces with a toothed blade that sliced through bone as well as tissue. 'Traces of flunitrazepam [Rohypnol] were detected in the body, but it's unclear at what quantities this drug was present and how long before her death the victim took the drug,' he said. Nor, he said, was chloroform detectable in the body, but it could have evaporated in the seven months that the body was in its seaside tomb. The specific cause of Ms Blackman's death could not be determined.

In autumn 2004, the court's attention had returned to the fate of Carita Ridgway. On 2 December Obara spent ninety minutes on the stand insisting that the relationship with her was consensual, that she had contracted food poisoning and that he had taken her to hospital.

In a statement for the defence later posted on the Internet site 'The Truth Of Lucie's Case', he would set out his own version of events. They had first met in 1991 when Carita Ridgway was working at a small bar called Takagi. She moved to another bar, frequented by Obara and some of his acquaintances, 'including the general manager of the bank branch Obara had dealings with'.

She and Obara developed 'a sexual relationship, as a bar hostess and her customer,' said the statement. She visited Obara's room at Zushi twice, so the Obara-friendly website claimed. She had 'play' with the accused on her first visit but not on the second, which took place several weeks later. The same statement blamed Hideshima Hospital for treating her with painkillers that caused 'serious liver problems'.

In April 2006 Lucie's parents were invited to Tokyo to give what were called family victim impact statements. Struggling to control her emotions, Jane Steare told the court:

> I spent seven months praying [Lucie] be found [alive], but my worst fears came true when she was found not only dead, but her beautiful body had been chainsawed into pieces, her beautiful long blonde hair had been shaved off and her head had been encased in concrete.
>
> I used to believe that the sorrow of any parent losing a child is the greatest sorrow anyone can know. I was wrong. To lose a child and know her body was desecrated in such an inhuman way is the greatest and most unrelenting pain I have ever had to endure. It is with me day and night.

The statement Lucie's mother gave to a press conference afterwards was equally moving, perhaps more so. She spoke of her gratitude to the 'ordinary Japanese people here in the streets of Tokyo who have come up to me to say how sorry they are that this has happened'. She spoke of her concerns when Lucie had first left home and described how she had filled 'her handbag with guardian angels and crystals that I had bought her to keep her safe'. She went on:

The last time I heard from Lucie was two days before she died. Her message began, 'I am still alive.' She had been ill with a cold and been cooped up in her room. She asked if I could send her a remedy for cold sores.

When I received the telephone call from her best friend, Louise, to tell me that Lucie was missing, I felt I would die. I often awake again in the early hours and begin wondering if this was the time of night she died. I wonder if she suffered. Did she feel any pain? Did she call out my name? I will never know.

Annette Foster, Carita Ridgway's mother, told the court that it was two years before Robert Finnigan could even say her name without breaking down. Samantha somehow blamed herself and had tried to kill herself in 1994. She was 'still haunted by the loss'.

'Owing to Joji Obara I almost lost both my daughters,' she said and told the court of her own decade-long struggle

333

with depression and physical illness. 'I loved Carita intensely and when she died I also wanted to die. I was bereft; there was no other person on this earth that I was closer to,' she said.

'My preference in Obara's sentence is that he should be executed,' she said. 'However, in the circumstances that is not possible. He should be imprisoned until he dies.'

Joji Obara was not in the courtroom to hear the statements. He would tell his prosecutors why: 'The mothers just wanted to take out their emotions on the alleged perpetrator and because I am innocent it was irrelevant for me to face them.' He had stripped naked and somehow attached himself to the washbasin in his cell.

Tim Blackman was not in Tokyo at the same time as Jane. His statement was read to the court:

Her death has left me shattered, empty and numb, as her precious life has been torn away from me.

I had dreamed of her wonderful future; her wedding day – the day she would have felt her most beautiful and most happy; the day she would bear my first grandchild. But now this will not happen . . . I see the pain and despair in the faces of Sophie and Rupert, knowing I can only comfort them with words, as I worry how their future will be affected by the loss of their sister.

After the internment of Lucie's ashes my daughter

Sophie . . . could no longer sustain the grief and trauma caused her by the death of her beloved sister and she attempted to commit suicide. Since then she has been under psychiatric observation and is currently an inpatient at a psychiatric unit.

The Blackman family was buckling under the mental strain, but at least, like the Ridgways, they maintained a fragile unity on the surface in their desire for justice for Lucie. However, that unity was already being tested by an extraordinary new challenge. It was coming from 'friends' of Joji Obara.

CHAPTER 23

Joji Obara was now in the fifth year of the legal process weighing his innocence or guilt. The defendant himself had consistently maintained his line – that the women he was accused of drugging and raping (in two cases leading to their deaths) had submitted to his alleged assaults consensually. They had done it for money. Now he did not have any money – or so it seemed.

Proceedings had long been in hand to wind up his tangle of property interests and declare him bankrupt. His mother was said to have kept him afloat financially in the past. But he had, it seemed, other friends with wealth and influence, who thought his case worth fighting.

In November 2005, Tim Blackman was shopping in Newport on the Isle of Wight, when his mobile phone rang. A thin, reedy voice at the other end of the line said in broken English that he was representing the Obara defence team and wanted to discuss the possibility of making what he called *mimaikin* – condolence money. This was different from the concept of *tsugunaikin* (atonement money), which implied an admission of guilt, and could be offered by any charitable person who took pity on the principals in a case for whatever reasons.

There had already been approaches to the Blackmans (and to the Ridgways) in a similar vein: keep quiet, go away, have money in return. In September 2005 a Tokyo-based British journalist with contacts in both camps had told Tim Blackman that 'Obara's defence lawyers have asked me a couple of times, in vague terms, what I thought your attitude would be to some kind of payment from him. I answered that . . . they'd have to ask you directly. I could put you in touch. Families of crime victims do win damages from time to time, but you'd have to talk to a Japanese lawyer to find out how difficult the process is and what your chances might be.'

But Obara was on the point of being declared bankrupt with colossal debts (one estimate put them at £122 million). So where was the money coming from?

Tim Blackman would eventually admit that the offer came from a friend of Obara's, 'an industrialist with businesses in Japan and Britain'. And, Lucie's father would further claim, such a move would not have an influence on the trial where prosecutors were due quite soon to start giving their closing statements.

Jane Steare had also received a similar approach, via her new husband. That was some strange piece of Japanese etiquette, apparently. Phone calls had been made and e-mails had arrived, matter-of-fact in tone, offering money and persistently spelling Lucie's name incorrectly. In return for a payment of two hundred thousand pounds, Mrs Steare had been invited not to give a victim impact statement. She had refused outright and already been very publicly furious about it. She'd then been offered double the sum. She had refused – of course. Still the chivvying e-mails kept coming.

As they did on the Isle of Wight. 'The defence lawyers were suggesting we write to the court to say that we forgive the defendant, that we are sorry for him or we don't think he did it, which obviously we couldn't do,' Tim Blackman said at the time the offer of condolence money first became public. Meanwhile Obara's lawyers had set a deadline: accept before the end of September or the offer would be withdrawn.

With just a few days to go, on 28 September Tim Blackman signed a document confirming his acceptance of 100 million yen (at the current exchange rate, around £420,000) 'representing the family of Lucie'. At the same time he signed a document prepared by Obara's defence, questioning the accuracy of much of the evidence put forward by the prosecution. He did it, so he was to explain, simply to 'highlight inconsistencies in the case'.

Phrased by Obara's lawyers in painfully fractured English, the statement called into question the cause of death: 'Hereinbefore and as father of Lucie Blackman I would like you to please inspect the most important these three points supposed to be able to clarify the cause of death and this case,' it began.

Tim Blackman said in his deposition that he had not known 'that the cause of death of my daughter . . . was unknown' and that 'the DNA or so on of defendant Obara were not detected from the body of my daughter at all'.

'I did sign certain documents pertaining to prosecution questions, but they were elements that would never have arisen in the final judgment anyway,' he would tell a Sunday newspaper. 'They pertained to the fact that we do not know how Lucie died – whether she was killed by a fatal dose of recreational drugs, whether she died from too much chloroform or Rohypnol . . . We shall never know these things.'

But the document raised detailed questions about the state of Lucie's body, about the concrete in which Obara, it was claimed, had encased her severed head, and the means by which he is alleged to have transported her dead body to Aburatsubo. And that was not all. He had not known, Mr Blackman said in the statement, that 'the defendant Obara lodged at the Japanese-style hotel on the day and at the time supposed when my daughter would have been dismembered and abandoned' (5–6 July 2000, when, Obara told investigators, he was carousing at a county inn in Miura, testimony about which had become a major plank of his defence).

Tim Blackman's move took the conflict with his ex-wife across a new threshold. After so long, the prosecution case was nearing its end. Then it would be the defence's turn. They would surely seek to use Tim Blackman's statement. Jane Steare acted with urgency. As she told a sympathetic reporter:

I e-mailed the British Embassy in Japan, who have been wonderful, explaining my position.

Given the time difference, we were working in the early hours of the morning because we knew the prosecution were summing up that day. And I was desperate to make sure that whatever Tim had done could not be taken as representative of the family's wishes.

After my dealings with the embassy, the prosecution team was able to convince the judge that because he was not a representative of the family, Tim's statements were inadmissible and he could not be called as a witness for the defence. Otherwise, we could have been looking at a disaster in terms of the outcome of the case.

The judge did indeed agree to prosecution requests that the statement be excluded from consideration in the trial. Cynics might point out that Tim knew that would happen before accepting the money. But whether he knew that would be the case or not, Tim Blackman's actions did seem extraordinary – like a gross act of betrayal by a man who, thus far, had commanded the respect of all those who had encountered him on his unlooked-for quest as a man of endearing honesty.

Tragic Lucie's unstoppable dad, valiant for the truth, seemed a bigger villain than the man who allegedly caused her death. He seemed to want it all ways. He had taken the money for the work of the Lucie Blackman Trust (formally set up in summer 2005, although it had been collecting funds since 2001) to promote the safety of women and young people abroad, and for the good of the wider Blackman family, he declared. At the same time, he sent a message to the bemused detectives of the Tokyo Metropolitan Police department: 'I believe the defendant to be guilty of all charges . . . I do not forgive the defendant in any way whatsoever. The condolence from his [Obara's] friend is accepted just as we have received condolence from around the world.'

Jane Steare continued to denounce her ex-husband's move in excoriating terms. She described it as 'obscene'. 'He is conducting these negotiations against my wishes and the pleas of his children,' she said. 'Lucie's loyal family and friends are sickened by Tim Blackman's utter betrayal.' She asked Hampshire police to investigate the legality of his actions. She'd been made executor of Lucie's estate by the High Court three years before. How dare he negotiate or accept anything on her daughter's behalf.

She told a newspaper: 'As far as I am concerned, Tim accepted one hundred million pieces of silver . . . Judas was content with just thirty.' And as for the Trust, she said: 'I am content for public opinion to decide whether it's right to support a personal safety charity founded and led by a man who negotiated for six months with those representing a convicted killer and serial rapist.'

Tim Blackman returned to Tokyo that October of 2006 to oversee details of the hugely contentious payment. Indeed, as Jane Steare had predicted, Obara's defence lawyer requested his appearance in court to explain why he had accepted it. The judge disbarred such a move.

'I know my ex-wife referred to it as blood money but I do not understand that or see that at all. I think it is through lack of information,' Tim Blackman told a reporter. 'The majority of the money will be put into an account somewhere and we will see how everybody feels about it at the end of the trial. It is really difficult as a parent and head of a family to make decisions sometimes when people have lots of different views about it,' he said. 'My most important reason for accepting it was my family. If there was going to be a row, I was prepared to face it. Whether Obara gets five, or one hundred and fifty, years does not make the slightest difference to me, or to Lucie either now. I looked at it from a number of angles and made a decision, rightly or wrongly.'

Most of the media and the public, as expressed in Internet forum posts, thought that he was wrong. Utterly and completely so. He was variously a 'pathetically addled dad', or a 'rat'. It did not help when he reportedly paid £55,000 for a vintage, American-built racing yacht two months later. It was all he could do to keep smiling and carry on calling for justice. He told an interviewer, meanwhile, that his payment was like a fine, except that it was one collected by him and not the state. That hardly helped.

Tim himself admitted that he had accepted the offer when he did because the deadline for a payout would have expired at the end of September 2006 and if Joji Obara was found guilty, a civil suit would have been meaningless because he would already have been declared bankrupt. But there was clearly a big seam of Obara-linked cash still being mined somewhere. The tragedy of Lucie Blackman had turned into venal farce.

Joji Obara made what would turn out be his final set-piece statement in the Tokyo District Court on 11 December 2006. Still he denied anything to do with the death and destruction of the body of Lucie Blackman.

In his testimony thus far in his defence, the story about the mysterious Mr A had become ever more tortuous. There was a long, bizarre interlude about Mr A burying items from the Zushi apartment on an island, Oshima, off the coast of the Miura peninsula. They included a bottle of Christian Dior perfume ('Poison') similar to one that he had given to Lucie on 1 July (and which the police had coincidentally found in the Zushi condo). There were various tablets and medicaments, cosmetics and a pair of earrings. He had intended to take his newly acquired motorboat to the island on Sunday 15 October – but on the twelfth he had been arrested. In 2002 the items had been recovered, buried near a tree on the island by private investigators acting for the defence. The same investigators had identified Mr A as someone called Saturo Katsuta who had 'been a yakuza boss's car driver'. Mr Katsuta had died of a drug overdose in 2001.

Obara also had detailed rebuttals for each prosecution allegation. For example, there had been an admission along the way that Obara knew Lucie had a pierced navel. But this didn't mean he had seen her naked; she often wore tops short enough to show her navel.

Of the prosecution's claim that he had searched Internet sites soon after Lucie disappeared looking for information on how to dispose of a body with acid, he claimed that this was inspired by a conversation he had had with Lucie on how to remove a tattoo from 'her hostess friend'.

Of the phone call to Louise Phillips on 3 July, claiming that Lucie had gone off with a newly risen religion, Obara denied flatly that they had come from him. 'I don't have any memory of naming myself Akira Takagi,' he said. 'The person who said that must have meant it as a joke.'

Of his movements on the night of 6–7 July from midnight to seven o'clock the next morning, he said he had gone for a long walk because 'Hirokawa and Abe, caretakers of the Blue Sea, said there were policemen still there. I didn't want to see them. He kicked my [dead] dog.'

'You could have gone back to the Ryokan (the country inn) and had some rest,' it was suggested. 'And the typhoon was coming the next day. Why did you take a walk?'

'In the early morning of the sixth I went back and stayed there and had some rest – sometimes the strong wind of summer typhoon makes it comfortable,' he replied.

'I went back to the Blue Sea before six in the morning.

I thought that police were still there and they might come to see me. But they didn't. So I went out to the convenience store to buy some newspapers. On the way there I met Katsumi Iida, a senior policeman. On the midnight of 6 July I met the caretaker on the street. I noticed the smell of alcohol on his breath when I met him. So I think he was drunk.'

He had gone back to Tokyo and resumed his shadowy affairs. It would seem that the frozen Irene had returned to the city with him. Joji Obara still had an answer for everything.

CHAPTER 24

When Lindsay Ann Hawker got on the plane for Narita Airport in October 2006, the attractive young woman from the Midlands was well aware of the fate of Lucie Blackman. The name of the dead nightclub hostess had been in the British newspapers off and on for the past six years. The story of her warring parents, their rows about money and a contentious trial of her alleged assailant had flared up yet again in the press and on television lately.

All that was ancient history as far as the twenty-one-year-old with a first-class degree in life sciences from Leeds University and a boyfriend who she seemed set to marry was concerned. But she had a reason to be interested. She too wanted to live and work in Japan, if only for just a few months. It was part of growing up.

Lindsay had been fifteen when the Lucie Blackman drama had begun. It was all so long ago – before 9/11, before the world had changed in so many ways. But lots of things were the same. For Sevenoaks substitute Coventry, for fee-paying, ambitious Walthamstow Hall school for girls substitute fee-paying, ambitious co-ed King Henry VIII school. Lindsay was bright, independently minded and she was adventurous. Just like Lucie. Only Lindsay Hawker had a different plan on how to finance her post-uni travels. She was going to teach.

But she too was up for fun. A contemporary at Leeds University would post a description of her on Facebook, the social networking site. 'We called her "party girl" because every day Lindsay came into the lecture theatre looking like she was just popping in before a party – like a model in her skirts and scarves and confident style,' she said.

Lindsay's father, William (Bill) Hawker, ran a driving school and her mother, Julia was a transport economist. Home life in Brandon, a suburb of Coventry, was as comfortable and supportive as they could make it. Her parents just wanted to do the best by their three daughters, Lisa, twenty-five, Lindsay, twenty-one, and Louise, twenty. For Lindsay, leaving home and going to the other side of the world was not a retreat from a domestic battlefield, as it might have been for Lucie. It was a timely way of coming into full adulthood.

Lindsay had won a place at Leeds University to read life sciences. Her special interest was botany. That summer of 2006 she had graduated. At the recruiting fair one stall in particular had caught her imagination – that of the Nova English language school of Kyoto, Japan.

Nova was a national phenomenon. Over a quarter of a century since its foundation it had grown to be the biggest Eikaiwa (English conversation school) in Japan. It hired 2500 foreign teachers a year, mainly from the UK, America and Australia, with intense targeting of colleges and campuses. A cute pink rabbit was the cuddly face of the company. The recruiting pitch was seductive: 'Nova Group offers motivated people interested in teaching English in Japan the opportunity to chase their dream through employment within an established organisation . . . If you desire the experience of being part of an Eastern culture and are ready and willing to blend in the cultural dynamics of the familiar and unfamiliar in Japan – Nova Group will help you take that first step.'

And it was true. If hostessing was not for you, teaching was the next best way for a gaijin girl to survive. Sometimes it seemed that every foreigner in Japan was working for an English school or a hostess bar (or both). And Nova had a reputation for looking after its staff, finding and paying for accommodation for example, although it could be tough in that Japanese paternalistic way. Drug testing was mandatory (but only for foreign teachers); in January 2007 a clutch of staff were sacked after they had been busted in Roppongi for possession. Relations outside the classroom between student and teacher were banned – and giving lessons outside of the Nova system was a breach of contract. This was to protect the company's revenue certainly, but also to stop male teachers 'hitting on' young female students. There was a joke among Nova staff (not without foundation) that it was really to stop female instructors who were also working in hostess bars from enticing their students to meet them after work.

Lindsay bought into the whole package. She arrived in Tokyo in October 2006, ready to work at the Keiwo branch. She shared a flat in Funabashi City in Chiba Prefecture with two other teachers. The work was hard, but her pupils were terrific. Japanese people were so nice and the streets were safe, safe, safe. There were some strange goings-on, but mostly it was just hilarious. Still, Lindsay knew that it was better to be careful, to leave notes for her flatmates saying where she might be going on a night out.

Lindsay liked to party. The best scene was at Hippy Dippy Do, the expat bar run by Robert from Essex next to Gyotoku station. It was twenty minutes on the subway from the flat. Or she might go to The Other Side, a darts bar across the street which was much more Japanese, but Itto, the manager, really liked foreigners and made them more than welcome. And the Japanese liked her. One guy in particular seemed to like Lindsay a lot. Too much, perhaps.

On 20 March Lindsay sent a message via Facebook to her boyfriend, Ryan Garside, in England.

> Love u lots dont worry abt the guy who chased me home, its jus crazy Japan. miss u xxx

It was the beginning of a new tragedy – a missing gaijin girl, distraught friends in the city, calls to the family home, to the embassy and to the police, pleas to politicians and a father desperately setting out to find his missing daughter. Except Lindsay Hawker's body was found pretty quickly.

This time, it was her apparent killer who would be at the centre of a media frenzy and a story that, like Lucie's, seemed to expose Tokyo's dark side as a place of stalkers, sexual menace and English roses in peril. 'Are there any new developments in the case?' a newspaper correspondent in Tokyo would be asked by his editor in London soon after the story had broken. 'It's simply impossible to overestimate the degree of interest there is in this creature, with his fascination for white women.' But it was more complicated than that.

Lindsay Hawker was a teacher. What she was doing in Japan was completely different from Lucie. But both were nice girls from middle-England who had sought out the great Japanese cultural adventure in their own way. Lindsay had gone through the same crash course of do-they-really-do-things-like-that as every other newly arrived gaijin. The Tokyo subway was staggering, so were prices. The flat in Funabashi was miniscule. Did all those salarymen have to get so drunk at night and read manga-porn on the subway the next morning? It seemed that they did.

At New Year she had showed the city to her parents and her younger sister who had flown out to celebrate her twenty-second birthday on 22 December 2006. They had drunk champagne in the rooftop bar of the Tokyo Park Hyatt hotel. It was fabulous.

Lindsay had been in Tokyo for almost six months (that was twice as along as Lucie Blackman) when on 20 March she encountered the guy who 'chased her home', the one she referred to in the Facebook message. A friend had seen her with this man travelling on the train together. They had both got off at Gyotoku station, where she had picked up her bike and pedalled off. But he had chased after her, running like an athlete, all the way to the apartment. Because one of her flatmates was at home, she agreed to let him in when he asked for 'a glass of water'.

'He drew a picture of her in felt-tip pen and gave it to her at the same time as he gave her his home address and phone number,' it would later be revealed. One source described the blobby pictorial tribute as 'manga-style'. It seemed that the eager stranger had insisted she give him private English lessons. She, with a certain reluctance, had agreed. It was against Nova's rules, although many people did it to make extra cash. What harm could it do?

A surveillance camera picked up Lindsay and a man at a café near Gyotoku station on the morning of Sunday 25 March 2007. They sat at a table for about an hour before the man got up and made a seemingly deliberate fuss of searching for change to pay for their coffees. In the sequence Lindsay was wearing a knee-length white coat and could be seen repeatedly adjusting her hair.

Staff at the shop remembered the couple and said that an English lesson appeared to be taking place between them. Perhaps doing it in a public place with this near stranger was a safety precaution. Perhaps Lindsay had been taught something. The next thing, they got into a taxi. That was safe enough. The driver would be tracked down to tell reporters that the pair had travelled without saying much to an apartment block in Ichikawa. When they got out, the man had told the driver to wait for a few minutes. They had gone off together (not so safe). Time passed. The taxi company was very busy that day so the driver had driven away.

Lindsay had been booked for a teaching shift later that Sunday morning. She didn't show. Nova staff rang her on her mobile phone with some concern. There was no reply – but no need to report it, even though it was totally out of her work pattern thus far to let students or colleagues down. Julia Hawker also rang from home in England: 'I called her on Sunday morning, which was her Sunday evening. I thought she might be somewhere where the reception was poor, but even so I was worried. I made seventeen calls to her mobile,' she would tell a reporter.

It was now Sunday night in Tokyo. Lindsay did not return to the apartment. Unlike Lucie Blackman on that fatal July day seven years before, there had been no calls saying what Lindsay was doing or where she was going. It was unusual but there was no cause for alarm – not yet.

The following morning her flatmates rang to tell the language school they thought she might be missing. By then Lindsay had not been seen for nearly twenty-four hours.

Julia Hawker went to work as usual but at about midday on Monday, Bill arrived at her office in Coventry. He told her that Nova had called from Japan to say that Lindsay was missing. Lindsay's mother recalled what happened:

We went home immediately and called the Foreign Office. Louise and Lisa also came home and Lindsay's boyfriend, Ryan, came up from London. We all knew something was very wrong . . .

That evening Warwickshire police came to see us. I remember them describing it as an abduction, which made us even more worried.

Bill Hawker booked three tickets to Tokyo – for himself, for Ryan Garside and for a family friend who had offered to help. It was decided that Lindsay's mother would stay at home while they went to do what they might. But at 3 a.m. on Tuesday – mid-morning in Japan – the phone rang. It was the British Embassy. Lindsay had been found dead.

Where? How? When? It was impossible to take in.

Lindsay had taken the precaution of leaving with her flatmates the address and number of the man she had agreed to meet. At around 3:30 p.m. Tokyo time on Monday 26 March, one of them had gone to raise the alarm at Funabashi police station and produced the name and the address.

Nine police officers had gone that evening to a fourth-floor flat in Ichikawa. It belonged to a twenty-eight-year-old Japanese horticulture student. His name was Tatsuya Ichihashi.

As the *Mainichi Shimbun* newspaper would report, 'Officers visited Ichihashi's apartment in Ichikawa, Chiba Prefecture, at about 9.40 p.m. on Monday, just as the twenty-eight-year-old was preparing to walk out the door. One of the officers accosted him, asking "Are you Mr

Ichihashi?" Ichihashi answered affirmatively but escaped down the apartment's emergency stairway and fled in the direction of Gyotoku station. The fugitive was not wearing shoes. He was seen running toward Gyotoku station on the Tokyo Metro Tozai Subway line.' He was an athlete, faster than any puffing cop. The mob-handed arrest attempt had been farcical. As it would be dispassionately reported a little later:

Ichihashi lost both shoes while scaling the fence behind the condominium. His discarded socks were later found along the road leading to the station. Prefectural police pursued with scent-sniffing dogs, but lost Ichihashi's trail. The bicycle used by Ichihashi to go to and from Gyotoku station was found parked at the station.

Ichihashi also dropped a backpack containing underwear when he encountered investigators in front of the building. Police believe Ichihashi was planning to destroy evidence and was preparing his escape before they arrived.

Inside Ichihashi's apartment, police found a garbage bag containing Hawker's clothes and an empty plastic bag of gardening sand, used to bury Hawker's body in a bathtub found on the balcony.

That was the bit that got news editors in Britain excited. A bathtub full of sand (actually there was only one bag, bought from a nearby garden supply shop early on the evening of 26 March) was terrifyingly reminiscent of Lucie in her seaside tomb. It was some sort of shrine, it was reported; the suspect had planted it with the seeds of exotic trees. Was it exquisitely oriental or was it just plain barking mad?

No one could ask Mr Ichihashi because he had vanished without trace.

CHAPTER 25

For Bill Hawker, what he'd thought would be a frantic bid to search for his daughter had instead become a grief-laden journey to identify her body. He was taken from the airport to a funeral parlour. Her battered face and body had been rendered doll-like by cosmetics. 'I knew it was Lindsay because she was so tall and because she was my daughter, but she was so badly beaten,' he would tell a reporter.

'Her hair was wrapped in gauze, her body in a Japanese gown and they'd had to put a lot of make-up on her. They let me say goodbye and I just stayed there, holding her toe under the cover.'

It had taken the personal intervention of Lucie Blackman's family to compel the Japanese to take notice of

a missing gaijin girl. Bill Hawker gave emotional statements to the media, but this time it was to appeal to the
police and the public to do everything they might to find
his daughter's killer.

The local media were all too ready to pursue a new sex-
murder sensation. Some reporters combed the bars of
Ichikawa and Gyotoku looking for evidence that Lindsay
Hawker and Ichihashi were romantically involved. Nova,
for their part, strenuously denied reports that Ichihashi was
a student at one of their schools who had been dating Ms
Hawker. She had in fact, so it seemed, been teaching him
privately which was against their rules.

Meanwhile, details of Lindsay's last hours alive, the
manner of her death and the life and times of her alleged
killer (the official crime of which he was posted as being
suspected was 'illegal disposal of a dead body') came tum-
bling out through media leaks as the Chiba prefectural
police sought to redress the acute embarrassment of losing
the barefoot suspect on the streets of Ichikawa.

Lindsay had been killed by strangulation and had also
suffered a frenzied battering. Her father would be given the
eventual autopsy report on how his daughter had met her
death. He relayed its contents to a newspaper in stark detail:

It was an horrific murder. There was literally not a
square inch of her body that wasn't badly bruised.

He tied her up with horticultural tape. This is dreadful to say, but he punched, kicked or used a blunt instrument throughout her body. This could have gone on a day and a half possibly, before the poor thing eventually died.

There was total bruising of the front of the body, defensive bruises on her arms, which were dreadfully knocked about, all of her back, the inside of her legs. It was as if he'd systematically injured every part of her body.

When I had to identify my daughter, the Japanese had her so that I could only see the top of her head and her face. I didn't want to see the rest of her body. Her face was badly beaten. They had put on a lot of make-up and my daughter never wore make-up. So we never realised the extent of her injuries.

He also cut her hair off — the final indignity for her was to have her hair cut off.

But where the hell was Ichihashi? Who was he? Had he done anything like this before? The Japanese media foamed with speculation as their English-language counterparts flew out to pick up the trail of another dead gaijin girl.

On 29 March love hotels in Funabashi were searched. The next day, the Tozai subway line was shut down and

Ichihashi's bicycle was discovered in the parking area of the subway station closest to his apartment, but nothing more. He had vanished. It was variously rumoured that he had committed suicide or was being protected by the yakuza.

The Ichikawa apartment itself, containing little more than a table, chair, futon mattress, laptop computer (devoid of clues), a television and a few clothes, did not reveal much. His passport was found in a drawer. Getting out of the country and into another would be very difficult. The British press reported that 'piles of manga comics, which feature stories of rape and torture, were found at Ichihashi's flat'. The Japanese press, however, did not bother with that. Any youngish Japanese male living alone would have piles of manga comics featuring extreme sexual violence.

The apartment's resident had lived by himself and there were no indications that he had ever had any kind of job. There was no police record other than when he had been given a caution for stalking a female student and taking a ten-thousand-yen note from the coffee shop where she worked.

He was the son, it turned out, of wealthy physicians from Gifu Prefecture in central Japan. His father was an eminent surgeon, his mother ran a dental clinic. It was they who held the lease on the flat in Ichikawa. They paid the rent and deposited a large monthly allowance in his bank

account. He had an older sister 'who he doesn't contact –
he didn't even go to her wedding in January'.

'The father is a warm, gentle type, even though the
mother is a bit snappy,' a neighbour told the women's
weekly magazine *Josei Jishin*. Now they had retreated into
their 'palatial' home in Gifu with a police tap on their
phone in case their allegedly murderous son should ring.

On 3 April Ichihashi's parents' phone did ring, but the
caller remained silent. In circumstances eerily similar to
those in the hunt for Akira Takagi seven years before, the
call was traced to a public telephone kiosk in the Nishinari
ward of Osaka. Investigators were unable to attribute any
fingerprints to Ichihashi and the episode was put down to
a malicious prank.

Where was he? There was no electronic footprint, no
cash or credit card transactions for the days and weeks
since he had disappeared down the back stairs of his apartment block. If he was not already dead (thought by police
to be highly unlikely) the authorities had to assume that he
had an accomplice or a girlfriend, someone who might be
hiding him or at least supplying him with food or money.

The Hawkers, like the Blackmans before them, were
doing their best to raise the media profile of the hunt. This
time the police seemed to need less prompting, releasing
CCTV footage taken in the café and caught by a security
camera in the lift of Ichihashi's condominium some time

between 20 and 25 March, showing clear images of the prime suspect. Three hundred thousand 'Wanted' posters were printed and distributed with the appeal:

Help Find a Criminal!
Wanted For Illegal Disposal Of The Body Of A British Female Teacher
Warrant For The Arrest Of Tatsuya Ichihashi
28 Years Old
180cm (5' 11") Tall
Slim Physique
Characteristics:
Single-edged eyelids
Prominent Lower Lip
If you have any information regarding the case of the British female teacher whose body was found on March 26 in Ichikawa City (Chiba), please contact the police.
Gyotoku Police, Chiba Prefecture

A month after its discovery, Lindsay's body was flown home to England. Just like Lucie, she would be buried in circumstances that were a combination of intense private grief and public spectacle. Hundreds of mourners would have to be accommodated, as well as television crews, photographers, officials; the Japanese ambassador expressed a desire to attend with his wife. It was decided to hold it in

Coventry's cathedral, famously reborn out of a blitzed wartime shell. The dean readily agreed and the service of remembrance and thanksgiving for the life of Lindsay Ann Hawker was scheduled for Thursday 26 April 2007.

CHAPTER 26

The last act in the fight for justice for Lucie Blackman (and for Carita Ridgway – and for the eight other women whose alleged assaults were components of the indictment against Joji Obara) was rapidly approaching. The saga of crime, detection and criminal justice, Japanese-style, had proceeded so languorously for so long. Now it was almost clattering to a conclusion.

On Tuesday 24 April 2007, reporters and cameramen thronged outside the main gate and a chosen few within the precincts of Tokyo District Court to record the arrival of two grieving families at the end, it might seem, of a long road in their search for justice.

Just before 10 a.m. Judge Tsutomu Tochigi, Justice Yoshihi Nakao and Justice Kenji Nagaike solemnly took their place in Criminal Bench No. 5.

Tim and Sophie Blackman had flown in for this, the climax of their long, long quest. Tim's girlfriend, Josephine Burr, was with them. Jane Steare had chosen to stay in England because, as she said, she 'could not face seeing Obara across a courtroom'.

Father and daughter had spent the night before in a Tokyo hotel, confident, happy almost, remembering those chaotic days seven years earlier when they had first arrived in the sweltering, overwhelming city, praying that Lucie would turn up alive. It had all been so strange then. Now it was achingly familiar. They rehearsed what they would say to the press when Joji Obara was sentenced for the rape and killing of Lucie Blackman. Then they would celebrate the guilty verdict with champagne.

Carita Ridgway's parents, Nigel Ridgway and Annette Foster, were in the court – with Nigel's second wife. Their mood was sombre. Ushers seemed eager to keep them separate from the Blackmans. They met them fleetingly in the lift. Samantha Termini (her married name), Carita's sister was also in the courtroom; she had flown in to Tokyo with her husband Richard and two children. The kids were back at the hotel with their father, who was watching the proceedings on live TV news. Samantha took her place with her parents and stepmother plus an official and translator from the Australian Embassy. As she recalled the scene:

Obara was sitting directly in front of us all with his back to us, facing the judge (first row Tim and family, second row embassy staff, third row Ridgway family).

Obara looked old, thin and weak and he was wearing large, thick-lensed glasses. He clutched a small blue towel in his hand. Occasionally he wiped his face with it. His hair was longish with grey streaks and the judge made him stand up in front of the whole court while he spoke to him at length. He wasn't speaking kindly and the interpreter would shoot out some translations every few minutes. He was so close I felt like jumping up and leaping over the barrier and strangling him in front of everyone.

Judge Tsutomu Tochigi began in the Japanese way by pronouncing the sentence: 'The accused is sentenced to life imprisonment. Sixteen hundred days of pre-sentence detention time is to be counted in . . .'

The Blackmans' hearts leapt. This was justice at last. In the matter of the rape leading to the death of Carita Ridgway he was guilty. In the matters of eight further charges of rape – including two leading to injury – guilty. Then the bombshell:

Out of each fact regarding the offence charged regarding abducting for indecency, drugging and raping resulting

367

in death and destroying and abandoning the corpse of
Lucie Jane Blackman, the accused is acquitted.

There was a collective intake of breath. The prosecutors
stared at the floor. The police looked baffled. Joji Obara
stared ahead impassively. Tim Blackman clutched Sophie's
hand. What the hell was happening? As Samantha Termini
remembered the moment:

> When the judge read out the not-guilty verdict for
> Lucie, everyone was shocked and swearing under their
> breath. Tim and Sophie looked especially horrified and
> were turning round looking at us and others. Reporters
> ran out of the courtroom with the news.
>
> Rich said the Japanese TV was reporting it as a real sur-
> prise – that Obara got off for Lucie and then 'pulled out of
> a hat', so to speak, life in prison for Carita's death and the
> eight other rape victims. He said it was reported like a
> game-show format. It seemed that the Japanese people had
> been in the dark about all his other victims other than Lucie
> until the breaking news of the verdict. I'm sure that they
> are not being reminded that there are at least two hundred
> plus other victims who have not been investigated at all.

The presiding judge gave a summation of their reasons.
'There is nothing to prove that he was involved in the

rape and her death. The court cannot prove he was single-handedly involved in her death,' he said. 'What is clear is that the victim acted together with the accused and then vanished and, following that, she was found dead.'

Tim Blackman stared ahead in stunned silence as an interpreter provided by the embassy beside him scribbled down an English translation of what was being said.

'There is no doubt [Obara] was involved in one way or another, but there is no evidence to link the defendant directly to the crime,' said the judge. 'But the possibility that the act may have been committed by a third person cannot be denied and the purpose of dismembering [the body] has not been explained, so there remains reasonable doubt in terms of recognising it as the defendant's crime.

'The defendant is recognised as being involved in the damage and abandonment of Lucie's dead body in some form,' he said. 'That the defendant . . . gave false information as if Lucie was alive, trying to cover up Lucie's death, supports such recognition. Then the problem is how the defendant was involved in the death of Lucie . . .'

Tim Blackman was fighting to control himself. How was Obara involved in the death of Lucie? Wasn't that obvious?

'Unlike the case with the other victims, there was no video recording of the alleged rape of Lucie Blackman and no direct evidence to prove that the defendant administered any drugs to her or assaulted her,' intoned the judge as he continued with his ruling. In spite of the similarities between her case and the others, Justice Tochigi pronounced their collective view that the court was unable to determine that Obara had raped Lucie – as long as the cause of her death remained unknown.

That was particularly wounding. When it was found in the cave on that dreadful day when Tim had watched it on live TV, Lucie's body was too far decomposed to deliver a conclusive forensic narrative. And why was that? Because the police had taken seven months to find it. And although flunitrazepam was detected in the autopsy, neither the amount nor the timing of when it was taken could be determined. 'There was a period when Lucie was distressed on her arrival in Japan,' according to the judgment. 'Even though it required a doctor's prescription to obtain it in Japan, it could not be affirmed that she had never taken flunitrazepam on her own.'

And what about the charge of abduction for indecency, the very act of taking Lucie to the Zushi apartment? 'Because he had taken women to Zushi for wining and dining and normal sexual intercourse under agreement from women, it cannot be asserted beyond reasonable doubt that he intended to conduct an indecent act against Lucie's will,' said the judge.

There was not enough evidence. In the matter of Lucie Blackman, Obara was innocent.

Regarding the nine other cases, the judge described them as 'abnormal crimes involving unilaterally assaulting victims whose consciousness had been impaired due to drugs'. According to the ruling, Obara had brought the eight women, four Japanese, two British (excluding Lucie), one Ukrainian and one Australian (Carita Ridgway) to his apartment in Zushi, Kanagawa Prefecture, between February 1992 and June 2000, and there he had raped them after drugging them. He had inserted his fingers and objects into their vaginas and anuses. It was 'strongly to be presumed and acknowledged that he did so without consent from the victims. The victims stated they never approved having sexual intercourse with the accused.'

The judge continued, 'The drugs were ready, as was the video equipment . . . his plans were deep-laid and pre-prepared.' Once the women were insensate there was 'no attempt to secure their airways other than removing vomit'.

In the case of Carita Ridgway, it was the court's judgment that she had suffered fulminant hepatitis and subsequently died as a result of the use of chloroform administered by the defendant. The medical evidence derived from the liver biopsy was conclusive. In the video taken around 15–16 February 1992, a bottle of what an expert witness identified as chloroform could be seen in the background.

So what of the condolence money, accepted by Tim Blackman and offered to the Ridgways and others? Had that had an impact on the Lucie verdict? Apparently not. The judge told the court: 'There is a limit to how far one can take such matters into consideration.'

Obara's defence team had offered Annette Foster condolence money and she had refused. But now Carita's family and her one-time fiancé Robert Finnigan had, in his words, 'retained a Japanese lawyer to advise and prepare civil proceedings against Obara'. They were told the prospects of succeeding against in a civil action were very good; however, while Obara appeared to be well funded with access to significant financial assets, those assets were not held in his name.

Was Obara crazy? At no point in the trial had psychiatric reports been asked for. No expert medical opinions had been sought or offered on a man who had declared his inability to have sex with a woman unless she was in a coma.

Jane Steare had referred to her daughter's alleged

killer (this was before he had been charged) as 'a perverted psychopath, a lunatic'. Sophie Blackman, for one,
recognised the tragedy of his condition when she commented to a reporter: 'The first time I saw him in court,
I had an overwhelming feeling of absolute pity for a man
whose only sexual activity has been when he has drugged
someone.'

Japanese tabloids had suggested from the beginning that
he had begun to show signs of a 'sexually predatory nature'
as a young adult. The prosecution had described him as
'nothing but a cunning beast – who had shown not a piece
of human nature nor any sign of contrition'. Indeed, in
spite of the condolence payments, he seemed utterly without remorse.

Was it something in his childhood and adolescence? His
friends and supporters (and he had some such from his
days at Keio University and his tightly knit business circle)
suggested that his strange upbringing may have played a
part in forming his personality: a pampered child of exiles,
who lost his father when young, inherited a fortune,
changed his name and nationality and frolicked in the
bubble years.

His unrelenting protestation of innocence seemed perverse – un-Japanese even. But his nerdish self-obsession
was very recognisably so. He was an Obara-*otaku*. 'The
Great Plan' revealed in his notebooks and scraps of memoir

for some sort of global business conquest, was fuelled by narcotic self-experimentation. He was clearly intelligent – and proud of the fact. When his shadowy supporters produced a book in his defence (very similar to the 'The Truth Of Lucie's Case' website) it was subtitled 'the struggle of Joji Obara (who has an IQ of 180) vs an elite prosecution team'.

In 2006 Richard Lloyd Parry (still in Tokyo but now of *The Times*) had graphically described Obara's strange condition as he awaited judgment in his cell at Kosuge:

> Few battle so hard to prove their innocence. At the detention centre where he lives, documents relating to the trial stand in piles almost to the ceiling of his small cell. One of his team of ten lawyers visits him almost every day. Apart from the criminal charges against him, he is involved in [bankruptcy] litigation involving his companies.
>
> Apart from his lawyers, only his mother, now in her eighties, is allowed to visit him; for the past few months she has been too unwell to make the journey from Osaka. He gets on fine with the guards ... but rarely smiles or makes a joke. He seldom speaks of the past or of his family, and never about friends.
>
> 'My impression is that he is totally sane,' says one who knows him. 'There's nothing crazy about him,

except the way he treats women. He's very, very clever but very selfish, totally convinced that he is right, and he never listens to the opinions of other people. But I don't think he ever had a true friend he could rely on, and he doesn't now. He is a very lonely person. Apart from his lawyers, there's no one he can rely on or consult.'

Only once had Obara himself conceded that his behaviour might be in some way deviant, when he admitted through his lawyers in his final statement for the defence in December 2006 that 'although he might have problems with his personality due to the circumstances of his upbringing, his action concerning Lucie was not planned'.

And there was also the revealing testimony when Obara was questioned about his 'play' notebooks. One entry referred to SMY – code, it was alleged, for a particular anaesthetic that, according to the prosecution, he used to induce a state of coma in his 'partners'.

'To have play without SMY didn't work at all,' Obara explained, 'because the woman I had play with did feel things (had an orgasm) and enjoyed it.' Asked what was wrong with the woman enjoying it, he replied, 'If the woman I had play with enjoyed it, it does not mean play.'

It fell to Judge Tochigi to comment on the defendant's

place on the spectrum of sexual 'normality', if that is what it was. He said:

> You treated these women as sexual objects to satisfy your lust. Your behaviour is not healthy sexual behaviour, but a filthy crime. Furthermore, you used lethal drugs such as chloroform that can cause death due to disordering of the liver function.
>
> One opinion might be that these women were careless, but I believe that they could not anticipate your deviant behaviour . . . You repeated the same routine over eight years, treating their lives and their bodies carelessly.
>
> It is rooted in your self-centred attitude based on your perverted sexual tastes, and deserves the most severe reproach.

Obara, he said, had 'trampled on the dignity of women'.

Two families, two tragedies. Justice for Carita but not it seemed for Lucie. It was a horrible twist in the story. The British Embassy phoned Jane Steare in the early hours of the morning with the news. 'I'm heartbroken, just heartbroken. I just can't believe this verdict,' she told reporters. Tim and Sophie huddled with their lawyers, promising a press statement later in the day.

Obara's counsel, Yasuo Shionoya, announced they intended filing an appeal against all the guilty charges and that Obara felt 'very sorry' over Lucie Blackman. 'He understands that Lucie was found in a sad situation, but please read the court's decision – this was not Mr Obara's crime,' he said.

The Ridgway family gave a statement: 'The sentence handed down by the court ensures that Obara will never be allowed to harm others. This, in itself, is of some comfort to Carita's family,' said her mother, Annette Foster. She went on:

> Carita's family do not understand how, despite their concerns raised with the police about Obara's involvement with Carita's death, that the police did not even interview Obara in 1992.
>
> Carita's family firmly believe that if Obara had been interviewed and properly investigated in 1992, he would have been stopped at that time.

Tim and Sophie Blackman faced the cameras later that afternoon. They were satisfied that Obara had been sentenced to life imprisonment, the maximum penalty possible in the cases, but they were also deeply disappointed that the defendant was found not guilty over Lucie's death. There was, they had discovered, decisive evidence linking Obara to the crime, but which the prosecution had inexplicably failed to present; they declined to say exactly what.

It was not quite over yet.

CHAPTER 27

On 26 April 2007, two days after Obara's acquittal in Tokyo in the matter of Lucie Blackman, almost nine hundred mourners, family, friends and the public, packed into Coventry Cathedral for a service of remembrance and thanksgiving for the life of Lindsay Ann Hawker. The Japanese Ambassador, Yoshiji Nogami, and his wife attended. The coffin was covered in white lilies and at the end of the service a white dove was released in the square outside the cathedral before the family left for a private committal.

There were tears and there were tributes for a young life cut short. The thoughts of many mourners dwelled on how that had come to be. Another month had passed with no sign of the prime suspect. The Chiba police at first assumed that Ichihashi was still somewhere close to the scene of the crime. Empty apartments were searched, open ground scoured, even a private duck-hunting park used by Japan's Imperial Family was brought into the trawl.

The search for Ichihashi spread to the margins of Japanese society. Osaka's *doyagai* (skid row) district of Kamagasaki, full of cheap lodging for day labourers and homeless where the mystery phone call to the suspect's parents had originated, was turned over.

It was reported that he was subsisting in all-night Internet cafés, 'capsule hotels' or *manga kissa* – cafés in which you paid a small number of yen by the hour to sit and read manga comics. The *Shukan Post* claimed that investigators were 'looking into the possibility of Ichihashi being disguised as a drag queen'. Women's wigs and cosmetics had been found in the apartment apparently and now the runaway suspect was reportedly earning a good living in a Kabuki-cho cabaret.

For the English-language media the case was a chance to lambast the Japanese police for their incompetence, to do another take on Roppongi club life and to report on general Japanese sexual wackiness. Life as an English-language-teaching gaijin girl was as perilous as a hostess, it quickly emerged.

The ubiquitous former police inspector Dai Davies led

a probe for a Welsh television documentary. He 'discovered the pressure English teachers come under to ditch language lessons and work as hostesses'. Operating alongside an undercover TV reporter, Davies saw 'wealthy businessmen trying to lure Western girls into the seedy trade'.

'It is about more than being a waitress,' he said. 'And English girls are particularly popular. They are targeted as they walk out of language schools after work.'

Maybe so. A former Nova teacher in Osaka posted this revealing blog. And there was an extra twist. Japanese sought to learn English, it seemed, because they were mentally ill:

Many times fellow colleagues would report flashings, gropings and stalkings to police there and meet indifference, and/or 'you were asking for it' attitudes.

Japanese society has a skewed idea about women, and a love hate relationship with foreigners. If you are both, you may receive a lot more attention than you bargained for.

It is worth remembering also that the populace is large, and a care in the community policy is in place. Students once advised me of doctors recommending individuals with mental health issues to take up hobbies like flower arrangement, or learning a foreign language.

A British tabloid, meanwhile, found the story of Sharon, a twenty-six-year-old business studies graduate from Inverness who had taught English in rural Japan. She told how, because she was 'taller and curvier than Japanese women, the local men can be a little bit leery'. A 'stalker' had begun a campaign of posting admiring notes in her letterbox. 'I felt utterly sick because I was all alone,' she recalled. 'Out of my window I could see nothing but rice paddies . . . suddenly, home felt a very long way away.'

The police had proved pretty useless, while 'every night [she had come] home with a sense of dread and I was only ever slightly relieved when I saw my doormat empty. It was like a ticking bomb, I knew there was another letter on its way, I just didn't know when.' Her narrative continued in an even more alarming vein:

After another week of anxiously looking out the window, letter number three arrived – again by hand. This time the translation was more sinister. It read: 'Do you like tea or coffee? If I am ten minutes late for our date will that be acceptable? Are you lonely? Do you cry when you are in your house alone? Do you prefer sex with English men or Japanese men?'

Compared with the smutty talk in hostess bars this was pretty tame stuff. But English-language teachers, it seemed, generated the same kind of erotic appeal as the gaijin sirens of Roppongi. 'Even slim girls are voluptuous in their eyes,' said Sharon, 'and as we are so much taller than Japanese men and also seem more unavailable, the differences are fascinating to them.'

The presiding media myth of white women being stalked by oriental males had come down intact from the days when Lucie went missing in the stews of Roppongi. That the suspect in the Hawker case was a manga-loving layabout with wealthy parents was one thing. Were sinister establishment forces (or the omnipresent yakuza) protecting him? The display of police incompetence added to the weary stereotyping. But actually it was all rather like that.

After three months, still Chiba detectives had failed to apprehend the prime suspect. And just as it had with Lucie, after this lapse of time and with this degree of press coverage, the case was getting political. On 26 May, the then British foreign secretary Margaret Beckett, on a visit to Tokyo, urged the Japanese media to give it more coverage. The ambassador, Graham Fry, expressed pious hopes that the police would soon get their man. But he also defended the Chiba police's efforts, saying they were 'doing their best' and remarking favourably that more than a hundred officers were still working on the case.

The Hawkers themselves found it more than appropriate to return to Tokyo to keep the media profile high. They made a direct appeal to the suspect's parents. 'Somebody's supporting him,' said Bill Hawker. 'His father has refused to come out of his palatial home. The family have not offered any help towards the capture of their son.'

Lindsay's parents appeared on a live Saturday-night TV show that featured over-the-top contributions from psychics and a lurid reenactment of their daughter's murder that left the family in tears.

At least, however, the reclusive Ichihashi parents, the good surgeons of Gifu, had not tried to offer the Hawkers money by way of atonement for their son's alleged crimes. In the whole sad story of Joji Obara's predations on young women, money had proved a corrosive influence. And now it was rearing its ugly head again.

In February 2008 Nigel Ridgway flew to Tokyo at the Obara defence team's expense to negotiate a condolence payment. The interior ministry in Tokyo told him that he was not eligible for government help for crime victims because his daughter was not a Japanese citizen. Lawyers had advised that a private civil case would be cripplingly expensive. Obara, in his prison cell, had refused to meet him.

A statement was presented which he found unable to sign. At the time, Carita's mother Annette Foster publicly denounced her ex-husband's actions and spoke of her anxiety that the convicted Obara could win early release as a result.

Over several anguished months in the late spring of 2008, the Ridgway family began to concur, as Tim Blackman had before them, that accepting money from the Obara camp would not have any substantial effect on a judgment in the pending appeal (by the defence against the guilty verdicts), and that this was their last chance to get a payment of any kind. The sum being offered was a hundred million yen (£450,000), the same as Tim Blackman had accepted.

In March prosecution launched an appeal against Obara's acquittal in the Blackman case. His lawyers, in turn, announced that they were appealing against his conviction in the rape resulting in the death of Carita Ridgway.

'If the circumstantial evidence is evaluated appropriately and comprehensively, it is certain that the defendant committed the [Blackman] crime,' the Tokyo prosecutors said in a statement presented to the High Court on 25 March. Obara's chief defence lawyer said: 'We will keep rejecting the prosecutors' allegations . . . Regarding the case of Ms Ridgway, we seek an acquittal.'

The Obara camp seemed confident. On 26 May 2008 the Tokyo High Court ordered the publishers of *Shukan Shincho* and a reporter to pay 200,000 yen in damages for libellously reporting in July 2006 and February 2007 that Obara had 'murdered' Lucie Blackman.

Obara's lawyers announced on 13 July 2008 that Nigel Ridgway was going to take the condolence money on behalf of his elder daughter, Samantha, and his ex-wife, Annette Foster. It would be paid just as Obara's appeal against the sentences of a year before was about to have its second hearing in the Tokyo High Court. A statement by Mr Ridgway would be part of it. He was understood to have signed a document stating that he believed Obara was capable of rehabilitation and which questioned some of the evidence used to convict him in his Tokyo trial of raping and killing his daughter sixteen years before. First one father, now another.

Asked for her response to the move, Jane Steare remained magisterially aloof. 'All I sincerely hope is that the judges in this appeal and any subsequent appeal rightly disregard the actions of Lucie's father and of Carita's parents,' she told a London newspaper.

But Carita's family could not see it in quite such stark terms. After what had clearly been a long period of high emotion and deep soul-searching, they had at last found solidarity in doing what had seemed so repellent. On 17

July 2008 they jointly addressed a letter to the prosecutors in Tokyo. It explained their reasons:

The family of Carita Ridgway wish to advise you that we have accepted a sum of money from Mr Joji Obara as a 'condolence' offer.

However, because we have accepted this payment it does not mean that we consider that Mr Obara is not guilty of his crimes. We would support the Appeal Court's decision to continue with the life sentence that was handed down to him in April last year.

Our reasons for this are that Mr Obara has never confessed his crimes to the family, has not said sorry for the awful things he did to Carita and has shown no remorse.

We were persuaded to accept the payment of 'condolence' on the condition that Nigel would sign 'statements' which Mr Obara hopes will lessen his sentence . . . With the assistance of our lawyers, Nigel was able to revise and edit the wording of the statements until he thought that, after legal advice, they would be of little value to Mr Obara in a court of law in Japan.

We humbly ask you to treat the statements with circumspection – especially as they were traded for the 'condolence' payment . . . In essence, Mr Obara did not give the 'condolence' payment to say sorry for what he did to Carita, but to make a 'deal' to give himself some advantage in court.

In the final analysis, who should pay compensation to the family of a victim of crime? Should it be the Japanese people, or government agencies? We concluded that the person who committed the crimes against Carita, Mr Obara, should be the one to pay . . .

We consider that Joji Obara is a dangerous serial criminal who should not be released back into society.

Robert Finnigan added his own statement: 'I would respectfully submit that the payment Obara has made to Carita's family cannot, in any way, mitigate the sentence handed down to him,' he said, adding: 'Obara has now made payments to most of his known victims. I would submit that he has done this, not out of a sense of remorse or compassion (he has shown none of these qualities), but rather in order to advance his own self interests . . . In these circumstances, justice, and Japan, is better served if Obara is incarcerated for the maximum period the law allows.'

The horrid legal bickering dragged on. Pretty soon it would be ten years since Lucie and Louise had arrived full of worldly wisdom at Narita Airport and more than two decades since Carita had flown in from Sydney. It was all a long time ago. How many generations of ninety-day butterflies would have done their stuff in the meantime? Gaijin girls still came and sought work to pile up some money – although not so many from Sevenoaks. More from Sverdlovsk. And 'host' bars, like hostess bars except with the genders reversed, were now the big news in party-loving Tokyo.

And Roppongi? On an early summer's night in 2008, Exotic City boasted 'white, black and yellow ladies. All of staff speak English. Very different from American gentlemen's club & you must enjoy!' Cleopatra was bursting with 'beautiful hostesses from Russia, Ukraine, Colombia. You'll be relaxed in the international, sophisticated hostess club.' And outside McDonald's a desperate-looking Taiwanese girl in a utilitarian quilted jacket was trying to hustle *massaji* customers. The *fuzoku-annai* – a kind of garish shopfront offering a computerised entry point into the bizarre array of sex establishments stacked up high in the entertainment buildings – were booming as Russian men hustled dopey-looking Westerners inside. Nigerian touts glowered from across the way. This used to be their exclusive turf.

In Geronimo's, where Lucie had sought her own kind of after-work oblivion, thirty-something, vodka-shotting

British bankers were going the same way. And good old Greengrass (formerly the Casablanca) was 'now hiring female English speakers and international ladies'. The money looked pretty good.

AFTERWORD

On a June day in 2008 I stood in the garage of a fine Victorian house on the Isle of Wight as Tim Blackman dug out boxes of old papers. It was a year since I'd set out on my own quest, and almost eight years since his life had been turned upside down by the disappearance of his eldest daughter from Sendagaya, Tokyo.

'It's just so sad, isn't it?' he said, his voice breaking as he handed me bundles of e-mails and scribbled notes that told the story of Lucie's disappearance – or rather that of his and Sophie's frantic attempts to find her – and the grindingly drawn out judicial process that had followed. It suddenly all seemed a long time ago. In that awful newspaper cliché, he had done his best to move on.

The following day, 22 June, Tim would be getting married in Holy Trinity Church, Ryde, to his long-term partner Jo Burr. A marquee was being erected in the garden of the former vicarage where they now lived. Bees buzzed in the hollyhocks and the house was full of sunlight and pink roses. 'This should be one of the happiest days of my life,' said Tim. 'I am about to marry the woman I love, with my son, Rupert as best man and my daughter, Sophie, standing beside me. Jo's four children from her first marriage, Ryan, Luke, Alicia and Rosie, will all be there too.

'But, without Lucie, there is always that sense of someone missing, a space that simply cannot be filled ever again. Often I will invite Sophie or Rupert for the weekend and they say they'll come, only to ring up and confess that they can't face it because being together without Lucie always makes them desperately sad.'

Tim Blackman's family, sundered first by divorce and then shattered by violent crime, looked like it would never recover. It was a tribute to Tim that his children had stood by him, and him by them. He had taken on a big step-family and made that work. It had taken years but the signs were good. As he told me:

Even in a normal family a daughter's death would be terrible. In our case Lucie's story has remained in the news, constantly reminding us even if we could forget.

But I am beginning to have hope and a sense of renewal. Sophie, who suffered terribly through her sister's loss, becoming so desperate that she attempted suicide [she took an overdose of her prescription anti-depressants] in 2005 when Lucie's ashes were interred at last, is now a beautiful twenty-eight-year-old, a qual-ified cardiac technician. Since meeting Alwyn, her thirty-three-year-old boyfriend, I have seen her slowly blossom and come back to life.

I can't say how much this means to me. When we were in Tokyo looking for Lucie together, Sophie used to say to me that she would never leave Japan until Lucie was found.

Rupert is now living with his gorgeous Dutch girl-friend Moneik in Holland. We are doing well, but nothing will ever make it completely all right again. Nothing could.

So why was Tim marrying now, after twelve years of living with Jo? 'I am aware that what I went through in searching for Lucie and discovering the truth has left me a sad and maybe difficult man,' he said. 'I didn't want to put that on to somebody else at first. Now it feels right.'

Tim Blackman, in his own strange way, had felt it right

to go to the beach at Aburatsubo where Lucie's body had been found, and drink champagne in her memory. A little while before our meeting on the Isle of Wight I had been there too; when I told him this he seemed profoundly moved that anyone should still care.

What I found there was deeply affecting. A plain wooden crucifix by the high-water mark. Some fresh spring flowers placed in a Nescafé jar. It was the simplicity of these tributes to the memory of Lucie that really played with the emotions. But their very modesty bore testimony to the way that some ordinary Japanese people felt about the slur that the rape and death of a young Englishwoman had brought upon their national honour.

I was told on many occasions that the Japanese would prefer the world to forget that Lucie met her death here. One former mama-san of a hostess bar told me: 'You must not write that Japan is dangerous. Such things have never happened before!' Smiles froze whenever I brought up the matter. It seemed an embarrassment, an insult almost, to mention Lucie's name.

Perhaps that explained the intimacy of the tributes at Aburatsubo, the humble flowers in their improvised vase, driftwood and seashells arranged like a child's seaside garden at the entrance of the now empty cave. They may have been put there by other bargirls who had come from Tokyo, thought my Anglo-Japanese friend who had brought me here. But there was no one on the beach to ask. As a child, he said, he'd often been here with his family for bucket-and-spade holidays. He came here now sometimes because it was just a nice place on the coast, he said, and that 'Lucie's story is quite a legend still'.

All I could feel, looking out over the Pacific Ocean, was the unbearable sadness of the deaths of Lucie and Lindsay – and of Carita and Tiffanny before them – and the utter tragedy of any young life cut short.

On 16 December 2008 the prosecution's appeal against the acquittal of Joji Obara in the matter of Lucie Jane Blackman came to judgment in the Tokyo High Court. This time, her mother was in Tokyo. Tim was in the mid-Atlantic, taking part in a yacht race.

Obara reportedly avoided looking towards the public gallery where Mrs Steare sat with her eyes fixed upon him. His head bowed slightly as the tribunal chairman, Judge Hiroshi Kadono, read out the verdict.

Jane Steare wept quietly as it was delivered. Obara did abduct Miss Blackman, drug her and cut up her body with a chainsaw. But the cause of Lucie's death could still not be identified. 'The use of chloroform in raping the victim cannot be determined. These crimes, using drugs to hurt a number of victims, for the purpose of satisfying his desires, were unprecedented and highly malicious,' said the judge. Obara said he would counter-appeal.

'Truth and honour have prevailed, not only for Lucie, but for all victims of violent sexual crime,' said Jane Steare. It was enough.